SPENSER STUDIES

SPENSER STUDIES

A Renaissance Poetry Annual

X

EDITED BY

Patrick Cullen AND *Thomas P. Roche, Jr.*

AMS PRESS, INC.
NEW YORK, N.Y.

SPENSER STUDIES
A RENAISSANCE POETRY ANNUAL

edited by Patrick Cullen and Thomas P. Roche, Jr.

is published annually by AMS Press, Inc. as a forum for Spenser scholarship and criticism and related Renaissance subjects. Manuscripts must be submitted *in duplicate* and be double-spaced, including notes, which should be grouped at the end and should be prepared according to the format used in this journal. All essay-length manuscripts should enclose an abstract of 100–175 words. They will be returned only if sufficient postage is enclosed (overseas contributors should enclose international reply coupons). One copy of each manuscript should be sent to Thomas P. Roche, Jr., Department of English, Princeton University, Princeton, N.J. 08544 and one copy to Patrick Cullen, 300 West 108th Street, Apt. 8 D, New York, N.Y. 10025.

ISSN 0195-9468
Volume X, ISBN 0-404-19210-6

Contents

dino and Badius. These Virgilian references in "Aprill" of *The Shepheardes Calender* and variously throughout *The Faerie Queene* explore Venus-Virgo's association with the forest, with *materia* or *hyle,* as extensively posited by the commentaries on the *Aeneid.* By doing so, the poetry opens up enigmatic and turbulent perspectives upon interpretation, especially the symbolic or "integumentive" style of reading practiced by the commentators who split Venus into different personages. The changing contexts of these allusions also create undermeanings clearly problematic to imperialist readings of Spenser. The essay provides access to this Virgilian background and examines its implications for interpreting the poetry.

E. K., in his letter to Gabriel Harvey, predicted that readers of the *Shepheardes Calender* would find Spenser's language the "straungest" part of the work. Modern readers of the poem, however, have disappointed him: Citing the many precedents for Spenser's use of archaisms, neologisms, and other variant forms in sixteenth-century literature, recent critics agree that E. K. greatly exaggerated his case. Modern efforts to demystify the language of the *Calender,* however, begs the question of why E. K. insisted so strongly on its strangeness, and why Spenser's earliest critics concurred with E. K.'s view. E. K. described Spenser's language as graceful, majestic, and full of "auctoritie" on the one hand, and base, rude, and rustic, on the other. These contradictions, overlooked by modern readers of the poem, reveal a bold poetic strategy: Spenser, setting archaisms and other "literary" forms alongside rustic dialect, created a language calculated to disturb and provoke his audience. The inclusion of northern English in the *Shepheardes Calender* reveals how far the new poet was willing to travel in order to create the impression of novelty, and difference, even at the risk of alienating his "southern" readers. In an innovative scheme to manipulate the reception of his inaugural work, Spenser encouraged our sense of "estrangement" from the poem.

In *The Shepheardes Calender,* parenthetical phrases produce fleeting illusions of voice that induce us to experience the formal structures of the *Calender* as figuring arbitrary,

explains. Yet despite the Letter's provenance as Spenser's most complete literary critical statement, and despite its dynamic role in a notable publishing event of unparalleled significance to Spenser's career, it has not received the searching and comprehensive analysis it deserves. Too often assuming the Letter's transparent and unmediated relation to *The Faerie Queene,* critics either dispute the Letter's "accuracy" or, more commonly, mine it piecemeal as an authoritative source of evidence to support interpretations of *The Faerie Queene* or readings of Renaissance critical theory. In my essay, I treat the Letter not primarily as a commentary on *The Faerie Queene* but as an independent pluralist text born out of a matrix of personal and professional responsibilities and animating a carefully planned and executed publishing event: a complex politico-literary act of damage control, cultural criticism, and rhetorical play by an inspired and informed Renaissance intellectual. I focus on a few literary, critical, and historiographical cruxes of the Letter in order to explore the ways they illustrate Spenser's masterful manipulation of his cultural personae.

Book I Canto x of *The Faerie Queene* begins with what many critics take to be the most theologically Protestant, not to say Calvinistic, stanza of the entire poem, yet the canto goes on to present the most blatantly Catholic images in Spenser's epic. The combination of Calvinist theology and Catholic imagery forms part of a larger pattern of divine predestination and human effort in Book I, a pattern in which predestination and free will paradoxically work together in the process of justification and sanctification. Whenever Spenser shows Red Cross Knight putting forth effort, the poet adds a phrase or a passage which reminds the reader of God's sovereignty and initiative. Canto x reverses the pattern, beginning with a stanza emphasizing God's sovereignty, then proceeding to suggest, through the most convenient imagery available, the contribution that human effort and free will have to make. Spenser found Catholic images suitable vehicles to suggest human effort because Catholicism insisted so strongly, through its doctrines of free will, sacramental efficacy, and salvation by faith *and* works, on human effort cooperating with grace. The paradoxical coexistence of predestination and free will came to Spenser from St. Paul by way of St. Augustine. If my thesis is correct, the theology of Book I is more Augustinian than specifically Calvinist or Catholic, for Calvin denied free will, and Catholicism, by the time of the Council of Trent, had deemphasized (though not denied) predestination; but Augustine's theology contains a strong emphasis on both.

That Spenser was unaware of the discrepancy between the Calvinist opening and the Catholic content of Canto x seems unlikely, for he was well-versed in the theological disputes of the Reformation. Spenser wrote his epic hard on the heels of Calvin's revised *Institutes of the Christian Religion,* the Thirty-nine Articles of the Church of

England, and the Canons and Decrees of the Council of Trent. *The Faerie Queene* responds to those texts not by denying predestination or free will but by juxtaposing them, thus suggesting that they are not mutually exclusive.

Astrophil and Stella is the work of an author keenly sensitive to time's constraints and the hazards of missed occasions. The sequence's thirty-third sonnet focuses a unique predicament which I propose governs Astrophil's pained self-revelation: he stands pathetically aware of his status as a lover who has had the chance to gain his lady, but has unwittingly allowed the opportunity to pass. This peculiar twist transforms the poems from conventional exercises in courtly seduction to components in a poignant and emotionally complex project of recovery, a quest shadowed by the bitter recollection of past failure. The approach helps delineate time's subtle yet pervasive role in the sequence, and glances finally toward the circumstances which perhaps inspired Sidney to organize his persona's psyche around this distinctive armature.

Most accounts of John Skelton's anti-Wolsey satire *Speke, Parott* acknowledge the confused and chaotic nature of the text, but see its apparent incoherence as simply tactical, a shield to conceal the poet's dangerous political intentions. This essay, while accepting the care and subtlety with which Skelton created the text, looks more closely at the nature of the disorder exhibited in the poem, and examines the opposition enacted within Parott's monologue between authorities of various kinds and the notion of "riot," or anarchic disorder. It examines the parallels which the poem draws between events in the political world and those in the world of philology, chiefly between the rise of Wolsey as Henry VIII's chief minister and the expansion of humanist Greek scholarship in the schools and universities. This essay claims that the struggle between authority and riot, rationality and wilfulness plays a fundamental role in the poem's political strategy. Yet ultimately, it is suggested, Skelton was forced to watch the political instrument which he had created turn in his hand. So resistant is the sense of crisis within the text that it finally frustrates the attempt to use Parott as an effective political mouthpiece.

Calling Colin Clout

ROLAND GREENE

229

John Skelton's "Collyn Clout" delivers a number of important literary and cultural issues to its audience's attention, even apart from its polemical mission against Cardinal Wolsey. "Collyn Clout" fashions a deliberately factitious and empty speaking voice—the speaker named Collyn Cloute—through whom the poet shrewdly manages the play of credibility and authority needed for a potent indictment of ecclesiastical and political abuses; its foregrounding of Collyn Cloute indicates the social and institutional marginality of the English poet in Skelton's time, and makes bringing this poet-speaker nearer to the center of things part of its program; and the poem reminds us at every turn that its workings are entirely a textual effect, in which by the end the distances between the various standpoints—poet, speaker, object, and audience—have been rendered shorter. Through an approach on these terms, one begins to see what Spenser saw in Skelton's poem that compelled him to use the same fictitious speaker for his own purposes near the end of the century.

Misogyny and Economic Person in Skelton, Landland, and Chaucer

ELIZABETH FOWLER

245

John Skelton's "The Tunnyng of Elynour Rummynge" cites *Piers Plowman* and Chaucer's Wife of Bath and Shipman's Tale in order to establish its metaphorical structure, in which economic value and women's sexuality work in tandem to degrade human agency. In a series of transactions that liquidate commodities into instantly depreciating value. Elynour's ale stands in for the economic general equivalent. Skelton's misogynistic tirade develops into a critique of the model of person usually adopted in economic writing: with its dramatization of the market, the poem counters canonical economic texts by portraying economic person in terms of drunken female consumers rather than the traditional male producers of useful commodities. The topos of Skeltonic economics is consumption rather than production. The marketplace encounter with the general equivalent is not the socially binding, productive moment described by canon law: instead, economic exchange causes a degradation of value and an impairment of the subject, whose agency is adulterated by the agency of money. Similar kinds of partial subjects reappear throughout Skelton's poetry, providing models for Spenser's investigations of the social construction of person. Skelton's technically innovative voicing and characterization fragment the highly symbolic personification employed by Langland without recreating the unified, narrative interiority with which Chaucer endows the Wife of Bath. Skelton invents a representation of person that can express the effects of subjectivity while still retaining the capacity to combine and analyze distinct discursive traditions that was deveoped in allegorical personification.

Corrigendum

The table of contents in Volume VIII does not list under Forum and Gleanings the titles of the articles included. Under Forum, it should have read: A. Kent Hieatt, "Arthur's Deliverance of Rome? (Yet Again)," (pp. 243–48). Under Gleanings, it should have read: Ruth Samson Luborsky, "The Illustrations to *The Shepheardes Calender:* II," (pp. 249–53), and Alex A. Vardanis, "The Temptations of Despaire: Jeffers and the Faerie Queene," (pp. 255–57).

A. KENT HIEATT

The Alleged Early Modern Origin of the Self and History: Terminate or Regroup?

[The following reproduces the 1991 Kathleen Williams Lecture, in the program "Spenser at Kalamazoo" at the conference of the Medieval Institute, May 1991]

I BEGIN OFF-TOPIC, by reminding you of something familiar: there was a time when the educational statesmen came from English Departments, and when Matthew Arnold-type writers on culture and critical theory—even Lionel Trilling ones—held a general reading public. It's largely over, in spite of President Rudenstine of Harvard. We console ourselves with the reflection that, inside academe, our discipline is very attractive. Students love English departments. But do they love the Renaissance, and do they love Spenser? Not perhaps as much as some of us would wish. As we are all aware, some who may be present have undertaken NEH-financed steps in this direction. Aside from these steps, an incidental advantage of the development of theory within our corner of the discipline is that students learning how to think have found the drama of the mind entering Renaissance studies. Some of us will remember the B-52-strength impact of A. C. Hamilton's and Louis Montrose's audience here—the largest one for a Kathleen Williams lecture, or perhaps for any Spenser event since 1554.

The ability to arouse interest in our field through bold, far-ranging formulations is a matter of the bottom-line. As in other literary areas, so with us: administrators like theory. Outside literary areas, however, our formulations are beginning to draw less favorable attention. At Princeton's "Spenser 400" conference in September 1991, for instance, the non-literary academic commentators, laid on by the executive for the last day, expressed themselves with some acerbity, or worse, on the shakiness of much that had preceded them. The thoughts of one of those commentators, Anthony Grafton, on an earlier occasion get at something basic in the feelings about some of our work among some of the specialists in other fields who study the same cultures and time-spans that we do.

Renaissance Quarterly had published in Winter 1989 a "Recent Trends in Renaissance Studies: Economic History," containing three substantive studies. In summing up there, Grafton said (814–15):

> No tactic has been more commonly used in recent work on cultural history than that of juxtaposing a text on, say, family life from Renaissance Italy with a secondary work on, say, family life in Tudor England; the two are connected by a confident bridging statement to the effect that the text (1) exemplifies, (2) contradicts, or (3) subverts the social norms its author knew. All three of the papers published here show that when historians of culture conduct this kind of smash-and-grab raid on social and economic history, they violate the integrity of the evidence they claim to use. If we hope—as nowadays, surely, we all do—to connect social and economic with cultural and intellectual realities, we must replace this sort of intellectual booty capitalism with far more sophisticated ways of exploiting—and collaborating with—other disciplines.

Nothing is more striking about those three studies, and other non-literary ones, than their nearly complete refusal to take seriously most of the things that we have meant by the word "Renaissance." Even when they use the terms "Middle Ages" and "Renaissance," as the author of one of these studies says,[1] the words are just familiar ones, stripped of their roles in maintaining the dramatic organization of Western history and intended to rid historical scholarship of a "pernicious humanism."

On this scene breaks Lee Patterson, in a *Speculum*[2] article. By showing that our period was not nearly so innovative as we often claim, he was trying to induce Medievalists to theorize literature as the rest of us do, but it is his *premise* that I am concerned with here. It's true of course, what he says about Lyotard's *petits récits*—small-scale narrative generalizations, like feminist, ethnic, gay, multicultural ones preferred today—instead of stale *grands récits* like the evolution of Western culture to its present form.[3] Patterson naturally adds that something interesting can be said about novel developments, or quantitatively expressible tendencies, in our period; what he objects to is the notion that in stark contrast to the "Renaissance" the Middle Ages is totally corporate and never individual, or totally unaware of the otherness of far distant periods.

Surely the kind of thinking whose implications he attacks here—binary opposites or dialectical upshots—is rhetorically insidious for us. The applications of this partly philosophical technique to cultural history have a rich past. I was first captured by it in high school when I read Oswald Spengler's *Decline of the West:* an aristocracy as time, a priesthood as space; number as magnitude in the classical world, as function in western culture. For the Classical world, the limited, self-defined body; for the Arabic world, the cavern; for the West, infinity; for the Chinese, the landscape; for the Egyptians, the path. Macrocosm and Megalopolis; Portraiture, Contrition, and Syntax; Classical, Magian, and Faustian *numina.* And so on, in college, with Dilthey, Dagobert Frey, Worringer, Cassirer. Always reversals and somersaults. The dominance of this kind of thinking shows up in one of Patterson's hilarious shorter exhibits, this time from the direction of transatlantic, cultural-materialist New Historicism. Francis Barker, on the arrival of subjectivity in the Renaissance, says of the Middle Ages:[4]

> . . . place and articulation are defined not by an interiorized self-recognition . . . but by incorporation in the body politic which is the king's body in its social form . . . The social plenum *is* the body of the king, and membership of this anatomy is the deep structural form of all being in the secular realm.

"The figure of the king," Barker says, "guarantees, as locus and source of power and as a master signifier, a network of subsidiary relations which constitute the real practice and intelligibility of the lives of subjects." Thus no individual thought individually; the practice and intelligibility of Abelard, of Alison and Absalon in *The Miller's Tale,* of the writers of *The Paston Letters* are entirely within the anatomy of the king.

Patterson attacks secondly another component of the humanist notion of the Renaissance, the sudden arrival of the consciousness of history. The textbook humanist view is that, for the Middle Ages, Antiquity was contemporary—yesterday, when people thought and spoke exactly as they do today: triumphant anachronism. Only the Renaissance, in this view, grasped the *pastness* of the past. It identified, with more and more precision, the literary styles of antiquity; identified the otherness of cultural, legal, and political forms of ancient civilizations; and recognized the gulf—that is, the Middle Ages—which separated it from that more desirable time.

As a description of one among several tendencies, not a revolution, this usual doctrine cannot be criticized. Lorenzo Valla was philologically more accurate than Bede. Yet, as I'll show, it's a mistake to suppose that the Middle Ages lacked a sense of history. Their sense of a past was sometimes intense; alternatively their reason for contemporizing the past was not ignorance but a desire to comment on the present through the past.

The most striking recent updating of the now traditional notion of the novelty of the Renaissance, humanist sense of history is Thomas M. Greene's 1982 *The Light in Troy: Imitation and Discovery in Renaissance Poetry.*[5] Greene goes beyond the notion that the Renaissance recognized the distant otherness of Antiquity and that the Middle Ages did not. He sees Renaissance poets recognizing the supreme difficulty—in principle the impossibility—of recuperation, by imitation, of doubtfully recorded ancient artifacts whose *mundus significans* is alien to our own. Each of us is poignantly and permanently isolated, but historically separated periods all the more so. Although literary texts are the nearest to being recoverable of all artifacts of historical cultures, our modern sense of radical Derridean discontinuity and of the aleatory makes the recovery even of words hollow and highly problematical. Courageously but forebodingly, Greene presents us with what he sees as the only way of shoring up an at best disorderly literary continuity: doubtful but indispensable etiologies—relationships among successive uses of a word, of syntactic unity, of intertextual allusion, or of metaphor. For him the truth lies indeed in the healing power of *imitatio,* but rather more strongly in our tragic isolation, and the sundering of the culture of the Renaissance, and ours, from Antiquity by the abyss of the Dark Ages. "Humanist culture," he says, "had its mainspring . . . in the paired intuitions of rupture and continuity," (193) but what is really compelling about his book is the idea of rupture—of tragic irrecoverability. As Greene says in one of his set pieces, "The perception of cultural as well as linguistic distance . . . became for

Petrarch a certainty and an obsession; the discovery of antiquity and simultaneously the remoteness of antiquity made of Petrarch a double exile" (8). Greene attempts to impute much the same feeling to the entire, humanistically colored Renaissance, and his view has attained wide currency. It is a powerful fusing of recent critical thinking and detailed historical exposition. *Renovatio* as perilous and heroic, and likely to be tragic, appeals to us.

What I am now trying to say about Greene's emphasis is certainly not that Renaissance figures lacked a sense of the alterity of antiquity, but that the plangent accents of loss, the innermost realization of the extraordinary difficulty of recovery, are not really that often encoded. The true difference between the Medieval and Renaissance senses of history in terms of the conceived relation to antiquity and its artifacts seems to me to be more complex and equivocal than he allows. Two of the largest exceptions, singled out by Greene himself, are Erasmus (called "neomedieval" [183]) and Ronsard. I think there are others. A general "crisis" over the near hopelessness of recovery does not appear to correspond to what was really alive in the minds of most humanistically inclined figures of the Italian and Northern Renaissance. They theorized on the relation of meanings and words, starting with Plato's *Cratylus,* but were not driven to the shifts to which Deconstruction has reduced us.

One of Greene's set pieces is Joachim Du Bellays's sonnet sequence *Les Antiquitez de Rome,* which of course was translated by Spenser: the ruins of Rome, marvels of architectural culture which, having fallen prey to *tempus edax,* can never be resurrected, never be imitated. Their ruins bury the signifying worlds of antiquity, as Greene sees it, so that even the words of the Latin literary texts (which, Du Bellay hazards, will live forever) are perceived by Greene—correctly, of course—to communicate only through doubtful etiologies (221). "Because Du Bellay's situation became in so many ways exemplary," he says, "it is possible to speak of a larger crisis of the humanist movement precipitated in the life of one microcosmic individual" (221).

One notes Du Bellay's tentativeness, but I want to suggest an opposite tendency by looking at the *Hypnerotomachia Poliphili,* or *Polifilo,* of Francesco Colonna,[6] a most important romance, interesting in many ancillary ways, published by the Aldine Press in 1499. Unexpectedly, its linked preoccupations with both the words and architecture of Greco-Roman antiquity put it into counterpoint with *Antiquitez.* The *Polifilo* displays the robust conviction that, with little sense of blockage, concrete measures can *contemporize* antiquity. Verbally Colonna achieves currency by writing recognizable Northern Italian, but (rashly of course) he thinks to recover the antique *mundus significans* by Latinizing and Hellenizing this Italian to the point where it is nearly a new language. And not simply the words of antiquity; what seems so impossible in the Rome of Du Bellay's *Antiquitez,* the architecturally worthy edifices are resurrected as well. Although it attacks the architecture of its own time vigorously and praises a theoretically irrecoverable antiquity, in pragmatic fact this text erects, in its fictional present, structure after meticulously described classicizing structure. The theoretical understanding of classical architecture, derived from L. B. Alberti's enthusiastic recovery of, and competitive spirit towards, classical theory, is proudly realized in the narrative and its woodcuts. Like Du Bellay, Colonna responds to ruins, but in the sense that he feels he is ready to replace them, and responds to words, but in the sense that he believes, no matter how incorrecty, that he can revive them in the body of the contemporary Italian vernacular.

The most painful excisions in my early draft here concern the importance and character of the *Polifilo,* this orphan of nineteenth- and early twentieth-century Italian and French chauvinistic literary history. Let me say only that its importance is only beginning to be recognized today since the first and only critical edition in the nineteen-sixties. There is no nearly complete English translation.

It was translated and much read in successive editions in sixteenth-century France, as a romance as well as a treatise on architecture. Along with translations of Albert and Vitruvius, it found its own context in a number of sixteenth-century châteaux, beginning with Chambord, even before a translation existed. Its effect on Rabelais appears to have been remarkable. It is not difficult to find examples of the same robustness towards the imitation of classical texts in Britain, but the *Polifilo* itself, in the same company of architectural texts, exerted only a small, but interesting, influence there, to which I'll return.

The *Polifilo* establishes an antique world of pagan mythology in which its modern Polia and Polofilo live. It is not a question of a timeless, pastoral present, as in the less drastically paganized world of Sannazaro's nearly contemporaneous *Arcadia.* Colonna establishes Polia's antecedents in a family—the Lelli—living in contemporary Treviso. The entire body of concrete, supposedly classical objects in the text is almost effortlessly melded into a significantly insistent present. The myths of Jove, Venus, Mars, and Adonis function as though current; the espousal of Polia and Polifilo, accomplished by a priestess of Venus and female assistants, is imagined as a contemporary sacrament.

The architecture in the *Polifilo* is often misunderstood. Greene says casually, for instance, "So many of the colossal structures are surrounded with broken fragments of stone that the fragments almost seem necessary for the structures to achieve their effect" (235). Strictly speaking, this has to be denied. Only two temples in Colonna's architectural program show dilapidation of any kind, and only one of these significantly. On the other hand a bath, a palace with its subordinate structures, a centrally important temple, and a system of buildings on the island of Cythera, centered upon an amphitheater enclosing the stately bath of Venus, and including an elaborate funerary monument, are as though mint-new. They are described at just as great length as the former two temples, and with equally sedulous attention to design, architectural theory, and fictional purpose.

First (Fig. 1) the one with insignificant ruins. *Polifilo's* first architectural adventure is the discovery of an obelisk-temple. It is taller than one World Trade Center Tower piled on another. It is surmounted by a bronze Occasio-Fortuna, revolving thunderously on bronze bearings. You see some nugatory ruins in the foreground, but we feel no sense of immemorial antiquity, although some ruins are registered in the text here.

Figure 2 shows an elevation of the bath, with Polifilo and the Five Senses, from a woodcut of the first French edition. No ruin here, nor in the Italian edition. The exterior and interior are elaborately described. Bathed, the Senses and Polifilo progress from it to Eleuterilida's—Free Will's—palace, again elaborately described, but with no hint of ruins. Figure 3 shows the scene of her banquet. Another woodcut (82) shows her functioning, uneroded fountain, borrowed by Rabelais for the courtyard of his Abbey of Thélème. A ballet is also offered, three times at different speeds according to the three classical musical modes.

Polifilo and Polia are later espoused in the temple of Venus Physiozoa (Fig. 4), shown in an elevation combined with a plan. As you see, it is in perfect condition. It follows the best rules. It is described with numbing attention to every architectural and symbolically significant detail.

We next come to the only real ruin in the book (Fig. 5). Out of the 171 woodcuts in the *Polifilo* only two show edifices with ruins of any kind. The woodcuts were evidently designed by a Venetian, living in a city without Classical ruins. These ruins look like the result of a recent explosion, as in a contemporary drawing of the fall of the Tower of Babel (Fig. 6), not of immemorial process. A nearly contemporary representation of the Colosseum (Fig. 7), crowned with vegetable growth and partly submerged by the rise in the ground-level, shows what Roman ruins really looked like then.

Greene says of the narrative at this point, "When Polifilo . . . enters at his mistress's urging the ruins of a temple of Pluto, the visit ends in

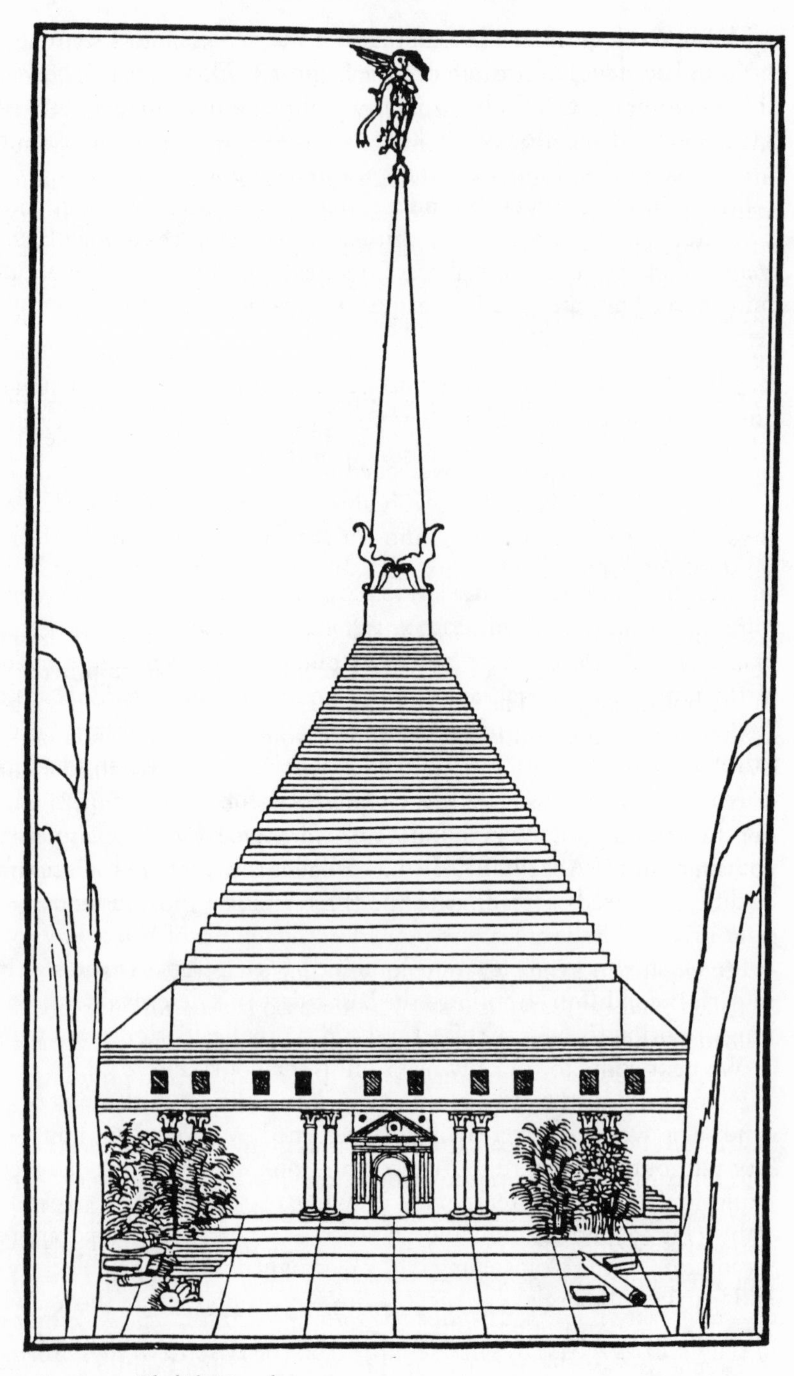

FIGURE 1. Obelisk Temple

Figure 2. Bath of the Senses (from 1546 French translation)

FIGURE 3. Eleuterilida's Banquet-Hall

Figure 4. Temple of Venus Physiozoa

FIGURE 5. Polyandrion

FIGURE 6. Fall of the Tower of Babel (1547, Cornelius Anthoniszoon, Copperplate)

FIGURE 7. Rome: Colosseum (Ca. 1508–9, Jan Gossaert, Drawing in brown ink)

FIGURE 8. Amphitheatre

FIGURE 9. Funerary Monument of Adonis

FIGURE 10. *The Barriers.* Inigo Jones's design for the central building.

FIGURE II. *Oberon.* Two designs by Inigo Jones

panic and flight" (235). This is a little skewed on two counts. Polia says that the temple was named, long since, "*Polyandrion*," "sepulcher of many persons." In it are entombed, with pathetic inscriptions, hieroglyphics, and statuary, lovers who misconducted their loves or died innocently. The interior, we are told in a three-word sentence, is dedicated to Pluto, but a temple of Pluto it is not. Some of the engraved Latin and Greek epitaphs, in which the quattrocento took such delight, are picturesquely dilapidated, but the majority of the funerary objects, including one huge monumental tomb, are as though new.

Polifilo's panic and flight from the Polyandrion are not, as I believe Greene likes to think, an effect something like the "*horreur*" which the speaker is made to express at sheer ancientness in Du Bellay's *Antiquitez*. Rather, Polifilo sees a depiction of Pluto's rape of Proserpina, and simply notes that his own love, alone on the neighboring seashore, might as easily be carried off by some god. His race out of the temple and back to her seems fictionally appropriate, considering that he will soon lose her to death. I'm not trying to say that the ruined *Polyandrion* is *nothing* but a foreshadowing of *Polia*'s and *Polifilo*'s imminent disaster, but it is that among other things including (admittedly) a strictly subordinated motif of the pathos of what time has long since devoured.

Landing from Cupid's boat on Cythera (after a voyage as elaborate as Guyon's to the Bower of Bliss), the lovers reach a whole symmetrical system of structures on this perfectly circular island, but principally two individual ones. The first is a huge amphitheatre (Fig. 8), in perfect condition. At its center, not illustrated in the *Polifilo,* but described through many pages, are the fountain and bath of Venus, untouched by time. Later the lovers adjourn, with attendant nymphs, to the elaborate funerary monument of Adonis, surmounted by a full-length, seated statue of Venus suckling Cupid (Fig. 9: one of three views, including an attached fountain and pool). It is as though carved yesterday.

Inadequacy to the complexity of the subject seems to me to be the weakness in Greene's drastic version of the theory that the Renaissance distinguishes itself from the Middle Ages in recognizing an historical abyss imperilling the imitation of even the words of antiquity. Many in the Renaissance felt not only that they could successfully imitate that part of antiquity whose physical embodiment persisted—the words—but also, even, that they could recuperate what in physical form remained only as ruins, if that: the edifices. They often lacked our tragic sense of loss. They did indeed acquire a much more just (although not more heartfelt or lively) concept of classical culture than anyone possessed in the Middle Ages. They avoided many medieval anachronisms. But, for instance, what Greene says about the later seventeenth century, that classical works became "the idiom of familiars who have lost their numinous ghostliness," is true, in the earlier, full Renaissance, of Alberti, Sannazaro, and Colonna as well, and, I think, of Erasmus, Rabelais, and Ronsard. Some of them resurrected old buildings; all of them maintained the possibility in their verbal imitations of rising to classical standards, not least, I think, in Du Bellay's own critical treatise, the *Deffence,* in spite of Margaret Ferguson's interesting deconstructive treatment of this work.[7]

Now for a transition. Considering the massive impact in France of the *Polifilo* itself—on Rabelais for instance (see Note 6)—and of the architectural thinking that animated it, particularly L. B. Alberti's confident recovery of the antique, it is strange that England shows little of such neoclassical, or Greco-Roman, architecture. Elizabeth's and James's lack of interest in it would have been quickly remedied if James's heir, the Protestant activist Henry Prince of Wales, had not suddenly died.[8] He was much interested in the architecture presented in the same constellation of architectural books so successful in France. Among his confidants was Richard Dallington, the translator of the first part of the *Polifilo,* who retained a strong interest in European neoclassical architecture. Ingo Jones attempted, not always successfully, to embody what Henry had in mind in the two masques which express his mature aspirations just before his death. The central building in *The Barriers* (Fig. 10) attempts to combine native Gothic with resurrected Roman elements. So does the one—in two designs—in *Oberon* (Fig. 11).

Henry's playing the part of Oberon speaks for his intention to continue the Arthurian imagery of *The Faerie Queene:* he becomes the successor of the elfin line—of the first Oberon and of Tanaquil-Gloriana—Henry VIII and Elizabeth—in the *Antiquitie of Faerie Lond,* which Sir Guyon reads in the House of Alma (II.ix.70–76) while Arthur is reading *Briton Moniments.* In assuming this name, and in his Protestant, activist policy of allying himself with other northern Protestant powers so as to crush the power of Spain and the Roman Catholic church, Prince Henry was the successor to those Elizabethan activists Leicester and Essex who stood closest to the queen. In his explicit decision to constitute himself in this way, he is a powerful self-fashioner, a case of the acutely conscious, individual, self-constituting self which it is normal today to consider a sign manual of the Renaissance.

This association with Leicester and Essex is particularly striking if what I have recently contended[9] is right: that Spenser aimed at a continuation of *The Faerie Queene* in which Arthur, associated in some real or symbolic union with Gloriana, would have led a coalition in crushing the power of Rome (for which read allegorically Spain and the Roman Catholic Church) and assuming the crown of the Roman Empire. Spenser no doubt bet initially on his patron Leicester as an allegorical stand-in for Arthur, but after Leicester's death, as I claim, he persisted in his notion, hoping against hope that Essex could be substituted, considering his relation with the Queen and his exploit of capturing Cadiz, mentioned in *Prothalamion.* Henry might be said to have wished to continue the tradition by other means, without a Gloriana.

In saying this I seem, like Stephen Greenblatt, to be presenting Machiavellian, acquisitive fashioners of invulnerability in the dynamically role-changing environment of the sixteenth century, starkly opposed to the fixed roles of a corporate Medieval society which lacked consciousness of the individual self. But actually Spenser got this powerful idea from sources as early as the twelfth century. We are speaking here of a battle of competing images nearly as strong as any in the Renaissance. The original British in Wales needed an historical myth to explain their defeat by the Saxons, but more importantly, as is shown by the persistence of "British history," so-called, in England, the English royal house needed a role adequately answering ancient Roman imperial hegemony and Charlemagne's assumption of the imperial crown in Rome in 800. Spenser's immediate forerunners in this *translatio imperii* were Hardyng in his fifteenth-century *Chronicle* and Malory; they, in turn, did no more than reverse the tragic last scene of politically motivated British, Arthurian, imperialist history, reworked since the beginning of the High Middle Ages,[10] which imputed a historical destiny to an English ruler by creating *ex nihilo* a usable past for him in the figure of an imperial Arthur. Hardyng turned his own earlier tragic story on its head, and made Arthur emperor of Rome, while fashioning his Lancastrian-inclined chronicle into a Yorkist one for the accession of Edward IV. Correspondingly, a Scots school of chroniclers refashioned Mordred, as a Scot, into the idealized hero, and Arthur into the villain, with role-consequences for the Scottish monarch.

All this undermines our current notion of completely innovatory Renaissance self-fashioning replacing a fixed concept of role in a traditionary, corporate Medieval society. A strengthened tendency—and the tendency *was* stronger in the Renaissance—is not a revolution. It will not do to say that the English, or the Middle Ages, had no sense of an historical past. They had an elaborate historical narrative going back to Brutus and Rome. What they lacked was *accurate* history, and a narrowing down of interest, as in the case of the humanists, to the classical world.

Before my last act, on self-fashioning in Spenser, I beg to direct your attention to a new book by a first-time author in which New Historicism plays a part and nothing is taken into account except what is socially and politically derived. I suspect that some of its argument is confused and contradictory, but it seems to me extraordinarily promising. This is *Shakespeare and the Dramaturgy of Power* by John D. Cox (Princeton, 1989). The book makes few of the standard, old-fashioned gestures at a lofty watershed separating Medieval from Renaissance consciousness of self.

Cox remarks (70) that the motive for self-fashioning as Greenblatt defined it is to gain social invulnerability against perceived mortal dangers. Its hard-carapaced self-sufficiency entails a kind of philosophical *Stoicism.* It also aims, of course, at gaining power: it is clear-eyed of Cox to perceive that a minority has always practiced self-fashioning. What was innovative in the Renaissance, he claims, was interest in the invulnerable self among a new class of the literate, instructed in the dissembling scramble for prestige by such readings as courtesy books.

But many of Shakespeare's heroes or protagonists fail to be "Stoic" in this way. The villains, like Richard III, are fully so, and such characters as Hal—Henry V—are so ambivalently. What protagonists like Lear attain, however, is "a quite un-Stoic sense of human selfhood as vulnerable, dependent, and paradoxically ennobled in the discovery of [their] limitations." (178) It is on this account, apparently, that various critics, most notoriously Roy Battenhouse, have tried to impute a Christian framework to Shakespeare's work. Cox does not do this. He starts with the notion of a dialectic: a residual "political realism" in Medieval mystery plays and popular preaching, which he identifies as Augustinian; a second stage—political idealism which exalts the ruler and class distinctions, finding in individually-isolating, Stoic dignity an escape from vulnerability; and a successor third stage: rationalism and materialism. He does not think of the second element—political idealism—as exclusively Renaissance; the idealization of rule is a developed feature of Aquinas's and Dante's earlier doctrines of Empire and Papacy. Equally he refuses to associate the vulnerability and abasement of monarchs and aristocrats in Shakespeare with the third-stage rationalism and materialism, as other Marxists have done. He associates it, instead, with the *first* stage, residual Augustinian distrust of earthly power, of the *libido dominandi,* as in Augustine's own *City of God,* in the Herods, Pilates, and self-fashioning opportunists of mysteries and moralities (here he's developing an idea of Emrys Jones) and in the by no means infrequent reduction of the high and mighty to mere forked humanitity in Medieval romances of the type of *King Robert of Sicily.*

Cox's dialectic enforces some overkill: intellectual structures proliferate beyond the ability of the perceived phenomena to carry them. But what he has to say is promising and suggestive. At one point, though, he is quite wrong. He recognizes that, at the same time that Shakespeare reveals the vulnerability of the mighty (something often revised out in the eighteenth century), he also ambivalently ratifies the class structure and power structure of Elizabethan society. But it doesn't occur to Cox to trace such ambivalence in Spenser. His Spenser is simply the defender of political idealism, the myth-maker of Gloriana and her court. He was of course that, but more. Cox specifies very shrewdly the "classic mystification of power that Augustine incisively identified and rejected" (he means Augustine's disposal in *The City of God* of the exaltation of imperial destiny that we are familiar with in Virgil), and Cox continues: "Analysis of the sixteenth-century political scene might well conclude that the Tudor penchant for assimilating English history to Roman imperial destiny deserved the same skepticism with which Augustine had surveyed the Roman exercise of power."

Beyond the exalter of imperial destiny, however, are opposite tendencies in Spenser. Cox neglects what probably occurs to all of you—the pessimism about earthly power in *Faerie Queene* VI and *Mutabilitie*. But, just as importantly, he neglects shrewd blows at the great and powerful in *Complaints,* published in 1591 and much of it written long before—the humbling of the mighty in the Vision poems and, most notably, I think, the ridiculing of the Lion, king of the forest, who sleeps in "Mother Hubberds Tale" through the loss of all his power to those self-fashioning courtiers the Fox and the Ape, and then loses all dignity—is reduced to mere forked felinity with no clothes on—when he awakes in confusion:[11]

> Arise, (said *Mercurie*) thou sluggish beast,
> That here liest senseles, like the corpse deceast,
> The whilste thy kingdome from thy head is rent,

And thy throne royall with dishonour blent:
Arise, and doo thy selfe redeeme from shame,
And be aveng'd on those that breed thy blame.
Thereat enraged, soone he gan upstart,
Grinding his teeth, and grating his great hart,
And rouzing up himselfe, for his rough hide
He gan to reach; but no where it espide.
Therewith he gan full terribly to rore,
And chafte at that indignitie right sore.
But when his Crowne and scepter both he wanted,
Lord how he fum'd and sweld, and rag'd, and panted;
And threatened death, and thousand deadly dolours
To them that had purloyn'd his Princely honours.
With that in hast, disroabed as he was,
He toward his owne Pallace forth did pas;
And all the way he roared as he went,
That all the forrest with astonishment
Thereof did tremble, and the beasts therein
Fled fast away from that so dreadfull din.
At last he came unto his mansion,
Where all the gates he found fast lockt anon,
And manie warders round about them stood:
With that he roar'd aloud, as he were wood,
That all the Pallace quaked at the stound,
And all within were dead and hartles left . . .
(Lines 1327–55)

His revenge is complete, but the execution of it has lacked Stoic dignity of the kind that Ben Jonson or Chapman would have furnished. Skepticism about earthly glory is a constant throughout Spenser's career, not just at the end of it.

In pursuing the matter of how consciousness of self, like consciousness of history, only tends to enter on a new stage in the Renaissance, not to invent itself, I need to turn to the central document of American New Historicism, Stephen Greenblatt's *Renaissance Self-Fashioning: From More to Shakespeare.*[12] New Historicists are likely to be very vocal about the wrongness of basing any conclusions on their earlier work, because they have now advanced so far beyond it. But on the subject of the arrival of individual consciousness in the Renaissance, Greenblatt's book is now a basic text. Cox, for instance, for all his disagreements with it, says that without it he could not have written his own book. While I apologize for mentioning anything eleven years old, I plead that it is still read; and although Professor Greenblatt has deepened and subtilized his notions of the negotiations between society and literature, nothing suggests to me that he now rejects what I am about to examine.

At the point in *Renaissance Self-Fashioning* which most concerns us in this group—the discussion of Spenser—there is a summing up of what has preceded and a fresh beginning (161), considerably less temperate than the opening pages on the subject of how the Renaissance introduces individual consciousness in the modern world: "despite its age and well documented limitations, one of the best introductions to Renaissance self-fashioning remains Burckhardt's *Civilization of the Renaissance in Italy*" (161). We learn from this whipping-boy of a book, long reproached for its unbalanced view of the transition from the Middle Ages, "that the political upheavals in Italy in the later Middle Ages, the transition from feudalism to despotisms, fostered a radical change in consciousness: the princes and *condottieri,* and their secretaries, ministers, poets, and followers, were cut off from established forms of identity and forced by their relation to power to fashion a new sense of themselves and their world: the self and the state as works of art."

This is the beginning of the doctrine of the intensely self-conscious act of self-fashioning. As Lee Patterson says of Greenblatt's book in another connection, the vigorous political speculation of the Middle Ages, and the frequent changes in the conditions of power, are not so much denied as swept under the rug. We are to remove our eyes from them.

Then, in a move which reminds us of Anthony Grafton's complaint that conditions in various parts of sixteenth-century Europe were not directly comparable, Greenblatt leaves Italy for the Spenser of the "Letter to Raleigh," saying "It is to a culture so engaged in the shaping of identity, in dissimulation and the preservation of moral idealism, that Spenser addresses himself in defining 'the general intention and meaning'" (169) of *The Faerie Queene.* "If it is true," Greenblatt says, "that we are highly sensitive to those aspects of the Renaissance that mark the early, tentative, conflict-ridden fashioning of modern consciousness, then *The Faerie Queene* is of quite exceptional significance, for Spenser's stated intention is precisely 'to *fashion* a gentleman or noble person' . . . This mirroring—the conscious purpose of the work seeming to enact the larger cultural movement—may help to account for the reader's sense of encountering in Spenser's poem the process of self-fashioning itself" (175). When Greenblatt says "conflict-ridden" he is thinking of

Freud. The episode he chooses in *The Faerie Queene* is the Bower of Bliss, in II.xii: Guyon's sea voyage to it, its profoundly erotic appeal, his chaining of Acrasia and destruction of the Bower, "the ontogeny of our culture's violent resistance to a sensuous release for which it nevertheless yearns with a new intensity. . . . We can secure [the] self only through a restraint that involves the destruction of something intensely beautiful; to succumb to that beauty is to lose the shape of manhood . . ." (175). Greenblatt properly wishes here to continue the discussion of sexual motifs which he had undertaken in earlier chapters. He defines the New Historical insight: the intricate game of denial and affirmation of competing desires, of tragic conflict (178), the notion that each constitutive act in the event is faulty, and must be followed by another. As here: "the uneasy, aggressive, masculine court identity fashioned by Wyatt: male sexual aggression—the hunt, the loathing, the desire to master—is yoked to the service of ideal values embodied in a female ruler, and it is through this service that identity is achieved."

I think my two objections to this position are that there is nothing uniquely Spenserian, Elizabethan, or Renaissance about a tempting seductress who disturbs the right course of action and against whom retribution is executed, *but* that Greenblatt has radically misidentified Guyon's reason for chaining Acrasia and destroying her bower. First off, the tempting seductress.

The notion of "sexual melt-down," as Greenblatt says, is unfamiliar in our personal experience. Who do you and I know who has been deflected from her/his proper life's work into constant carnality by a seducer/seductress? You and I tend to think in terms of Britomart-Artegall relationships, the union of *amor* and *amicitia*—as, for instance, the life- and work-enhancing union of a Renaissance specialist and, as it might be, a novelist, or another Renaissance-specialist and a Medievalist; and we all hope that the level of carnality remains constantly high. Yet, if not in our lives, then in our work we recognize that seductresses who lead heroes into harmful courses aren't confined to the Bower of Bliss. They are common to Sumerian, Assyrian, Hebrew, Greek, Chinese, and American Indian cultures. One of the closest fits to Guyon and Acrasia is the originally Semitic Samson and Delilah myth, which was much relished in the centuries before the Renaissance: she unmans him; with a climactic gesture he destroys her confederates and their no doubt aesthetically stirring temple.

So nothing uniquely Renaissance is going on here. Among the numerous Medieval instances which undercut the Renaissance-specific stipulation of self-fashioning in connection with Guyon and Acrasia, perhaps the most graphic case of self-righteous insistence on punishing the beautiful instead of succumbing to it belongs to a fourteenth-century Walloon chronicle,[13] contemporary with Chaucer. It describes a set of relationships (unlike those in Malory) among Mordred, Lancelot, and Queen Guenevere, after Mordred and Guenevere have become lovers and King Arthur, returning from foreign conquest, is killed in battle with Mordred. Lancelot, the former adulterous lover of Guenevere as we know, gathers an army, defeats Mordred, and captures him and Guenevere. Considering her unfaithfulness and unchastity (and forgetting his own) he puts her to death. Then, personally, he puts Mordred, with the corpse of Guenevere but without food, into a chamber so small that Mordred can neither stand nor sit, and locks the door. He opens this room on the sixteenth day. By this time Mordred, hunger-crazed before expiring, had eaten parts of Guenevere's limbs and her face. Sensationalistic of course; but surely the self-fashioning quality—the loathing of the female, and the imaging of a just, exemplary heroic gesture—is there in the spin put on the prose as strongly as in any Renaissance case. The same holds for the humiliating revenge upon the beloved in the more familiar fifteenth-century *Petit Jehan de Saintré.*

Obviously this sort of Aarne-Thompson *Motif-Index* approach uncovers plenty of material for a just feminist attack. It does not, however, support the notion that it is Spenser and the English Renaissance that are fashioning a newly developed modern consciousness of self.

I've said that my second reason for discounting Greenblatt's notion that Spenser is fashioning our culture's equivocal renunciation of pleasure in showing Guyon's destruction of the Bower of Bliss is that Greenblatt has misunderstood the story, has misidentified Guyon's main reason for chaining Acrasia and destroying her Bower.

I think that when someone of my generation makes this kind of claim, sophisticated hearers are likely to suspect that he has not read Fish, or has not heard of reader-response—that he is committing essentialism, as in a way I am. Perhaps an appeal to Umberto Eco's new "communal nature of the interpretive act" within certain interpretive communities and "internal textual coherence" controlling "the otherwise uncontrollable drives of the reader"[14] will help here, and Paul de Man's firm assurance that literary language has a referential, or deictic, aspect.[15] In any case Greenblatt has neglected données within the fiction which I think will bulk as large for you as they do for me.

He says that Spenser is telling us by Guyon's chaining of Acrasia that "A pleasure that serves as its own end, that claims to be self-justifying rather than instrumental, purposeless rather than generative, is immoderate and must be destroyed, lest it undermine the power that Spenser worships." The reason that Acrasia must be thwarted is that her sexuality does not "inspire virtuous action and ultimately, with the sanctification of marriage," result "in the generation of offspring." That is, Spenser is fashioning puritanism into the gentleman by showing Guyon destroying sex-for-sex's-sake-only.

To choose a lesser example among several available, I wonder what to make in this connection of Sir Calidore's courtesy in Book VI, when he passes by a succession of gentle couples canoodling in the forest without even trying to see out of the corner of his eye how far things have got. They are preoccupied momently neither with the promotion of virtuous action in Greenblatt's sense nor with generation.

The main reason[16] why Guyon embarks on vengeance against Acrasia in Book II is not, as Greenblatt claims, that her sexuality is self-justified rather than instrumental—that she and Verdant are simply enjoying themselves. It is, rather, that she had undertaken to defend her sexual primacy by murder, a point that apparently escapes Greenblatt entirely. At the end of the first canto, Guyon had vowed to avenge on Acrasia the deaths of two people whose orphaned infant he held in his arms. Acrasia's lover Mordant had been won back from her by his wife and child; Acrasia's reaction had been to poison Mordant and thereby to precipitate the panicked suicide of his wife, as Acrasia's verse had predicted would happen. The variant on this in the "Letter to Raleigh" is that the Palmer, carrying the child, seeks at the court of Gloriana an avenger of the two murdered parents, and is assigned Guyon to perform the quest.

The similarity of the names Mordant-Verdant for the two lovers of Acrasia known to us suggests a serial character to her behavior. We may not understand sexual melt-down, but the *crime passionnel* is well within our journalistic experience. In newspaper-speak, Acrasia poisoned someone else's husband because she couldn't keep him from going back to his wife; that's why the wife killed herself, and why her infant is left defenseless. That's why Guyon was put on the case to catch her.

Greenblatt devotes not one syllable to this murder. I suppose him to have been oblivious of it. Is it too much to say that his attributing Guyon's behavior to disapproval of non-instrumental sex is simply wrong, not an acceptable alternative interpretation? I do not see how it could have arisen except through lack of acquaintance with the text he was working with. That is why I've appealed, in Eco's new *Limits of Interpretation,* to his "communal nature of the interpretive act" within our *own* interpretive community and to his "internal textual coherence."

The principle entailed here is applied by us almost daily, at a lower level, in trying to teach students how to read and write about poetry and fictional narrative. We point out things they seem to have missed.

Or is the evidence for Acrasia's crime in Canto i too far away from Greenblatt's subject, the Bower of Bliss, in Canto xii? Too much narrative distance to assert continuity, so that we are being dealt a new Acrasia, with no connection with the old one? I think not. The evidence of her criminality is repeated in Canto xii. To make this clear requires an excursion.

One of Greenblatt's strongest points (171) is that the Bower of Bliss has more erotic immediacy—more bang—than any of Spenser's other large-scale amorous operations. A reason for this—perhaps the only reason—is that this scene, like "Ruines of Rome," "Virgils Gnat," and some of his visions, belongs to Spenser's laborious apprenticeship in turning himself into a laureate poet. It is a translation and adaptation, in this case of the similar episode of the Garden of Armida in Tasso's *Gerusalemme Liberata.* The reason for the more intensely erotic appeal of the Bower of Bliss than of the Garden of Adonis and the Isle of Venus is not, I think, that Spenser wanted the latter two to be less erotic, but that he was following Tasso in the former. In the same way, and for no fictionally discernible reason, the pastoral appeal in "Virgils Gnat" is much more intense than it ever is in *The Shepherdess Calender* or *Faerie Queene* VI or *Colin Clouts Come Home Again,* because "Virgils Gnat" is a translation of the classical *Culex,* attributed to Virgil. It is the immediate source of some of his best effects in the other texts. Accepted in the pastoral passage of "Virgils Gnat" are the little goats nibbling on the thickest grass, the bushy shrubs, the boughs of trees, the budding twigs, the soft willow, the goats chewing tender prickles in their cuds and looking at themselves in the brook. Rejected are: fleece twice steeped in Assyrian dye, glistering of gold, *pictured* beauty, gleam of precious stones, the cup embossed with vain imagery, the whelky pearls. Accepted: the pipe of fenny reeds, the looser locks wrapped in wreaths of vine, milk-dropping goats, darksome caves in pleasant vallies. Rejected: greedy riches, bloody strife, deadly fight of warlike fleets, foes' cruel knife, trophies of glittering spoil, frankincense from Panchaea. Accepted: "O flocks, O fauns, and O ye pleasant springs/ Of *Tempe,* where the country nymphs are rife . . ." caerule streams, rumbling in pibble stone, creeping under moss green as any gourd; wood-gods; satyrs; swift dryads; fairies; the streams of Hebrus and Peneus; one of the longest tree-catalogues in Spenser; small birds; silver springs; frogs with jarring voices, shrill grasshoppers; echo. All in one passage. Elsewhere he parcels them out among widely separated passages.

It is much the same with the Bower of Bliss. Elsewhere, running on regular intertextuality and not on premium source-translation, Spenser does not let himself go, or cannot go, in an incantation of particularities. The Isle of Venus and the Garden of Adonis, abodes of much erotic pleasure, are not like that. His virtues are manifold; inexhaustible particularity is not one of them. So that, to the same degree as in "Virgils Gnat," much of the Bower of Bliss is a very ingenious carrying over into English from another author.

So much for my excursion, and now for the evidence of Acrasia's murderousness in the Bower of Bliss itself. At only one point, where the context is translational to an intense degree, does Spenser explicitly reject Tasso for something else. It is as though Spenser had cut a hole in the paper. On the gate of the garden, Tasso gives us representations of Omphale humbling Hercules, and Cleopatra causing Antony to lose the Battle of Actium. *That's* non-instrumental sex for you; it would have fitted Greenblatt's interpretation excellently. Instead, Spenser substitutes a seductress who murders to serve her passion. In one image on the pure white ivory gates of the Bower of Bliss, Medea, fleeing with her lover Jason from her father, has killed her young brother Absyrtus and cut him into pieces, and now drops these behind her so as to deflect his and her parent. In another image Medea has sent the wedding-garment to her successor in Jason's love, Creusa, and this garment burns Creusa alive:

> And other where the snowy substaunce sprent
> With vermell, like the boyes bloud therein shed,
> A piteous spectacle did represent,
> And otherwhiles with gold besprinkeled;
> Yt seemd th'enchaunted flame, which did *Creüsa* wed.
> (II.xii.45)

So that the murderer (for the sake of her sexual primacy) of Mordant and his wife gets approximated in images of Medea murdering another male and another woman (for the sake of *her* sexual primacy). The obliqueness with which this is realized in Spenser's text is in tune with the obliqueness with which so much of the garden is shown to be a lie: most like nature, but a lying art.

(Incidentally, there is nothing any more innovatory—uniquely Elizabethan—about this true version of the story than about Greenblatt's mistaken one. Aside from Medea, consider Ishtar [3rd Millenium B.C.]: she lusts for Gilgamesh and offers herself to him. He berates her for her treatment of her former lovers. Enraged, she persuades a reluctant god to activate the Bull of Heaven. The bull kills hundreds of people. Ishtar indirectly causes the death of Gilgamesh's cherished friend, Enkidu.[17] Similar in telling respects to Acrasia's behavior.)

I have no time to consider how this fundamental exegetical error has skewed Greenblatt's discussion of love on the Isle of Venus, which I've elsewhere interpreted in terms of the art of heterosexual psychic comradeship, natural sex, and female freedom.[18] Let's turn, rather, to his notion of Spenser's fashioning—self-fashioning—of the modern consciousness, in Guyon's exploitation of the Bower as a surrogate for the modern Western World's response to the native cultures of the New World, and, more generally, for imperialism and exploitation of non-European populations. This, seeming to me the centerpiece of the book, is one of the first cases of what we now think of as characteristic of New Historicism: the juxtaposition of cultural items that at first glance appear to have no connection with each other.

Greenblatt picks out as common features of Guyon's actions and sixteenth-century colonial ventures, as described in their special literature, "the long, arduous voyage" to a paradisal "world of riches and menace," "accomplished with order, discipline, and constant labor," and "with an unspoken but powerful male bond." Greeblatt evokes the supposed dangers of immorality and idleness common to the New World and the Bower in more detail than I may take time for. Guyon's destruction of the Bower is related to "the way in which Europeans destroyed [American] Indian culture," "not despite those aspects of it that attracted them but in part at least because of them. The violence of the destruction was regenerative. . . . In tearing down what both appealed to them and sickened them, they strengthened their power to resist their dangerous longings, to repress antisocial impulses, to conquer the powerful desire for release. And the conquest of desire had the more power because it contained within itself a version of that which it destroyed: the power of Acrasia's sensuality to erase signs and upset temperate order is simultaneously attacked and imitated in Guyon's destruction of the exquisite Bower . . ." (183–4).

We now know that this will not quite do (and cf. Samson's destruction of a temple), because it is not mainly the sensuality but the vengefully homicidal aspect of Acrasia that impels Guyon to control her. Yet could we not perhaps salvage Greenblatt's politically correct picture of the white man's colonialism and imperialism by showing that the contemporary European literature on the New World described their inhabitants as savagely murderous as well as idle and lascivious? Indeed we could, and more, for we can say with complete political correctness that the very murderousness which Europeans so arrogantly condemned among the native Americans was blood and bone of European civilization itself and its detestable butchery in the service of barely distinguishable monotheisms.

But a more serious difficulty with the enterprise of associating Guyon's voyage to the Bower, and his behavior there, with colonial voyages and exploitation, is its arbitrariness. The text again resists the effort to associate the two things, although not so drastically as before.

Spenser had in mind two such trips to gardens of a seductress and her victim when he was creating the Bower of Bliss. Ariosto's enchantress Alcina, who had misled Ruggiero, had an island among the Canary Islands, which were admittedly an object of French and Spanish colonial conquest in the fifteenth and sixteenth centuries. The insuperable difficulty in trying to find a statement about colonialism here is that Alcina, while sufficiently idle and pleasure-ridden to suit the white man's idea of subject races, is only half the story: her sister Logistilla, to whom Ruggerio escapes, has another island across a channel from Alcina's, in the same archipelago, and Logistilla is all that her name suggests: as good as Alcina is bad. Besides, Ruggerio travels to and from the Canaries, not in a colonizing kind of boat, but by flying hippogriff, with whom he has no unspoken but powerful male bond. Tasso's garden of Armida is in the Fortunate Isles (which may be the Canaries) and the male saviors of Rinaldo, her victim, do indeed voyage there in a boat, in direct connection with Tasso's invocation of Columbus's voyage. The difficulty here is that when they arrive in the garden, what they find are not anything that can be equated with lesser breeds but only folks from back home. Armida is simply an adherent of the infidel's cause in keeping the Holy Land from the Crusaders; her lover simply belongs to the Christian side. She has set up housekeeping in a locale of exotic allure so as to achieve her ends. The two of them next meet in Jerusalem.

We are all agreed that the Odysseyan character of such voyages implies something about strangeness, or a move from the mimetic to an allegorized or codified realm, or at least to a *different* one, as in the case of Polia and Polifilo's voyage with Cupid to Cythera, which is as eventful as Guyon's to the Bower. But can such a voyage be made to convey something about European exploitation and colonization? Perhaps it can, but Acrasia's island seems to me an unlikely candidate because of the prevalence of two-way traffic; first Mordant gets there somehow; then his wife Amavia and their newborn child go there (and there goes Greenblatt's unspoken but powerful male bond), then Mordant, Amavia, and the boy travel back to the realm where Guyon and the Palmer can find them; then Verdant gets to the Bower somehow. Then, finally, Guyon, the Palmer, and the Boatman can strike out into the unknown, where Mordant, Amavia, child, and Verdant have already had their innings, not to speak of a large number of earlier lovers transformed into animals. Perhaps you can still visualize colonizing in this context. I find it difficult.

(Returning to one of the points with which I began, let me not refrain from the upbeat. We are devoted to maintaining English studies at a high level; we want to create a nurturing environment for future students of the Renaissance; some of us even view graduate programs as subject to capitalistic laws: expand or perish. The opposite position—what in 1990–91 might be called the Harvard syndrome—namely that we can afford to continue with literary studies as though it were 1958—is really a device of Franz Kafka's *Hungerkünstler,* the Hunger-Artist, although few at Harvard are going to starve: anyway, steps are supposedly being taken there. Yet the Anthony Graftons of this world are reminding us that as long as we only wing it, as long as we commit snatch-and-grab raids while playing the violin, we are living on already severely diminished capital. Some graduate students are ready for the onerous but not impossible combination of theory and philological knowledge which is properly our next step. That way lies self-respect. Truth is beautiful—truth of the interpretive community, with respect for textual resistances.)

I've tried to show that some recent efforts to establish the Renaissance as a period of uniquely evolutionary development of historical and individual consciousness exaggerate the true state of affairs. Briefly, in a very impressive book Thomas Greene tries to strengthen the idea of a *volte face* in historical perception between Medieval historical "metonymy" and Renaissance historical "metaphor." A more inclusive taxonomy would in my opinion emphasize an independence of spirit in both Medieval and Renaissance times. It might be hazarded that what was really entailed in the Italian fourteenth century through much of the European seventeenth century was a gradual, extremely uneven movement towards greater and greater historical precision, an extension from the generality of the moral and political in history to the specificity of the recovered image and word, and a narrowing down of the range of history—of usable pasts—from myth, mythic history, and any available chronicled datum or *récit,* to what was thought to be culturally and morally significant in the Latin, Greek, and Hebrew of what the humanists recognized as Antiquity—centrally, a few strategic centuries, flanked by less and less significant times. That, largely, remained the position until just before the arrival of Romanticism.

The degree to which something happened to the consciousness of an individual self in the Renaissance is a much harder nut to crack, in part because the terms of reference are vague. The difficulty is suggested by the existence of Joel Fineman's West Coast *Shakespeare's Perjured Eye: The Invention of Poetic Subjectivity in the Sonnets,*[19] according to which poetic self-consciousness in its most important sense arrives about 1600, and Paul Oppenheimer's East Coast *The Birth of the Modern Mind: Self, Consciousness, and the Invention of the Sonnet,*[20] according to which it arrives about 1220. "Self fashioning" is even vaguer. In common with Professor Lee Patterson, I see religious figures, and some political figures, of the Middle Ages in intensely individual terms, formulating new bases for living and agonizing over existential choices. Others (*Nota bene:* not many non-literary scholars) prefer to see a Medieval monolith. It is true that in the Renaissance a sizeable class of aristocrats and courtiers acquired a degree of learning and sensed the availability of many more roles than their predecessors had imagined. Yet I have already indicated how the English royal court made an early beginning on the fashioning of new roles for their central figure, but also for others, in order to validate or achieve power. Aside from the turn of an aristocracy, and those who aspired to their condition, towards humane learning and consequently greater self-consciousness, I fail to see significant change in the categories of consciousness with the coming of the "Renaissance" (as you and I insist on calling it).

University of Western Ontario

Notes

1. Jan de Vries, "Renaissance Cities," *Renaissance Quarterly* 42 (1989), 781.
2. "On the Margin: Postmodernism, Ironic History, and Medieval Studies," *Speculum* 65 (Jan. 1990), 87–108.
3. Jean François Lyotard, *La Condition Postmoderne: Rapport sur le Savoir* (Paris: Edi ions de Minuit, 1979), 63, 98–108. This is translated as *The Post-Modern Condition. . .* (Manchester, 1984).

4. *The Tremulous Private Body: Essays on Subjection* (London and New York: Methuen, 1984), 155–58 (quoted by Patterson, p. 97).

5. New Haven and London: Yale University Press, 1982.

6. The edition used here (the only satisfactory one): Francesco Colonna. *Hypnerotomachia Poliphili,* critical edition of Giovanni Pozzi and Lucia A. Ciapponi (2 vols, Padua: Antenore, 1964; reissued in 1980, in a smaller format and with corrections and a bibliographical update). The 1883 French translation by Claudius Popelin reproduces the woodcuts of the original, sixteenth century French translation. It is usable but contains many mistakes. My treatment of the *Polifilo* in this paper will be much extended in an article in *Word and Image:* "Contemporizing Antiquity: the *Hypnerotomachia* and Its Afterlife in France," by A. Kent Hieatt and Anne Lake Prescott.

7. "The Exile's Defense: Du Bellay's *Deffence et Illustration de la Langue Françoyse,*" *PMLA* 93 (1978), 275–89.

8. The points concerning Henry that follow depend largely on Roy Strong, *Henry Prince of Wales, and England's Lost Renaissance* (London: Themes and Hudson, 1986).

9. "The Passing of Arthur in Malory, Spenser, and Shakespeare . . . ," in *The Passing of Arthur: New Essays in Arthurian Tradition,* ed. Christopher Baswell and Wm. Sharpe (New York: Garland, 1988), 173ff. For a summary of this argument as presented in another paper, and for Thomas P. Roche, Jr.'s response, see *Spenser Studies VIII,* 335ff (in the "Forum" section, not itemized in the Table of Contents). For my answer see "Forum" in *Spenser Studies IX.*

10. This can be seen, among other texts, in Geoffrey of Monmouth, *Historia Regum Brittaniae,* and Wace, *Roman de Brut.* See now James Noble, "Patronage, Politics, and the Figure of Arthur in Geoffrey of Monmouth, Wace, and Layamon," in *The Arthurian Yearbook,* 2 (1991), 159–78.

11. All quotation and citations of Spenser here depend on the Variorum edition of his *Works. Complaints* is in Vol. II.

12. (Chicago: University of Chicago Press, 1980).

13. Jehan des Preis, dit d'Outremeuse, *Ly Myreur des histors, chronique . . . ,* ed. Stanislas Bormans (Brussels: M. Hayez, 1864–87), II, 242–45.

14. *The Limits of Interpretation* (Bloomington: University of Indiana Press, 1990), 40–42, 149, 213–14.

15. Not forgetting, of course, how wary we must be of assuming "that language functions according to principles which are those, or which are like those, of the phenomenal world." See his *Resistance to Theory* (Minneapolis: University of Minnesota Press, 1986), 11.

16. Some of what follows is traced in my *Chaucer, Spenser, Milton* (Montreal, McGill-Queens University Press, 1975), 169–214.

17. *The Epic of Gilgamesh: An English Version with an Introduction by N.K. Sanders* (Harmondsworth: Penguin Books, revised 1964), 83–93.

18. *Chaucer, Spenser, Milton,* 75–145. I now feel that I exaggerated the freedom, which goes only a litle further than freedom in choice of a mate.

19. (Berkeley: University of California Press, 1986).

20. (New York: Columbia University Press, 1989).

ANTHONY DI MATTEO

Spenser's Venus-Virgo: The Poetics and Interpretive History of a Dissembling Figure

> O—quam te memorem, virgo? namque haud tibi voltus Mortalis, nec vox hominem sonat; o dea certe!
>
> —*Aeneid,* Book 1, lines 327–28

> It is said I am not divine.
>
> —Queen Elizabeth I, Speech on "Marriage and Succession"

ALLUSIONS TO THE VIRGILIAN symbolism of Venus-Virgo in *The Shepheardes Calender* and *The Faerie Queene* comprise an increasingly complex inquiry into the relation of poetry, sexuality, and politics. To identify the intertextual play of these allusions requires knowledge of a specialized code of Renaissance literary theory, of what Sir Thomas Browne loosely calls "the Philosophy of Hermes," principally, an interpretive practice of reading *sub integumento* for hidden undermeanings. Browne pointedly describes this philosophy as a "stenography," a symbolic code in "short Characters."[1] As exercised on the *corpus* of Virgil, this exegetical shorthand developed a complex network of symbols, part of which we may conveniently call "Venus-Virgo," a symbolic yoking of opposed images that, in E. H. Gombrich's terms, performs in Renaissance art an "expressive evocation of a concept."[2] This "goddess" born of a hyphen appears through Spenserian allusions like a Socratic "provocative," a construct of the mind which brings its opposite with it, awaking the intelligence.[3] As W. J. T. Mitchell has described, such imagery encourages contradictory readings and perceptions that go against the grain of conventional attitudes regarding what and how things mean.[4]

In the works of Spenser, I argue, The Venus-Virgo network of meanings provokes critical reflection upon and tolerance of unresolvable ambiguities. It is a poetic way of envisioning love prominently directed at the Queen, instigating awareness of conflicting ways of seeing, opening a range of alternate paths for vision.

As part of a maturing poetic career, Spenser's repeated allusions to "Venus-Virgo" imply a sharp criticism, even a scrambling of the interpretive code that evolved in Virgilian criticism of Venus. This criticism represented her as an archetypal image of the ambiguity of things (of destiny, poetry, love, and human knowledge). Venus as Virgo is a dark, dissembling figure allegorically associated with the effect of embodiment upon the soul. The fact that the Spenserian use of the symbol is addressed conspicuously to Elizabeth needs to be critically explored against this critical background.

Spenserian poetry performs an ironic double function, both forwarding and less obviously derailing Virgilian symbology. Current readings of Spenser tend to overlook the subversive function, viewing the poetry as serenely uncritical of Elizabethan ideology.[5] We are admittedly well advised by John N. King not "to draw sharp distinctions among political, pietistic and aesthetic endeavors" in the Tudor period.[6] Yet poetry "clowdily enwrapped in Allegoricall devises," in the words of the "Letter to Ralegh," is arguably a method for creating multiple meanings with conflicting allegiances that play against each other.[7] True, as the frontispiece of Henry Howard's *Regina Fortunata* makes clear (see figure 1 and note 60), Venus-Virgo identifies a code name or semantic charter for the imperial cult of Elizabeth that Spenser is helping to shape. In Spenser's poetry, however, it is also a conflict-ridden signal of the poetry's multiple bodies of meanings generated by contrasting loyalties to political and imaginary dimensions of writing Elizabethan poetry.

As part of an interpretive code for reading Virgil, Venus-Virgo acquired a wide range of meanings—from Venus disguised as nymph of Diana in Virgil (Book 1), to Venus versus Diana and heavenly love versus earthly love oppositions. These divergent but tightly interwoven meanings develop in what has been called Virgilian "mystical" commentary and suggest a sustained exegetical project to control or limit the play of possible interpretations.[8] My chief focus will be Spenser's parodic use of this symbolic code that had evolved in mystical commentary responding to the sole passage in Virgil (Book 1 of the *Aeneid*) where Venus appears like Diana. I do not suggest that Spenser would

FIGURE I. Elizabeth I as Venus-Virgo, from Henry Howard, *Regina Fortunata* (Egerton Manuscript 944, fol. lv), ca. 1576. By permission of the British Library.

have restricted himself to this commentary as he shaped his own artistic program to adapt "antique praises unto present persons fit" (III. Pr.3), but he does display a striking indebtedness to Virgil regarding Venus-Virgo. Different techniques of allusion to the Virgilian passage imply that the poet is deliberately restaging the encounter of Aeneas and Venus for assorted rhetorical purposes. Venus-Virgo serves as Thenot and Hobinoll's emblem of "Elisa" in the April eclogue and as apostrophe and description in *The Faerie Queene* which depict a servant, squire, and witch echoing Aeneas' words to his disguised mother. These multiple allusions exhibit the intratextual patterning that A. Leigh DeNeef calls a "basic strategy of Spenser's poetry, suggesting "inadequacies in the reader's understanding of previous passages."[9] When directed towards readings of Virgil, this revisioning process involves a transvaluation defined by Barbara Bono as "an artistic act of historical self-consciousness that at once acknowledges the perceived values of the antecedent text and transforms them to serve the uses of the present."[10] Part of this transformed perceptual frame is the Virgilian commentaries that Merritt Hughes conjectured in 1929 "hovered on the fringe" of the poet's consciousness "whenever he brought Belphoebe into his story."[11] Probing this awareness will show a maturing complexity in the implied criticism of the commentaries especially activated by Spenser's portrayal of numerous female personages.

I. Venus-Virgo and the Commentaries

At the fount of allegorical reading of Virgil is Servius whose mystical approach holds that Virgil, like Homer, hid within his poetry multiple meanings of astrological, civic, and religious kinds. He introduces the word polysemy into critical language ("polysemus sermo est") to describe the poetry's mixed purposes of praise, prayer, and song.[12] His commentary on the *Aeneid,* which never uses the word allegory, is eclectic, not following "any single system or plan."[13]

Servius establishes a range of different meanings for Venus-Virgo endlessly explored in future commentaries. He asserts that Virgil signifies Aeneas' horoscope through the apparition of Venus disguised as a nymph of Diana encountered along a sylvan path leading to Carthage. The hero was born when the planet Venus voyaged through the constellation Virgo, an astral conjunction creating sympathy in women for men ruled by this sign, a reading that obviously extenuates Dido's star-crossed attraction to Aeneas. That the disguised goddess appears in the middle of a forested path receives complex cosmological reading. Because the Latin word for wood, *sylva,* derives from the Greek word for matter, *hyle,* Servius understands the woods to represent "the mass of elements from which all things are created."[14] The veiled apparition in the wood symbolizes the mystery of embodiment, of how spirit inhabits matter. It does so, to make explicit the master analogy of Servian exegesis, in the same way that multiple meanings inhabit or have been breathed into the speech (*sermo*) of Virgil's poetry. The goddess's concealment represents the difficulty that mortals have discerning their origin in the cosmos and that readers have comprehending the veiled meanings of Virgil's poetry. Her appearance on a sylvan trail intimates that all things within the material world follow a secret course of destiny.

Servius' mystical implications strongly influence subsequent reading that imposes a system upon the poem, attempting to unfold the mystery of the wood and the text.[15] Aeneas' story comes to be seen as paradigmatic of the courage of everyman's life. Fulgentius' fifth-century dialogue *The Exposition of the Content of Virgil* asserts that the story of Aeneas depicts, in the words Fulgentius gives to Virgil, "the complete state of man: first, his nature; second, what he learns; third, his attaining to prosperity."[16] Within this comprehensive reading that becomes commonplace in the poem's interpretation, the first book depicts the first age of human life, infancy.[17] The poem begins with a shipwreck to signify "the dangers of birth." Of the Venus-Virgo episode, Fulgentius writes, "As soon as Aeneas touches land, he sees his mother, Venus, but does not recognize her, indicating complete infancy in that it is given to newborn babes to see their mother from birth, but the ability to recognize her is not immediately added."[18]

The commentary attributed to Donatus posits moral meanings of the apparition. In the encounter with Venus of the wood, Aeneas exhibits a perfection of virtue: "Behold how in this passage Aeneas' virtues both of body and mind are enumerated." Specifically displayed is the chastity of Aeneas who does not respond to what in lesser men would have been an "incitement to lust." Despite the unknown maiden's beauty, attractive dress, loosened hair, exposed legs, and her loneliness in a desolate place, Aeneas responds respectfully. The episode shows that Aeneas has already been chastened by a cruel, pursuing destiny. Donatus writes, "So dire a sequence of evil events promotes chastity in men and recalls even the lustful from the pleasures of Venus."[19]

These three post-classical readings of Venus-Virgo obviously diverge, stimulating in *bonum* or *in malum* interpretations (to use Pierre Bersuire's term for the homiletic alternatives available for Christian moralizers of Ovid). The disguised apparition of the goddess reveals Aeneas' already acquired virtue or signifies the stultifying effects upon the soul caused by its entry into the body. Provocatively, the apparition serves as an analogy for the text itself that conceals meaning to make the pursuit of truth more valued. Further expanding the episode's range of senses is Servius' cosmic understanding of the sylvan path as a symbol of destiny, the great *inter drum* or "hard journey" Aeneas must undertake to the promised land of Italy. This hard road of destiny stands for "the disequilibrium between gods and men."[20] From the perspective of destiny and human inability to comprehend its "dark path," the disguise of Venus intimates an epistemology that disallows direct knowledge.[21] In the scholastic terms of Dante's *Purgatorio,* we never know *propter quid,* which is godly wisdom, but only *quid,* never the cause but only the effect.

This oblique knowing characterizes the way poetry is read in the next systematic Virgilian exposition after Fulgentius, Bernardus of Silvester's twelfth-century *Commentum.* The work's modern translators Earl Schreiber and Thomas Maresca describe it as perhaps "the most important literary critical document of the Middle Ages for what it tells us about poetry and the way it was read."[22] Adhering to Macrobius' description of Virgil in the *Saturnalia,* Bernardus in his preface calls Virgil *poeta et philosophus.*"[23] The *Aeneid* accordingly exhibits a double quality—its "fabulous" narration functions as a covering (*integumentum* or *involucrum*) for profound philosophical truths, a dissembling poetic style associated with Orpheus.[24] Like Servius on the *Aeneid,* Bernardus never once mentions the word allegory, replacing it with its synonyms "*in integumento*" or "*mystice*" whenever he reads beneath the surface of the poem. His preface states the poem's method and theme: "The mode of writing is this: under a cover he [Virgil] describes what the human spirit does and suffers when temporarily placed in the human body."[25] Accordingly, Aeneas' name suggests *ennos demas* or *habitator corporis,* "inhabitor of the body," since *demas* signifies *vinculum* or "chain," and the body is the prison of the soul. This "etymological play" first found in Bernardus will influence Renaissance Platonist reading[26]

Despite the poem's alleged indirectness, Bernardus' "Christianizing" program is aggressive and clear. He formulated in his commentary "the archetypal pattern of Chartrian allegory: the theme of what may be called an intellectual pilgrimage, the travail of the spirit attempting to rise above its earthly situation through an understanding of *naturalia* and attain a vision of truth."[27] In a reading central to his work, Bernardus glosses Aeneas' request of the Cumaean sybil to teach him the way ("doceas iter et sacra ostia pandas," Book 6, 109) as "the ascent through knowledge of creatures" to the Creator (understood as Anchises *sub integumento*).

But Venus notably is a strong point of figural resistance to Bernardus' transcendent Christian reading. He feels compelled to split her in two, using terminology that will be crucial to Spenserian poetry. The Venus encountered in the woods can be associated with *mundana musica,* "that is, the even proportion of worldly things, which some call Astrea, and other call natural justice." This sublime aspect of Venus "subsists in the elements, in the stars, in the seasons, in living beings" and is antithetical to the petulant goddess, the wife of Vulcan, mother of Cupid, who represents "carnal concupiscence."[28] Yet we can see that Venus of the wood, as she will prove to Petrarch in the *Secretum,* is a great source of interpretive anxiety. Bernardus doe not explicitly correlate this Venus with *mundana musica* or Astraea, making no clear statement about which Venus she is.

There are two reasons for this anxious silence. The Venus who appears to Aeneas shortly after the wood episode sends Cupid disguised as Ascanius to play havoc with Dido's emotions (Bernardus understands Dido as "libido"). The proximity of these "antithetical" Venuses tend to erase the Platonic distinction Bernardus wants readers to enforce between harmonious Venus (Aeneas' mother) and carnal Venus (Cupid's).

The second reason threatens even more his attempt to baptize the text, attacking the core argument of his reading. In his elaborate conversion of Book 6 to Christian meanings, Bernardus identifies four kinds of infernal descents: natural, virtuous, sinful, and artificial or necromantic. The second and fourth descents he assigns to Aeneas' underworld journey. However, the natural descent clearly pertains to the Venus-Virgo episode since Bernardus, like Fulgentius, reads the opening episode of Book 1 as an elaborate integument for the incarnation of the soul: "The natural descent is the birth of man, for by it the soul naturally enters the fallen region and thus descends to the underworld and recedes from its divinity and gradually declines into vice and assents to pleasures of the flesh; this is common to everybody."[29] This contemptuous reading of the first descent conflicts with Bernardus' "integumentive" reading of Aeneas' parentage: "Aeneas is the son of Venus and Anchises since the human spirit comes from God through concord to live in the human body."[30]

The problem is the reluctance to give the *materia/mater* complex of meanings the moral valence of concord. The fact that Aeneas' comrade Achates, whose name means "study," accompanied Aeneas during his underworld descent but not at Dido's palace encourages Bernardus to understand that "study" accompanies "the human spirit" (Aeneas) in its pursuit of "wisdom" (the sybil) on its spiritual journey to "the Creator" (Anchises) but not in the soul's dalliance with "libido" (Dido).[31] This is the major allegory Bernardus finds in the poem, and he clearly does not want it sullied by the contrary indications of heavenly Venus' presence together with that of Achates'("study's") at the moment of "natural" descent in the first book. These presences would not harmonize with the negative "common" reading Bernardus gives to natural descent, the declination of the soul away from God into the carceral body. Bernardus attempts to suppress the problem in Book 1 by giving general remarks about "multivocationes" when we clearly expect his specific commentary on Book 1 to continue. These remarks constitute in fact the major announcement of Bernardus' interpretive practice.

Ironically, given this context, his theory of multiple meanings appears primarily motivated by a desire to split Venus in two, the divided symbol of the "twin" desires of longing for God and the temptations of the flesh. If the task of the interpreter of poetry is to "break the code" of the poet as Bernardus strongly implies and Coluccio Salutati will directly state, Venus-Virgo is an instance where the code cannot be unravelled.[32] In the evolving history of interpretation, her associations with *hyle* or primordial matter, with beginnings, human birth and the incarnation of the soul, position her at a limit of explication (the passage provoked Servius into exclaiming, "all things within the material world follow a secret course of destiny"). Venus as Virgo is a contradictory identity, like a stationary point of turbulence or a darkened radiance that, as is the case with Aeneas, can be addressed only in retrospect and not fully grasped. Recognizing her only upon her fleeing, Aeneas cries out,

> Quid natum totiens, crudelis tu quoque, falsis
> Ludis imaginibus? cur dextrae iungere dextram
> Non datur ac veras audire et reddere voces?

[What, again proven cruel, deceiving your own son
With false images? Why can't we join hands,
Hear and speak true words?]

(Book 1, 407–9)

In this, the sole passage where Venus appears in disguise to Aeneas, the equivocal appearance of Venus ("falsis ludis imaginibus") offers itself as a symbol of the poet's technique in writing *sub integumento* (under a cover), echoing, as this passage does, the description of the sibyl's discourse, "obscuris vera involvens" (Book 6, 100), the other "virgin" who sends Aeneas through the dark wood to a destined path.[33]

Early humanist allusions to Venus-Virgo acknowledge and often suppress these darkly speculative qualities of Venus-Virgo that seem to mirror the effects of the poem itself.

In the *Secretum,* Petrarch deploys Venus-Virgo to represent the dangerous ambiguities of symbolic reading. As in the *Aeneid,* she stands at the head of the work and initiates the central conflict when Patrarch's own persona Francesco mistakenly addresses Truth as Venus-Virgo. Contemplating "our coming into this world and what will follow our departure," the melancholic Francesco suddenly sees "a fair Virgin" break in upon his solitude.[34] Not knowing what to call her, he uses Aeneas' words to his disguised mother, "what name to call thee by, O Virgin fair?" The "Virgin," however, objects: she is that "Lady whom you have depicted in your own poem *Africa,*" and Francesco then calls her "Truth," who, like Dame Philosophy to Boethius, has come to Francesco to teach him to contemplate God. That Francesco first addresses her with Aeneas' words indicates his distraught state of mind too preoccupied with the glory and love of Laura and the laurel, which to Augustine, Francesco's interlocutor who accompanies Truth, are only fortune and worldly delights. Francesco will later tell Augustine that he has long been aware of how "carnal passion" distracts the mind from contemplation. Even where this warning against passion "lurks in the forests of other writers," Francesco has acknowledged its pertinence to his life. The writer of such hidden messages in a forest is specifically Virgil who showed that wherever Aeneas was accompanied by Venus, "he had understanding only for things of the earth." "Commerce with Venus takes away the vision of the Divine."[36] Augustine admires his ability to perceive the truth "shining out through the crevices" of the poets' thoughts, but again reproves Francesco.[37] His love for Laura shows "the flames of desire" are still too strong. Again the lines from the Venus-Virgo episode are quoted to indicate the wrong state of mind—"were she a queen, a saint," chides Augustine, "'A very goddess, or to Apollo's self/His own sister, or a mother of the nymphs,' yet all her excellence will in nowise excuse your error."[38]

Repeatedly, the Venus-Virgo passage indicates the blindness of Francesco whose soul is jeopardized by his lover's habit of seeing the divine in terms of earthly beauty.[39] This habit detours vision of the truth and is notably not undone by the end of the third book despite the strong remedies Augustine has tried. Petrarch never went on to complete his plan of writing three more books describing the peace of mind Francesco allegedly attained.

The Venus of the *Aeneid* likewise proved problematic to Boccaccio, whose interpretation also reads her from a negative, "misleading" perspective albeit far less ambiguously than Petrarch. In his chapter of the *Genealogiae* given to Aeneas, Boccaccio dwells on the human culpability of Aeneas, whose concupiscible inclinations drive him through the sea, that is, lustful passions represented by Venus (a metaphor for sea spume). By having "a Venus" appear to Aeneas, Virgil is representing Aeneas' longing for sexual satiety. She does not appear to him in Italy, asserts Boccaccio, indicating that Aeneas in Italy has his desire quenched by Lavinia—he has no more need for Venereal apparitions.[40] Significantly, Boccaccio's attempt to turn Venus into a projection of Aeneas' lustful mind leads to a misreading, the suppression of Venus' Book Eight appearance in Italy to Aeneas in her immediately recognizable godly form ("seque obtulit ultro," *Aeneid,* 8. 611) when she gives her son Vulcan's gifts, the famous shield and arms. Boccaccio even "cites" Servius as agreeing that Venus never appears to Aeneas in Italy.

From material darkness (Servius), implied source of temptation (Donatus), the mysteries of birth (Fulgentius), to silently but strongly implied conflicted reading (Bernardus), consciously ambiguous "misnaming" of truth (Petrarch), and now clear misreading, the Venus of the *Aeneid* has divided and troubled its interpreters. Most importantly, interpretation haltingly evolves from reading her Book 1 appearance symbolically to an inquiry into what symbolic reading is.

High Renaissance reading of the Virgilian Venus (Venuses?) confidently believes in the powers of symbolic interpretation even as its practice raised more and more questions about the nature of a symbol.

Cristoforo Landino's allegorical reading of the *Aeneid,* Books 3 and 4 of the *Camaldulensian Dialogues* first published in 1480, understands the epic as tracing the progress of the ideal man from the active to the contemplative life, that is, from immersion in the senses (represented by Aeneas' life in Troy) to victory over the body and sin through the attainment of *vera sapientia* (represented by Italy). Departing from Fulgentius and Bernardus' "everyman" reading, Landino sees Aeneas as the exceptional man.[41] Michael Murrin summarizes Landino's interpretation: "Aeneas' many voyages, his battles, his love, all figure forth an inward reality, the psychic drama of a man's growth out of this world."[42] The Venus-as-Diana figure, however, only ambiguously fits into this transcendental progress and, as it did Bernardus, prompts Landino to launch a defense of his interpretive method.

Throughout the dialogue, Landino's spokesman Leon Battista Alberti will be concerned with only allegorical reading "which happens when we do not comprehend merely what the words signify, but something also hidden under a figure."[43] In contrast to Alberti who seems to have complete access to the poem's submerged meanings, Lorenzo de'Medici, Alberti's main questioner, is puzzled by contradictions. He asks why is Aeneas praised for following Venus but Paris condemned?[44] Of course, Alberti resorts to Plato's doctrine to "resolve" the problem—there are two Venuses, heavenly (Aphrodite Anadyomene) and earthly (Aphrodite Pandemos). Yet Venus-Virgo is a perplexingly transitional or median figure between these antithetical versions. As the darkest manifestation of heavenly Venus, she both puzzles and guides, frustrates and inspires.

Like Bernardus, Landino presents a long excursus before elucidating the meaning of the disguised goddess. *Silva* or "matter" occupies the lowest place in the cosmic chain of being whose origin is the essence of God.[45] Accordingly, as Erwin Panofsky has shown drawing upon Pico, Ficino, and Landino's cosmology, "the realm of matter" is understood ambiguously by the Florentine Neoplatonists, both a cause of celebration, since the spiritual is present even in that which is most removed from deity, and of lament, matter being the prison in which celestial form is hopelessly and unrecognizably detained. Understood morally, matter cannot be in itself evil since it is part of the golden chain of existence and yet, because of its negative position in the cosmos, it "can, in fact, must, cause evil, for its 'nothingness' acts as a passive resistance to the *summum bonum*."[46]

Venus-Virgo symbolizes this contradictory doubleness of matter:

> Matter impedes and disturbs our minds; in fact, all vice flows from it. For it is inexperience, or ignorance, that gives birth to

> vice; but ignorance itself comes from the density and darkness of the body, according to Plato . . . Is it thinking of this kind which makes Virgil introduce Venus in mortal form and induces him to place her in the woods, since everything we do is immersed in matter; after all, he who wants to be ruler of the republic is inflamed with a love of human affairs, which are in no sense removed from the body and which therefore are involved with various errors. Nor does Virgil disguise her as a huntress without reason, for he who will go correctly about the business of getting food for his people must set himself the task of chasing down the beasts.[47]

The disguised Venus stands for "a love of these things corporeal and for the most part immersed in matter."[48] Only at the end of her speech does Venus reveal herself as goddess and mother to indicate that we are led to the divine only after we have "cultivated the honest and the upright in civic life," the earthly images of things divine.[49] But how can Aeneas be "inflamed with a love of human affairs . . . involved with various errors" and through this very engagement led to a vision of the divine? Landino does not have Lorenzo ask this question because consideration of it would work against the vulgar versus heavenly distinction of the two Venuses. The apparition in the wood will not be tidied up.

The last commentary we review is that of Jodocus Badius Ascensius (Josse Bade van Assche), Flemish poet, scholar, and famous printer whose press in Paris issued some of the first printed editions of classical literature. In his commentary on the disguised apparition of Venus in the wood, Ascensius approvingly cites Donatus on how this episode demonstrates the chastity of Aeneas. He adds that men must indeed interrogate Venus who can mislead imprudent men "not only by appearances but by words."[50] While this comment stems from Donatus, it concurs with the moral emphases of a writer who satirized the vices of women in his poem *Navicula Stultarum Mulierum.* Venus-Virgo represents a seductive reality beyond male control which must be scrutinized in word and deed lest she prove a rosy path to hell. Paradoxically, she is not only a confirmation of Aeneas' moral frame of mind, but an obstacle in his quest of the golden bough, which for Ascensius can represent wisdom or virtue.[51] That Aeneas encounters his mother in the middle of the sylvan path is another way of saying that the planet Venus was in the middle of Aeneas' horoscope and presided over the heavens at the time of his birth. Thus, calling Aeneas the son of Venus is only a way of saying that fortune at the time of his birth favored Aeneas, Anchises' illegitimate issue, a child of common Venerean passion. That he meets his mother on a sylvan path has the force of a pun on Venus' name—Aeneas came upon her ("obvenisse") in the middle of the forest. Beside having astrological significance, Virgil intimates philosophical truth because "silva" signifies "hyle" (Ascensius obviously drawing on Servius) which is the confused mass of all things and is "derived from prime matter." "The forest signifies to us the diversity of influences which make it so difficult to come upon the golden bough."[52] Like Bernardus, Ascensius notes that the golden bough is hidden in a forest because wisdom and virtue are hidden in our concerns for the world and therefore are difficult to come upon unless "the doves of Venus" lead us there, that is to say, "the grace of the Holy Spirit" or "desire" ("cupiditas") translated to mean virtuous "diligence."[53]

The commentaries clearly establish a conflicting range of meanings: Venus-Virgo is impossibly both an apparition that disturbs or interrupts Aeneas' course and a projection of Aeneas' internal qualities that confirms his leadership abilities (he is an example of "vir perfectissimus," to cite Julius Caesar Scaliger's description of Aeneas in his *Poetices*). She represent both immersion in the body, the vehicle through which the soul takes on the prison of matter ("hyle"), and the sign of favor, of grace, which redeems humanity.

Of foremost importance is how meditation on Venus-Virgo in the wood evolves, especially in the *Secretum,* into a contemplation upon the diverse meanings of poetry itself. Reflecting upon the analogy between allegorical reading of poetry and multiple understandings of desire (heavenly and lustful) undermines Christian-Platonic reading which attempts to see the poem as a paradigm of salvation. Bernardus outrightly cautions readers of Virgil against uniformity of approach when he comes to reading (actually avoiding reading) Venus as Virgo: "The diverse reflexivity of poetic veils and multiple designations in all mystical works must be respected because in all of them no one truth (single way of reading) will be feasible."[54] Of this unruly multivalence, Landino would say with Plato, "the symbol is the imperfect reflection of the higher reality which arouses our longing for perfection."[55] Hence, symbols ultimately silence the volubility of discourse. But the longing to pin down and exhaust the protean implications of the text tends to outstrip the very awareness that cautions against doing so. In the *Secretum,* this interminable will-to-know is a consciously represented problem. Petrarch has the figure Augustine warn Francesco: "Though desire is only one word, it involves countless things."[56] As Victoria Kahn has argued, Petrarch's dialogue displays a troubling awareness that desire undermines reason and right reading. By misnaming Truth Venus-Virgo, Petrarch stresses "the willfulness or eroticism of interpretation."[57] This waywardness of the human mind that has the ability of free choice brings about Francesco's enslavement by the two *nodi* Augustine identifies as *amor et gloria.* Thomas P. Roche, Jr. identifies this problem of the use or abuse of what is in itself good as central to the *Canzoniere* and the "Letter to Posterity" as well as the *Secretum:* while *caritas* and *cupiditas* are "in reality one," man in his fallen condition, "given a choice between a higher and lower form of love, upsets the hierarchy of love by choosing the lower, cupidinous love in the form of enjoyment."[58]

In view of the interpretive history of Venus-Virgo, it is no wonder that Petrarch selected this figure to represent the ambiguous effect of the will upon reading—like the *Secretum* itself, she "reflects two contrasting positions: an hedonistic *amor sui* [love of the prison of the flesh] and a *conversio ad Deum.*"[59]

II. Spenser and the Commentaries

Approaching Spenser's allusions from the perspective of Virgilian commentary complicates the regal associations of Venus-Virgo with the queen established by the scholarship of John King, Frances Yates, and Roy Strong.[60] Venus-Virgo as an imperial symbol, clearly in the ascendant in the April eclogue, is a major frame of reference that increasingly falls away in the allusions to her in *The Faerie Queene*, allowing other philosophically dark and morally divided aspects critical of the commentary on Venus to come into play.

In the April eclogue, Aeneas' address to Venus in disguise serves as the verse for the emblem concluding the poem. The emblem is part of an elaborate iconographic program for praising Queen Elizabeth. Within the context of the cult of the queen, the Venus-Virgo emblem can be linked to the maiden figure of imperial reform, the virgin Astraea. Astraea, already established in Virgilian commentary (Bernardus) as another name for the good Venus, is bluntly described by Yates as "the key to the complex symbolism used of this queen."[61] This complexity stems from the way the symbolism generates political, Christian, and poetic or Orphic readings.

Recent critics have read "Aprill" for Christian undermeanings. Exploring the Queen's dynastic cult, L. Staley Johnson and King have shown how the imagery of late Tudor Reformation politics frequently compared Elizabeth to King David and King Solomon, the main branches of the genealogical tree of Jesse leading to Christ. As the head of the Reformed Church of England, the Queen (like her father Henry VIII) was compared to David, establishing the right prayers for the true worship of God, and to Solomon, for she was seen as responsible for building the true temple of God. Johnson convincingly argues that the April eclogue "resonates with associations that reflect the ideals of English Protestantism in the early period of her reign when speakers addressed Elizabeth as an English Solomon whose virtue and wisdom had created a pastoral paradise."[62] If, as King argues, "the fundamental issue of late Tudor iconography is the constitutional problem of the capacity of a queen to govern," clearly such Biblical imagery helped allay distress about the rightness of a woman to rule over Church and State.[63]

Colin's hymn to Eliza stages a like pacification of anxiety, culminating with the epiphany of Venus-Virgo in the "embleme." Peace is described within the vision of Eliza as "for a Princess bene principall" ("Aprill," 126). The Venus-Virgo emblem connects with the motif of peace since Venus is traditionally the pacifier or bridler of Mars, who, as Lucretius describes in his prayer for peace, is "wholly vanquished by the ever-living wound of love."

Within this political program, the emblem has prophetic meanings. It engages the interpretive history of the Virgilian passage, symbolizing an implied apprehension of divine providence that strikes Thenot and Hobbinol dumb with admiration. Through its interconnections with Elizabeth as Astraea and the Virgin Mary (this latter linkage overtly posited by the Howard frontispiece as part of the range of associations current in the Elizabethan court), the emblem symbolizes crucial turning points in the spiritual pilgrimage of humanity on earth—the founding of Rome, the establishment of the *pax romana* by Augustus at the time of the birth of Christ allowing for the spread of Christianity, and the reign of Eliza bringing about the reestablishment of a true Church and the envisioned return of the golden age. If we take into account Dante's unorthodox or non-Augustinian chronology, Venus-Virgo even more directly connects with the incarnation of Christ. According to *The Convivio,* "It was all at the same point of time wherein David was born and Rome was born, that is to say Aeneas came into Italy from Troy, which was the origin of the most noble city of Rome."[64]

Associated with Astraea, the "virgo" of Virgil's Fourth Eclogue who would return to earth with the golden age of Augustan empire and who is routinely interpreted as a proleptic figure for the virgin Mary in Christian commentary on Virgil, Elizabeth as Venus-Virgo is a prophetic image for the coming of a new imperial city, replacing Rome as the true seat of Church and imperial empire.[65]

But the poetic context of the allusion to Virgil complexly supplements the symbolism of Elizabeth as bringer of justice and peace. Not formally part of Colin's hymn, the emblem describes Hobbinol and Thenot's reactions to the poem's recitation. This usage has crucial importance for understanding the broad resonance of the emblem's meanings, pertaining to the implied vatic function of poetry.

As Thomas Cain has argued regarding "Aprill," this function can be described as the poet's "Orphic" mission to civilize humanity through his rapturous song.[66] When the shepherds at the end of "Aprill" suddenly speak in heroic verse, it indicates the elevating effect of Colin's hymn and can be viewed as evidence of the poet's ability to draw men from their rustic or "uncouth" ways by teaching right living. This taming effect is associated especially with Orphic poetry as famously described by Horace in *The Art of Poetry:*

> Silvestris homines sacer interpresque deorum
> Caedibus et victu foedo deterruit Orpheus.
> (391–92)

As we have seen, the Venus-Virgo passage in the Virgilian commentaries is considered paradigmatic of an Orphic style of writing *sub integumento.* In that most influential of all Renaissance handbooks for fashioning a gentleman, *The Courtier,* this style of expression is associated with the "salutary deception" or "veil of pleasure" the ideal courtier must use to guide his prince on the "austere path of virtue."[67] Spenser's use of Venus-Virgo creates a similar deceptive veil of pleasure. As a description of the hymn's effect on readers, it indirectly but strongly indicates the authoritative Orphic role of the poet to instruct his sovereign—Cain observes, "only when he articulates her praise can she discern her ideal form and possess enduring fame."[68]

Further pursuing Orphic associations of "Aprill's" imagery, we recall how in mystical commentary on Virgil, Venus-Virgo symbolizes "natural" descent into the underworld or the descent of the soul into the body and the obfuscating effect this "incarceration" in matter has on the mind. Bernardus contrasted this "common" descent from Orpheus' descent through virtue which involves coming to mundane matters to contemplate them and thereby gain knowledge of God. Colin's love for Rosalind, stressed at the beginning and end of the eclogue and thus "framing" the hymn to Eliza, threatens any such poetic mission. The frame complicates the majestic aspects of Venus in the emblem through its radical difference from them. Analyzing the design of "Aprill," Patrick Cullen characterizes the conflict in terms of the frame's "iron age" and the lay's "golden age" perspectives on love, "one of the central contrasts, that between Colin and Eliza, upon which the eclogue has been structured."[69] Rather than the Venus of the hymn's peace and graceful harmony, the Venus that reigns over Colin's life can be aligned with what E. K. in the "Dedicatory Epistle" describes as "the common Labyrinth of Love" in which Colin in "his unstayed youth had long wandered." Colin has not come to fruitful terms with the soul's embodiment in the flesh and the desires this state generates, mortal conditions traditionally symbolized, as we have seen, by Venus-Virgo.

From the perspective of Colin's tragic love, the emblem's chastened Venus seems to break out of her virginal containment, endangering the poet's attempt to erect a lasting monument. Unlike the "Lauretta" of E. K.'s notes, "the divine Petrarches Goddesse," Rosalind silences Colin's poetry because his unbridled love of her blocks his Orphic quest for poetic virtue and, ironically, for her and true love. These dark undermeanings of the Virgilian Venus who is gloriously envisioned at the end of "Aprill" are acknowledged indirectly the next time Colin is encountered in the *Calender.* At the beginning of "June," Colin describes himself in terms that echo the opening lines of the *Aeneid:*

> But I unhappy man, whom cruell fate,
> And angry Gods pursue from coste to coste,
> Can nowhere fynd, to shroude my lucklesse pate.
> (14–16)

Like Aeneas, *fato profugus* (*Aeneid* I, 2), Colin can go forward in his career only when he has come to understand correctly the impulses or promptings of love so that they lead him beyond imprisonment within the dark wood of the flesh.

Given the narrative frame of "Aprill" and the poetic or Orphic associations of Venus-Virgo, it can be argued that Venus, not Eliza-Astraea, presides over the eclogue. Cain points out, drawing from Isidore of

Seville, "By traditional etymology, April is the month of Venus and of flowers . . . named after Venus or Aphrodite."[70] Insofar as the apparition of Venus-Virgo connects with the theme of cruel, divisive love, the emblem represents how the poet must come to terms with Venus or love and follow on the Orphic "sylvan" path, driven by a disciplining vision of love. It also warns against the false consolation of resting on past accomplishments, such as the writing of Eliza's hymn, recalling the poet's need to go on and avoid the fate of Petrarch's Francesco in the *Secretum,* imprisonment by a melancholic ardor blinding the soul to a more truthful or heroic understanding of love. As in the story of Aeneas, Venus-Virgo marks the humbling beginning of a heroic quest, in this case Immerito's career commenced by *The Shepheardes Calender,* which initiates the *rota Virgiliana* and is metaphorically described by E. K. as "the maydenhead of this our common frends Poetrie." Cain observes that by making the Virgilian emblem "serve as the shepherds' wondering response to Colin's poem, Spenser not only blatantly salutes his own achievement as Elizabeth's encomiast but also claims an identification with Virgil and so implicitly promises a poem to rival the Roman poet's."[71] Indeed, keeping in mind the history of this symbol in Virgilian commentary, we can see the poet emphatically pursuing an analogy: Venus-Virgo represents the body of the poetry itself, a symbol for the "integument," the multiple meanings "hidden" by the surface of the writing. Like Venus-Virgo looked back upon by Aeneas, *The Shepheardes Calender* makes truer or complete sense only when viewed retrospectively from the Lavinian shore, the "laborum via" of epic poetry. The Venus of "Aprill" can indeed be seen as a "complicating" figure in the technical sense given this term in Florentine Neoplatonism, representing a "conversion" in which the soul, having been sent forth by God, comes to live in the body, or, to use literary equivalents, in which a poetic career has taken on distinct form.[72]

* * *

These prophetic meanings of the Venus-Virgo symbol in "Aprill" (prophetic in relation to both political and poetic themes) are continued by *The Faerie Queene* along with a growingly pronounced emphasis upon the fractious materiality of human enterprise registered by the spirit's dark attraction for the things of this world, *silva* or *hyle.* The Venus of *The Faerie Queene* is turbulent and enigmatic, partly a mocking presence in the poem (the Venus *ridens* of the Temple of Love in IV. x) as well as a nurturing or sustaining goddess who inspires epic poetry (the Venus *alma* of the Proem to IV). The critical task is to respect the density of the symbol's relations that defy predictability.

Venus sets the poetry in motion, the reason why she symbolizes the response to the poetry of "Aprill." We must recognize her darkness before we are able to see her light.

Book I, Canto VI offers us a simple model, comparable to that in "Aprill," of the Venus-Virgo imagery as treated by Spenser.[73] Again, the Venus-Virgo complex symbolizes a way of seeing or of reading, this time not the poem itself but Una. More directly than in the eclogue, the symbol plays against the Virgilian passage and the complex commentary it received. The "secret course of destiny" (to use Servius' terms for the goddess' sylvan appearance) as manifest in the forest, in matter, *silva* or *hyle,* and the Orphic role of poetry to tame a wild humanity are motifs associated with the effect of the apparition of the "heavenly virgin" (I. vi. 5. 7).

In "a forrest wilde," Una is miraculously saved ("Eternall providence exceeding thought") by "the wyld woodgods" from Sansloy's attempted rape. The indirect allusion to Venus-Virgo in stanza sixteen describes "the salvage nation's" confused attempt to perceive or comprehend Una:

> The woodborne people fall before her flat,
> And worship her as Goddesse of the wood;
> And old Sylvanus selfe bethinkes not, what
> To thinke of wight so faire, but gazing stood,
> In doubt to deeme her borne of earthly brood;
> Sometimes Dame Venus selfe he seemes to see,
> But Venus never had so sober mood;
> Sometimes Diana he her takes to bee,
> But misseth bow, and shaftes, and buskins to her knee.
> (I. vi. 16)

As in Petrarch's *Secretum,* Venus-Virgo is a misnaming of the Truth. "Old Sylvanus," whose name may pun upon the original Virgilian context of the sylvan epiphany of Venus as a nymph of Diana, is a pagan without access to the truth of Christian revelation. "Vewing that mirrhour rare," Sylvanus is goaded only into reviving his "ancient love" for Cyparisse, in contrast to Aeneas' "chaste" response to the disguised Venus in the *Aeneid.* Shining more brightly because of the uncomprehending blindness surrounding her, Una, the Woman of faith, is turned into "th'Image of Idolatryes." The Orphic role of civilizing a wild humanity living in the forests is assigned to Una as she attempts "to teach them truth, which worshipt her in vaine" (I. vi. 19. 6). But the "trew sacred lore, which from her sweet lips did redound" (I. vi. 30. 9) falls on deaf ears.

The next use of Venus-Virgo again coincides with a male misperception of another "mirrhour rare," an alternate poetic example of saintly womanhood, Belphoebe. The Virgilian allusion in Book Two, Canto Three announces Belphoebe's entrance into the epic ironically heralded by Trompart, Braggadocchio's servant. The extended description of Belphoebe preceding her encounter with the false knight and squire displays what Harry Berger aptly calls a "conspicuous irrelevance," which he argues is "the basic strategy of Spenser's allegorical method."[74] In II. iii. 33, Trompart incongruously blares out the words of Aeneas to his disguised mother:

> O Goddesse, (for such I take thee to bee)
> For neither doth thy face terrestriall shew,
> Nor voyce sound mortall.

This address in the mouth of Trompart suggests equivocation, a darkness of meaning directing the reader's gaze to the obliquity of the poem's design that serves as an analogy for the embodiment of the spirit and its ambiguous longing for glory and love. We recall that in relation to the Venus-Virgo passage, Bernardus had described the effect of poetic integuments in terms of "equivocationes et multivocationes." Spenser underscores the ambiguity and resonance of his poem's design by heralding Braggadoccio and Belphoebe into the poem together in the same canto and by building up carefully and subtly throughout the canto a network of Virgilian associations.

As with Book One, Canto Six, the sylvan location of the apparition is stressed repeatedly. Disturbed by the sudden disappearance of Archimago, Braggadocchio and Trompart flee,

> Till that they come unto a forrest greene,
> In which they shrowd themselves from causeless feare;
> Yet feare them followes still, where so they beene,
> Each trembling leafe, and whistling wind they heare,
> As ghastly bug their haire on end does reare:

Yet both doe strive their fearfulnesse to faine.
At last they heard a horne, that shrilled cleare
Throughout the wood, that ecchoed againe,
And made the forrest ring, as it would rive in twaine.
(II. iii. 20)

The undermeanings of the forest dwelt on by virtually all the Virgilian commentaries subtly come into play before the apparition of goddess-like Belphoebe: the forest as *materia,* allegorically understood as the darkness of the material world or as the cares for the world that confront and block the soul in its attempts to contemplate reality. This stanza alludes indirectly to these wider connotations of the forest of the *Aeneid,* Book One, which the commentaries linked to the primordial forest Aeneas must enter en route to the underworld in Book Six. The references to the men who "shrowd themselves," "each trembling leaf," the "ghastly bug" making their hair stand on end and the horn sounding in the hunt ironically evoke as a subtext the "antiqua sylva" Aeneas and his comrades fearfully broach, described as "the deep of lairs of beasts" ("stabula alta ferarum," *Aeneid,* VI, 179), where they must go to pluck Proserpina's golden bough before entering Hades.

The extended description of Belphoebe conspicuously connects her to the forest and, more ominously, to Dido. Traces of the forest "enwrap" Belphoebe's hair (echoing and contrasting with the shrowding of the men in the forest and their hair on end):

And whether art it were, or heedlesse hap,
As through the flouring forrest rash she fled,
In her rude haires sweet flowres themselves did lap,
And florishing fresh leaves and blossomes did enwrap.
(II. iii. 30. 6–9)

Immediately following this description, we receive the comparison of Belphoebe to Diana closely echoing Virgil's comparison (*Aeneid,* I, 498–502) of Dido to Diana:

Such as Diana by the sandie shore
Of swift Eurotas, or on Cynthus greene,
Where all the Nymphes have her unwares forlore,
Wandreth alone with bow and arrowes keene,
To seeke her game: Or as that famous Queene

Of Amazons, whom Pyrrhus did destroy,
The day that first of Priame she was seene,
Did shew her self in great triumphant joy,
To succour the weake state of sad afflicted Troy.
(II. iii. 31)

The departures from Virgil are as striking as the borrowings: in contrast to Virgil's Diana "guiding her dancing bands" ("exercet Diana choros," *Aeneid,* I, 499), Belphoebe is "forlore" (ironically Braggadocchio is also described in the canto's epigrammatic couplets as "fowl forlorne"); the second comparison, welded to the Diana comparison and linking Belphoebe to the slain virgin Penthesilea, likewise implies Belphoebe's mortality and vulnerability.[75]

Another departure deserves recognition: whereas Venus in her Book I apparition in the *Aeneid* is seeking a sister, this Venus-Virgo is seeking "a bleeding Hind," reminiscent of the deer Aeneas slays in the wood upon reaching Africa prior to his mother's apparition. Dido, of course, will be thrilled by the arrows of Cupid disguised as Ascanius in Book I. True, Belphoebe is the hunter here, not the hunted, but the "filthy lust" her appearance stirs in Braggadocchio momentarily makes her the prey in the "soft" hunt spurred on by Venerean impulses, the same hunt that will bring about Dido's ruin. That Belphoebe first mistakes the hidden Braggadocchio as the hind she seeks brings to mind Landino's reading of why Venus in her entrance into the poem appears as a huntress in a wood: as ruler of a state, she is immersed in matter, involved with various errors, and hunting down the beasts to feed her people. Admittedly, Belphoebe in the allegory stands for Elizabeth's private person; both the "Letter to Ralegh" and the Proem to Book Three stress that Belphoebe represents "a most vertuous and beautifull Lady," the private chaste "body" of Elizabeth in contradistinction to her public "body" of ruler "figured forth" by Gloriana. Yet the symbolic reverberations of Venus-Virgo here and in the next appearance of Belphoebe entangle and submit the Queen's private and public "bodies" to the dark ways of the cruel but sustaining Venus.

In the larger mythographic structures of the poem, Venus ultimately contains Belphoebe-Diana. In Book III, Canto 6, it is she who instigates the search for Cupid leading to the discovery of the new-born twins Belphoebe and Amoret. It is she whom we glimpse only retrospectively and indirectly in Colin's Book VI vision of the dancing Graces on Mount Acidale. Only within this restless dynamic of poet and

and Venus do we understand the full import of the description of Belphoebe and the apostrophe to her. They point towards the spiritual and the intransigent which will not concede to mortal determinings. The hyperbolic and ironic aspects of Belphoebe's description signal that there are no certainties or untroubled equivalences in a poem dominated by Venus and heroic love.

While the "fear and hope" (II. iii. 32) Trompart sees in Belphoebe's face express the oppositional valences of the Venus-Virgo image, the next narrative episode that the image begins probes an even deeper contrariness. In Book III, Canto 5, Timias, Arthur's squire, awakes from his wounded condition to see his nurse Belphoebe for the first time. Nearly repeating Aeneas' words to his unrecognized mother, he exclaims in wonder, "Angell, or Goddesse do I call thee right?" (stanza 35). The Virgilian mortal or divine alternatives have been radicalized, suggesting the extreme divisions or conflicts developed in this episode.

Like the poet of the "Cynthia" poems, Timias will experience Belphoebe as one "wounding my mind with contrary conceit."[76] Unknowingly fueling such contradictory fire in Timias, Belphoebe's reaction to Timias' Venus-Virgo apostrophe ironically includes an emphasis upon the word "desire." Its meaning is carefully limited by the speaker only to nursing Timias but is momentarily unrestricted by the poetic placement of the word at the end of a line where it acts as the close of a metrical unit and can be ironically misread as the name of Belphoebe's mother:

> Thereat she blushing said, Ah gentle Squire,
> Nor Goddesse I, nor Angell, but the Mayd,
> And daughter of a woody Nymphe, desire
> No service, but thy safety and ayd;
> Which if thou gaine, I shalbe well apayd.
> (III. iii. 36)

The "Providence heavenly" (III. iii. 27) that provides for this chance meeting of Belphoebe and Timias leads to painful and anxious emotions that will test the merit of Timias. Belphoebe can heal the body of Timias, but she inflames his soul, which is tortuously poised, like the emotions Trompart sees in the virgin's face, between hope and fear. To Timias, the different kinds of desire Belphoebe distinguishes confusingly spring from the same source: echoing the ambiguous Virgilian tag "amor omnia vincit," he laments, "Of all love taketh equall vew" (III. v. 47).

These conflicts develop from a clash of multiple perspectives upon *eros* signalled through the Venus-Virgo allusion. The episode with its ironies operating in different directions plays simultaneously against the acquired meanings of the symbol: Servius' reading of the darkness of destiny symbolized by Aeneas' sylvan encounter with his mother; Donatus' moralizing about Aeneas' chaste response; Ascensius' implied mistrust of venerean sensuality; and Landino's reflections upon the darkness of matter as the place of the beginning of life, as both *mater* and *materia.* These ideas at cross purposes are spliced together in the "chance" encounter in the woods of Timias and Belphoebe, who, like a mother, will nurse the squire and is forbidden from sexual love for her ward. The Venus-Virgo image, rather than symbolizing the dividedness of the different types of loves (the commentaries routinely assigned different genealogies to the heavenly and the earthly Venues), reiterates the universal aspect of love described by the opening stanza of Canto V:

> Wonder it is to see, in diverse minds,
> How diversely love doth his pageants play,
> And shewes his powre in variable kinds:
> The baser wit, whose idle thoughts alway
> Are wont to cleave unto the lowly clay,
> It stirreth up to sensuall desire,
> And in lewd slouth to wast his carelesse day:
> But in brave sprite it kindles goodly fire,
> That to all high desert and honour doth aspire.
> (III. v. 1)

Belphoebe's "rare chastitee" must be seen within this all-encompassing perspective of love as Venus-Virgo. Chastity is a beatitude conceived ideally in Renaissance Platonism as the reconciliation of virtue and pleasure.[77] In Spenser, it is also inspirational, but unresolvably beset by conflicts; not a cool abstraction, chastity is a human aspiration in life deriving from our attitude towards our own embodiment and the dark nurturing "wood" from which we enter the world.

The virginity of Belphoebe itself is connected with female creative power. Timias desires but learns to serve the sanctity of Belphoebe and what her virginity represents, female power and integrity beyond male possession. The miraculous conception of Belphoebe and Amoret, in which the sun acts as a nonhuman father, intimates the sacred origin of honor and chastity. It also suggests the awe surrounding the creation of life as well as providing a genealogical sign for the holiness of virginity and marriage.[78] Timias' bittersweet service to Belphoebe indicates that honor requires acceptance of what both effaces and cultivates the self. Deference to Belphoebe's will against defloration reflects the poet's complex sense of what the origin of male honor is and casts the prime representation of Elizabeth's private person, Belphoebe, in a moral light relevant to all sexuality, male and female.

Spenser's fourth allusion to Venus-Virgo, the second in Book III, is beyond doubt the most complex because of the varied allegorical functions the image is made to serve.

In Canto 7, a witch discovers Florimel who has sought refuge in her hovel situated "in a gloomy hollow glen" (III. vii. 6), a sylvan geography we have come to read for Virgilian connotations. The allusion occurs through description of the witch's reaction to Florimel as she watches Florimel compose herself after her wild flight through the woods:

> Tho gan she gather up her garments rent,
> And her loose lockes to dight in order dew,
> With golden wreath and gorgeous ornament;
> Whom such whenas the wicked Hag did vew,
> She was astonisht at her heavenly hew,
> And doubted her to deem an earthly wight,
> But or some Goddesse, or of Dianes crew,
> And thought her to adore with humble spright;
> T'adore thing so divine as beauty, were but right.
> (III. vii. 11)

The witch's responses to Florimel have been carefully ordered so that they change from an initial dread of Florimel's intrusion in stanza 7, followed by wrath in 8, then pity or compassion in 9 and 10 and finally, in stanza 11 above, astonishment and adoration. The Venus-Virgo allusion, crowning the sequence of the hag's emotions, has an allegorical resonance the commentators, especially Landino, have taught us to read. The "vile Hag, all were her whole delight / In mischiefe" (9. 8–9), remains part of God's created world, and thus, like the realm of matter itself, symbolized by Venus-Virgo according to Landino, still retains "an innate faculty for receiving unto itself" the influence of heavenly form.[79] The allusion carries a weighty Platonic and theological import, momentarily directing the witch's gaze and ours towards the splendor of divine goodness manifested even in this most wicked "mother" and this most desolate place of the forest.

However, the allusion can also be read negatively from a moral perspective. It is Florimel's "golden wreath and gorgeous ornament" that specifically prompts the witch's attention to the maid's "heavenly hew" eliciting the brief wonder as well as, ominously, the adulation of the witch, who in canto viii will concoct false Florimel, a parodic version of the soul's fortunate fall into matter, a living idol made to console her lewd son. As with Sylvanus' false assessment of Una, the witch cannot read aright because of her thralldom to false gods. The Venus-Virgo reference thus serves a double, conflicting function: it registers an evil, idolatrous assessment of beauty as worldly splendor and expresses how great the power of virtue is, even an evil witch involuntarily acknowledging Florimel's goodness.

But besides pointing outward, if I may speak this way, to the moral universe of Christian values, the allusion also points inward, to the structure of the poem itself. The allusion's context has a wider and ultimately puzzling resonance that broadly directs attention to the interlaced design of Book III. The flight of Florimel bringing her to the witch's hovel was originally motivated by an attempted assault upon her by the "fowle foster" whose brother wounded Timias in the left thigh, a "sexual" wound that Belphoebe will heal and then cause. This fraternal connection of the two interlaced narratives that "frame" the Garden of Adonis (Canto VI) subtly underscores an obvious moral contrast between Timias and Belphoebe's relationship (Canto V) with Florimel's impending one to the witch's son (Canto VII). While Timias responds honorably, the witch's son shamefully indulges desire. Spenser seems to suggest that the use of or response to desire, and not a difference in the kind of desire, distinguishes love and chastity from lust, an allegorical reading of a universal, single love specifically encouraged by Book III, Canto V's opening stanza. But it is the witch who echoes Aeneas' words to his mother rather than her lustful son, which would seem a more direct strategy for contrasting opposed responses to *eros.* The presence of the witch and the terms of the description, belonging to the narrator's perusal of the witch's thoughts, have a disturbing effect on the dualistic image of Venus-Virgo. Mortal, nymph or goddess are the three possibilities in mother witch's mind as she ponders the maiden. All aspects of life seem scanned in this brief passage. The cosmic aspect of Diana as the triple goddess (witch Hecate in hell, maiden Diana on earth, Lucina, patroness of childbirth, in the heavens as the moon) seems to peer at us obliquely within the text. This alternate mythographic image is aligned not with moral hierarchies, but with a plenitude beyond good and evil, suggestive of destiny and the triple division of the universe into heaven, earth and hell. Natale Conti's reading of the triple goddess as the force of an unfathomable providence working its way from the heights to the depths of the universe comes to mind.[80] We seem to see both sides of the sacred, the blessed and the accursed, revealed simultaneously. The poet ironizes the Venus-Virgo image by offering another mythical representation created by an implied supplementary symbol which opens out to the narrative sweep of the poem designed to simulate the mystery of providence manifested to mortal eyes as chance, turbulence, randomness. We may think of illustrations of Petrarch *Trionfi* in which the triple goddesses of fate stand atop the dead figure of chastity.[81]

Of course, the Belphoebe and Florimel stories in which the Venus-Virgo reference occurs contrast with the more inclusive adventures of the Book of Chastity's hero Britomart. For Britomart alone does Spenser reserve the most complete representation of love and chastity. Belphoebe proves too martial, and Florimel too venerean, ultimately, when foiled against Britomart. Britomart's story alone includes both halves of the contrasting Venus-Virgo pair:

> For she was full of amiable grace,
> And manly terrour mixed therewithall,
> That as the one stird up affections bace,
> So th'other did mens rash desires apall,
> And hold them back, that would in errour fall.
> (III. i. 46)

Her story occupies the epic's middle books between extremes, between books of holiness and mutability. Like Aeneas' story, hers depicts the human struggle between destiny and design, freedom and responsibility, virtue and love.

In conclusion, we can readily see how the Virgilian commentary on Venus provides both a rich background for Spenserian poetry and a point of departure for investigating divergent and conflicting perspectives on love. Rather than tidy up through dichotomy or suppress aspects of Venus that do not conform to an idealized or sublimated reading of love, the poetry repeatedly acknowledges the ambiguity of love, both its radiance and its turbulence. The political or "public" theme of the imperial virgin and the "private" one of the chastity of the Queen give way, in an evolving complexity I have partially traced, to the greater, more inclusive issue of mortal endeavor confronted with and stimulated by desire, understood broadly as the ineradicable effects of matter upon spirit. The poetry subjects to irony the codes of mystical commentary by representing multiple, conflicting ways of envisioning love. By doing so, it warns of the dangers of semantic charters forged by a "this means that" commentary which, for purposes of systematic explication, reduces the referential powers of poetry and the way things can be seen.[82]

New York Institute of Technology

Notes

1. Thomas Browne, *Selected Writings,* ed. Geoffrey Keynes (London: Faber and Faber, 1968), p. 17.
2. E. H. Gombrich, *Symbolic Images: Studies in the Art of the Renaissance* (London: Phaidon Press, 1972), p. 129.
3. Plato, *The Republic* (523C), in *Great Dailogues of Plato,* trans. W. H. D. Rouse (New York and Toronto: The New American Library, 1956), p. 323.
4. *Iconology: Image, Text, Ideology* (Chicago and London: The University of Chicago Press, 1986), pp. 93–94.
5. Stephen Greenblatt's *Renaissance Self-Fashioning: From More to Shakespeare* (Chicago and London: The University of Chicago Press, 1980) argues that *The Faerie Queene* is"wholly wedded to the autocratic ruler of the English state" (p. 174). Greenblatt concludes that "Spenser's art does not lead us to perceive ideology critically, but rather affirms the existence and inescapable moral power of ideology as that principle of truth toward which art forever yearns" (p. 192). Greenblatt's position establishes a critical point of departure that sees the political function of Spenser's poetry as dominant and determining. In his important essay "'Eliza, Queene of shepheardes,' and the Pastoral of Power," Louis Adrian Montrose explores the poetry's ideological dimensions while he at the same time softens Greenblatt's politically "wedded" reading. Spenser's "pastoral of power," as the phrase partly suggests, has an ironic quality recognizing the priority of the poetic conventions of literary genre. Montrose observes, fresh meanings, the relations of "the poet and his muse," supersede historical and political implications as an imaginative image "new and complex" emerges. Montrose's essay is reprinted in *Renaissance Historicism: Selections from English Literary Renaissance,* ends. Arthur Kinney and Dan S. Collins (Amherst: University of Massachusetts Press, 1987). John D. Bernard reacts against what he sees as Montrose's and also Jonathan Goldberg's characterization of the poetry's conformance to the existing state order, arguing for a "pastoral of contemplation." Bernard sees *The Shepheardes Calender* as staging an "implicit contest of authorities . . . between political context and intertextuality." See *Ceremonies of Innocence: Pastoralism in the Poetry of Edmund Spenser* (Cambridge: Cambridge University Press, 1989), p. 49.
6. *Tudor Royal Iconography: Literature and Art in an Age of Religious Crisis* (Princeton: Princeton University Press, 1989), p. 3.

7. Edmund Spencer, "A Letter of the Authors," vol. 1 in *The Works of Edmund Spenser: A Variorum Edition,* ed. Edwain Greenlaw et al., 11 vols. (Baltimore: The Johns Hopkins University Press, 1932–57), p. 168. All quotations from the works of Spenser are taken from this edition and will be cited in the text.

8. Dominico Comparetti, *Vergil in the Middle Ages* (Hamden, Conn.: Archon Books, 1966), pp. 116ff.

9. *Spenser and the Motives of Metaphor* (Durham, North Carolina: Duke University Press, 1982), p. 94.

10. *Literary Transvaluation: From Vergilian Epic to Shakespearean Tragicomedy* (Berkeley and Los Angeles: University of California Press, 1984), p. 1.

11. *Virgil and Spenser* (Port Washington, N.Y.: Kennikat Press, 1969), p. 362.

12. All references to Virgil are from Virgil, *Opera* (Venice, 1544; rpt. in 2 volumes by New York and London, Garland Publishing, 1976). All translations of this edition are mine. Fol. 149r: "Cano"—polysemus sermo est. Tria nomina significat. Aliquando laudo, ut Regesque canebant; aliquando divino, ut Ipsa canas oro; aliquando canto, ut in hoc loco.

13. J. W. Jones, Jr., "Allegorical Interpretation in Servius," Classical Journal 56 (1961), 224.

14. Virgil, *Opera* (Venice, 1544), foo. 175r: "Media sese tulit obvia sylva"—quam Graeci *hyle* vocant, poetae nominant sylvam, id est, elementorum congeriem, unde cuncta procreantur.

15. William Nelson describes the Servian *hyle/silva* etymology as crucially important because it "becomes the basis for the new commentaries of the humanists . . . The reference to 'hyle,' a term of technical philosophy, linked the *Aeneid* with Platonic tradition, a connection particularly attractive to such scholars as Landino and Badius." See *The Poetry of Edmund Spenser* (New York: Columbia University Press, 1963), p. 159.

16. *Fulgentius the Mythographer,* trans. Leslie George Whitbread (Ohio: Ohio State University Press, 1971), p. 124.

17. Besides Bernardus (whose *Commentum* I will review at length), Dante subscribes to Fulgentius' "ages of man" reading in his tract *Il Convivio* (Book 4, Chapter 26) as does Coluccio Salutati in his *De Herculis Laboribus* (cf. Berthold L. Ullman, *The Humanism of Coluccio Salutati,* Editrice Antenore: Padua, 1963, pp. 55–56).

18. Fulgentius, trans. Whitbread, pp. 125–26.

19. Virgil, *Opera* (Venice, 1544), fol. 175r: Accedebat ad hominis castitatem malorum tantorum saeva congeries, quae etiam libidinosos revocata a Veneris voluptatibus.

20. Andrew Fichter, *Poets Historical: Dynastic Epic in the Renaissance* (New Haven: Yale University Press, 1982), p. 26.

21. Two recent studies have reached similar conclusions about the symbolic implications of Venus disguised as Diana. Studying patterns of poetic vision in Virgil, Spenser, and Robert Frost, T. M. Krier suggests that the meeting of Aeneas and his disguised mother is paradigmatic of an imaginative poetic process in which acts of recognition and loss occur simultaneously. Aeneas experiences the goddess' numinous presence as loss and absence. Her apparition intensifies his longing for certainty while she reveals the unclarity of things. See "The Mysteries of the Muses: Spenser's *Faerie Queene,* II.3, and the Epic Tradition of the Goddess Observed," *Spenser Studies* 7

(1987), 59–92. According to Rita Van der Steen Verbrugge's recent study of classical influences upon Spenser's concept of chastity, Spenserian chastity involves a similar poetic paradox of understanding uncertainty. She argues that Spenser's Book of Chastity "will demand tools beyond right reason; the comprehenion of 'Chastity' will require a knowledge of spiritual chastity as a concept involving man's potential to attain the divine and as a comprehensive virtue involving man's obedience to the providential law of God in all areas of life." See *Spenser's "Antique Praises of Chastity,"* (Ph.D. dissertation, University of Michigan, 1984), p. 80.

22. *Commentary on the First Six Books of Virgil's Aeneid,* trans. Earl G. Schreiber and Thomas E. Maresca (Lincoln: University Nebraska Press, 1979), p. XX.

23. *The Commentary on the First Six Books of the Aeneid Commonly Attributed to Bernardus Silvestris,* eds. Julian Jones and Elizabeth Jones (Lincoln: University of Nebraska Press, 1977), p. 1.

24. Although Bernardus does not mention Orpheus in his definition of *integumentum* (pg. 3 of the Latin edition by Jones and Jones), his wording follows almost verbatim Guillaume de Conche's definition in his glosses on Boethius which does attribute this kind of writing to Orpheus. Bernardus: "Integumentum est genus demonstrationis sub fabulosa narratione veritatis involvens intellectum, unde etiam dicitur involucrum"; Guillaume: "Integumentum vero est oratio sub fabulosa narratione verum claudens intellectum, ut de Orpheo." Guillaume is quoted by Winthrop Wetherbee, *Platonism and Poetry in the Twelfth Century: The Literary Influence of the School of Chartres* (Princeton: Princeton University Press, 1972), p. 267. Wetherbee notes (p. 110) that much of Bernardus' *Commentum* is taken often without acknowledgment from Servius, Macrobius, Fulgentius, the later mythographers, and Guillaume de Conche.

25. Bernardus, eds. Jones and Jones, p. 3: Modus agendi talis est: in integumento describit quid agat et quid paciatur humanus spiritus in humano corpore temporaliter positus. Schreiber and Maresca translate, "His procedure is to describe allegorically by means of an integument . . ." (p. 5).

26. Peter Dronke, "Integumenta Virgilii," in *Lectures Medievales de Virgile: Actes Colloque Organise par l'Ecole Francaise de Rome* (Palais Farnese: Ecole Française de Rome, 1985), p. 324.

27. Wetherbee, *Platonism and Poetry in the Twelfth Century: The Literary Influence of the School of Chartres,* p. 8.

28. *Commentary on the First Six Books of Virgil's Aeneid,* trans. Earl G. Schreiber and Thomas E. Maresca, p. 11.

29. Ibid., p. 32.

30. Ibid., p. 12.

31. Bernardus arrives at the reading of Achates as "study" through a typically playful etymology: "Achates quasi a chere ethis interpretatur, id est tristis consuetudo. A enim sine, chere leticia, ethis mos vel consuetudo. Hoc autem est studium quia ipsum est consuetudo et tristis." *The Commentary,* eds. Jones and Jones, p. 31.

32. For Salutati on interpretation, see Ronald G. Witt, *Hercules at the Crossroads: The Life, Works and Thought of Coluccio Salutati* (Durham, North Carolina: Duke University Press, 1983), p. 233ff.

33. The association of Venus with the declination of the soul into matter is reminiscent of the Venus of Epicurean philosophy. Lucretius' epic has recently been described

as exhibiting the kind of qualities that can be attributed to Venus-Virgo, who, in Book 1, after the fall of Troy and after shipwreck, paradoxically disguises herself to reveal herself and has proven so problematic to Platonizing commentary. Michel Serres observes of Lucretius' *De Rerum Natura,* "The poem's text is nature itself, that of Venus. The text loops back upon itself at the end of the martial events, but not in a perfect spiral." The Lucretian Venus represents the atomic "swerve" or *clinamen,* an atomic view of the universe that conflicts with the Timaean view of the cosmos based upon form rather than flow. Much like the effect of Venus-Virgo upon the *Aeneid's* commentators, the Venerean "declination interrupts the [Platonic and Martial] model as well as the theory, perturbing them, introducing turbulence." See Michel Serres, "Lucretius: Science and Religion," in *Hermes: Literature, Science, Philosophy,* eds. Josue Harari and David F. Bell (Baltimore: The Johns Hopkins University Press, 1982), pp. 98–124.
34. *Petrarch's Secret or the Soul's Conflict with Passion,* trans. William H. Draper (Westport, Connecticut: Hyperion Press, 1978), p. 1.
35. Ibid., p. 2.
36. Ibid., pp. 82–83.
37. Ibid., p. 83.
38. Ibid., p. 119.
39. D. C. Allen, *Mysteriously Meant: The Rediscovery of Pagan Symbolism and Allegorical Interpretation in the Renaissance* (Baltimore: The Johns Hopkins University Press, 1970), p. 140.
40. Boccaccio, *Genealogiae* (Venice, 1494; rpt. New York: Garland Publishing, 1976), fols. 51v–2v.
41. See Schrelber and Maresca's useful introduction to Bernardus' *Commentary on the First Six Books of Virgil's Aeneid, p. XXX.*
42. *The Allegorical Epic: Essays in its Rise and Decline* (Chicago: The University of Chicago Press, 1980), p. 27.
43. Cristoforo Landino, *Cristoforo Landino's Allegorization of the Aeneid: Books III and IV of the Camaldulensian Dialoques,* trans. Thomas Stahel (Ph.D. dissertation, Johns Hopkins University, 1968), p. 54: Christophorus Landinus, *Camaldulensium Disputatio* (Straussbourg, 1508), fol. F3v: Interpretamur postremo aliquid per allegoriam: quod tunc fit cum non quae verba significant intelligimus: sed quiddam aliud sub figura obscuratum.
44. Landino, trans. Stahel, p. 57.
45. Ibid., p. 140.
46. Erwin Panofsky, *Studies in Iconology: Humanistic Themes in the Art of the Renaissance* (New York: Harer and Row, 1972), pp. 134–35.
47. Landino, trans. Stahel, pp. 142–43.
48. Ibid., p. 140.
49. Ibid., p. 144.
50. Virgil, *Opera* (Venice, 1544), fol. 175v: Debuit Venus offerre loquendi fiduciam ne improbum videretur, quae cum virgine cum sola tunc esse putaretur, misceretur colloquium, sed ad fallendum quoque pertinebat, ut non solum specie, sed etiam sermone imprudentes traduceret, ut ad interrogandi necessitatem venire potuisset.
51. Ibid., fol. 329r.
52. Ibid., fol. 175v: Illucque matrem obviam habuit in media sylva: quae fictio astrologica, ratione non vacat: nam innuit Venerem fuisse Aeneae in medio Horoscopi,

et dominam coeli in nativitate eius. Unde Veneris filius, existimatus est. Ad quod accedit, quod dicitur obvenisee in media sylva: nam sylva ab hyle, quae est rerum omnium congeries, et prima materia deductam, plurimi attestantur. Per sylvam igitur, significatur nobis diversitas influentiarum, in qua difficile est illum aureum ramu, de quo in vi. mentio fiet, invenire. Quae ergo a poetis finguntur, altioris sapientiae medullas continent.

53. Ibid., fol. 329r: Opus etiam est, aureo ramo, id est sapientia, et virtute: quae in sylva, id est mundi latebris, difficilis inventum est: nisi nos Veneris aves, hoc est columbae, ducant: per quas intelligo, gratiam spiritusancti, qui in columbina specie nonnunquam apparuit. Vel, cupiditas, id est diligentia, nos ad virtutem ducat.

54. *The Commentary,* eds. Jones and Jones, p. 9: Hic autem diversus integumentorum respectus et multiplex designatio in omnibus misticis observari debet si in una vero veritas stare non poterit.

55. E. H. Gombrich, *Symbolic Images,* p. 150.

56. Petrarch, *Opere,* ed. Emilio Bigi (Milan: Ugo Mursia, 1968), p. 51: Quia hoc ipsum 'optare' verbum unum est, sed quod innumerabilibus consistat ex rebus.

57. Victoria Kahn, "The Figure of the Reader in Petrarch's *Secretum,*" *Modern Critical Views: Petrarch,* ed. Harold Bloom (New York: Chelsea House Publishers, 1989), p. 153.

58. Thomas P. Roche, Jr., *Petrarch and the Enlish Sonnet Sequences* (New York: AMS Press, 1989), p. 6.

59. Davy A. Carozza and H. James Shey, *Petrarch's Secretum* (New York: Peter Lang, 1989), p. 5.

60. The most explicit depiction of Elizabeth as Venus-Virgo is the illuminated frontispiece of *Regina Fortunata* by Henry Howard, which John King dates c.1580 in contrast to Roy Strong who prefers c.1576. The Queen is depicted seated on a throne, holding a scepter in her right hand and a globe crowned by a crucifix in her left. An open book rests on her lap with the inscription "pax tibi ancilla mea," alluding to Mary's response to the angel Gabriel. Beneath and between two white lions bowing down to the Queen at her feet is a banderole containing Aeneas' speech to his mother "O quam te memorem virgo" with the rest of the address altered to "O Dea digna Deo" from the original "O dea certe." King remarks, "The ambiguous sexuality of Howard's image derives from the iconography of the previous reign [Mary Tudor's] . . . by fusing the ideal chastity of the Blessed Virgin with the paradigmatic fertility of Venus." The iconography refers obliquely, King argues, to the personal situation of the queen (the marriage proposal by the Duke of Alencon)—"This illustration is poised at a liminal moment in the development of Elizabethan iconography, because its representation of the queen as a new Venus enhances her standing as an eligible woman at the last possible moment when she is still capable of marriage and child-bearing, even as her affinity with the Virgin Mary calls attention to the likelihood that she will retain her unwedded state." See *Tudor Royal Iconography: Literature and Art in an of Religious Crisis,* p. 259. Dame Frances A. Yates argues for connecting links between Elizabeth, Astraea and Venus—"There is yet another side to Spenser's Astraea, by which she becomes approximated to the Renaissance vision of beauty, of the celestial Venus." Evidence is found in Colin's vision of the Graces dancing around the "faire one" on Mount Acidale, a place sacred to Venus (*The Faerie Queene,* VI. x. 9). The allusion to Ariadne's Crown in stanza 13, according to Yates,

encourages association of "the Venus" of Colin's vision with Virgo-Astraea: "Spenser has fused this flowery Virgo, associated with Ariadne's Crown, with Venus and the Graces," and the whole network of symbols represents "the picture of Elizabeth seen by Calidore." See *Astraea: The Imperial Theme in the Sixteenth Century* (London and Boston: Routledge and Kegan Paul, 1975), pp. 73–74. Developing Yates's work, Roy Strong notes how John Davies in his *Hymns to Astraea* (1599) calls Astraea "Queen of Beauty," and Strong concludes, "In other words Elizabetha-Astraea-Virgo is also Venus, goddess of love and beauty, whose attribute, the rose, is another of Davies's themes, symbolic not only of the union of York and Lancaster but of her role as 'Beauty's Rose.'" Strong argues these mythological perspectives converging on the figure of the virgin Queen comprise the iconographic program of the painting *Queen Elizabeth going in Procession to Blackfriars* (1600). See *The Cult of Elizabeth: Elizabethan Portraiture and Pageantry* (London: Thames and Hudson, 1977), p. 47.

61. *Astraea: The Imperial Theme in the Sixteenth Century,* p. 28.

62. "Elizabeth, Bride and Queen: A Study of Spenser's April Eclogue and the Metaphors of English Protestantism," *SSt* 2 (1981), 75.

63. *Tudor Royal Iconography,* p. 212.

64. *The Convivio,* trans. Philip H. Wicksteed (London: J. M. Dent and Sons, 1940), p. 249.

65. For medieval and Renaissance readings of Astraea as the Blessed Virgin, see Frederick A. De Armas, *The Return of Astraea: An Astral-Imperial Myth in Calderon* (Lexington: University Press of Kentucky, 1986). De Armas cites among other writers Juan Luis Vives' "purely messianic" reading of the Fourth Eclogue—Virgo is both the justice of Christ and the virgin Mary.

66. *Praise in The Faerie Queene* (Lincoln: University of Nebraska Press, 1978), p. 14 ff.

67. *The Book of the Courtier,* trans. Charles S. Singleton (New York: Anchor Books, 1959), p. 294.

68. *Praise in The Faerie Queene,* p. 17.

69. *Spenser, Marvell, and Renaissance Pastoral* (Cambridge, Mass.: Harvard University Press, 1970), p. 119, 131.

70. *Praise in The Faerie Queene,* p. 22.

71. Ibid., p. 24.

72. For an explanation of Neoplatonic theory regarding the soul's incarnation, see Edgar Wind's explication of Botticelli's *Primavera* in *Pagan Mysteries in the Renaissance: An Exploration of Philosophical and Mystical Sources of Iconography in the Renaissance* (New York: W. W. Norton and Co., 1968), pp. 113–27.

73. I would like to thank Don Cheney for pointing out the relevance of this passage to my argument.

74. *The Allegorical Temper: Vision and Reality in Book Two of Spenser's Faerie Queene* (New Haven: Yale University Press, 1957), p. 123.

75. This is also Barbara Bono's assessment in *Literary Transvaluation,* p. 72. Thomas P. Roche, Jr., discussing the Dido-Penthesilea allusion, says that if within the historical allegory Braggadocchio portrays the Duc d'Alençon, then "Spenser may be presenting the queen with an image of her own potential downfall." However, this reading is not provable, and more importantly, obscures the "primary issue," which is, according to Roche, that Spenser uses Virgil's ambivalent presentation of Venus as

Diana, "that strange juxtaposition of normally conflicting tendencies," in his descriptions of Belphoebe to signal her transcendent status as a representation of "Heavenly Venus, eschewing earthly love." See *The Kindly Flame: A Study of the Third and Fourth Books of Spenser's Faerie Queene* (Princeton: Princeton University Press, 1964), pp. 100–103.

76. Sir Walter Ralegh quoted by Walter Oakeshott, *The Queen and the Poet* (New York: Barnes and Noble, 1961), p. 179.

77. See Edgar Wind's discussion of Neoplatonic chastity in *Pagan Mysteries in the Renaissance,* pp. 81–96.

78. Thomas P. Roche, Jr., *The Kindly Flame,* p. 88.

79. In his long section on *silva* introducing his reading of Venus-Virgo, Landino compares matter both to a mother and wood and God to a father and carpenter. The potency of matter is thus described: "verum innata sibi recipiendi facultate (et ut ita loquar) confuse omnes continere videtur" (*Camaldulensium Disputatio,* fol. H6r). This whole passage on the relations of matter and form in Landino in response to the valences of Venus-Virgo seems to have strong relevance to the allegorical meanings of Florimel. Consider the following passage from Landino in light of the various incidents associated with Florimel in Book III, specifically, the prolonged flight of this heavenly virgin, her miraculous retention of maidenhead despite two near rapes and her long imprisonment by Proteus, and finally false Florimel, who can be compared to Euripides' phantom Helen: "What has been set apart from matter is never destroyed, for it never takes to itself that which is contrary to it, but rather avoids and flees the contrary. That which is contained [*continetur*] within the womb of matter, however, falls into destruction on that account; it happens that matter, because it is found in all things which are spoken of as having material qualities, is like another Helen who throws open the doors and calls Menelaus within the house." *Cristoforo Landino's Allegorization of the Aeneid,* trans. Thomas Stahel, p. 142.

80. Consider Natale Conti's introductory remarks on the virgin goddess Diana who is considered the "same personage" as Luna, heavenly goddess of childbirth, and Hecate, guardian witch of the underworld: "Cum eadem Luna sit, et Hecate, et Diana, tamen non omnes hae vires, quae per has intelliguntur, uno nomine dicuntur, etsi ab uno fonte manant." Conti then identifies Hecate as "that power of fate springing from God" (illa sit fatorum vis a Deo proficiscens). *Mythologiae* (Padua, 1616; rpt. New York: Garland Publishing, Inc., 1979), p. 136.

81. See Lord Morley (Henry Parker), *Tryumphes of Fraunces Petrarcke,* ed. D. D. Carnicelli (Cambridge, Mass.: Harvard University Press, 1971), plate 15.

82. I would like to thank Patrick Cullen and Thomas P. Roche, Jr. for their rigorous support and gentle criticism throughout the writing of this essay.

PAULA BLANK

The Dialect of the *Shepheardes Calender*

IN THE FOUR HUNDRED YEARS since George Puttenham wrote that literary pastorals are composed "not of purpose to counterfait or represent the rusticall manner of loves and communication: but under the vaile of homely persons, and in rude speeches to insinuate and glaunce at greater matters,"[1] he has rarely met with any serious challenge. Louis Montrose has warned against treating Renaissance pastorals as "enamelled words" that transcend "rusticall" matters altogether. But even Montrose concedes that the realities of sixteenth-century rural life rarely find their way into works such as Spenser's *Shepherdes Calender,* and he concludes that Renaissance literary pastorals systematically suppress or displace material rusticity in order to glance at greater matters or, at least, at matters pertaining to the court.[2] For generations of critics, the *Calender* enacts a metaphorical excursion into the countryside that leads, finally, back to the centers of cultural power.

The *Shepheardes Calender* may avoid certain facts about sixteenth-century sheepfarming, but it does not eschew "real" pastoralism altogether. If the loves of Spenser's shepherds really concern the aspirations of gentlemen, their "rusticall manner . . . of communication" includes an important aspect of sixteenth-century country life. At the center of Spenser's pastoral experiment, as E. K. observed, was the compilation of an unusual poetic diction, a language that incorporated dialect words—"real" speech borrowed from the northern shires of England. Although northern English appears only sporadically throughout the eclogues, its presence repositions the poem beyond the borders of traditional courtly poetry. As unlikely a designation as it may seem, I would like to present the author of the *Shepheardes Calender* as a dialect poet, a "regional" author who (like those we meet in later centuries) self-consciously defined his work in terms of a marginalized, provincial culture. Instead of the courtly London poet we recognize at first glance, I would like to present a different Spenser, one who, like his protagonist Colin Clout, made a home in the north country.

* * *

The language of the *Shepheardes Calender* provoked controversy from the very beginning. The poem's editor and original commentator, E. K., identified Spenser's diction as the most problematic aspect of the work. In his letter to Gabriel Harvey, E. K. admits that there are many things about the Spenser's eclogues that will seem unfamiliar to readers, but "of many things which in him be strange, I know [the language] will seem the strangest."[3] E. K.'s prefatory remarks, along with his explanatory glosses, establish a critical approach to the poem that makes translation—the interpretation of strange or unfamiliar words—the key to Spenser's design. It is tempting to believe that the poet intended E. K.'s commentary to establish this orientation to his work.[4]

E. K. attributes the strangeness of Spenser's language to the fact that the poet borrowed so many words from Chaucer, words that have since become "something hard, and of most men unused" (5). He defends archaizing as an effort to recover an original English. Spenser, he says, "hath laboured to restore, as to theyr rightfull heritage such good and naturall English words as have ben long time out of use and cleane disherited" (11–12). E. K. assigns a political motive—the promotion of national interests—to Spenser's predilection for archaisms and, finding that the best defense is a good offense, he questions the patriotism of those who would attack native words. He forestalls the criticism of countrymen who "if them happen to here an olde word albeit very naturaly and significant, crye out streight way that we speak no English, but gibbrish . . ." with some ideological wrist slapping: "[Their] first shame is, that they are not ashamed, in their own mother tonge straungers to be counted and alienes. . ." (13).

E. K.'s apology for Spenser's poetry also appeals to the precedents set by earlier authors who made use of archaic diction. E. K. assures his readers that Spenser's antique language is "both English, and also used of most excellent authors and most famous poets" (5) and notes the archaisms of Livy and Sallust as examples. Quintilian, he reminds us, said that archaisms bestow majesty and dignity upon a verse. He predicts that Spenser will succeed Chaucer as "the Loadstarre of our language" (2), guiding English to new literary heights. Concerning Spenser's use of dialect, specifically, E. K. says nothing to Harvey at all, or at least, nothing explicit. We know that he observed the presence of dialect in the poem, since he marks several words as northern in his glosses, but he makes no mention of dialect in his prefatory remarks. The only unusual thing about Spenser's poem, it seems, is a preponderance of old words, words that have the sanction of literary history.

Because E. K. is Spenser's advocate, perhaps, few have noted that, for all his enthusiasm, he does not praise Spenser's archaisms unreservedly. Although he has the recommendation of Quintilian, the precedent of Livy and Sallust, and the nationalistic virtues of ancient Saxon on his side, E. K. does not rest there. Without stopping to evaluate the consistency of his proposals, E. K. offers a competing hypothesis: Spenser intended such diction to set off another, superior kind of language:

> But as in most exquisite pictures they use to blaze and portraict not only the daintie lineaments of beautye, but also rounde about it to shadow the rude thickets and craggy clifts, that, by the baseness of such parts, more excellency may accrew to the principall . . . even so doe these rough and harsh termes enlumine and make more clearly to appeare the brightnesse of brave and glorious words (9–10).

In a sudden reversal of judgment, E. K. determines that Spenser's unusual diction is neither "brave" nor "glorious," but rather "rude," "base," and "rough." E. K. adds that Spenser may have been following Horace's dictum of poetic decorum, prescribing a "low" language for low characters and kinds; the poet used old words "as thinking them fittest for such rusticall rudenesse of shepheards, . . . because such olde and obsolete wordes are most used of country folke" (6). By using the present tense, saying that such words "are" are not "were" used of country folk, E. K. suggests that Spenser deliberately set out to evoke the language of sixteenth-century peasants.

The several theories E. K. lines up to account for the diction of the *Shepheardes Calender* are conspicuously at odds. Was Spenser following a venerable theory dating back to the Latin classics, in which old words were said to endow poems with majesty and grace? Was Spenser, on the other hand, denying such language any "beautye" at all, implying that the baseness of such words compares unfavorably with something altogether better? Were Spenser's archaisms, in short, "brave and glorious" or "rough and harsh"? The fact that E. K.characterizes Spenser's language as at once majestic and low, authoritative and rude, points directly to the contradictions generated by the presence of archaisms and dialect words in the same poem. Although he does not address the effect of dialect words on Spenser's eclogues explicitly, E. K. identifies the source of the problem.

Spenser's early critics, in fact, are increasingly direct about the presence of dialect in the poem. Ben Jonson, to be sure, followed E. K.'s lead by singling out Spenser's archaisms for special consideration, although he arrived at a very different valuation. Jonson did not accept that the diction of the *Shepheardes Calender* was English at all, telling Drummond that Spenser, "in affecting the ancients, writ no language." Philip Sidney, on the other hand, objected to something more: "That same framing of his style to an old rustic language I dare not allow. . . ."[5] For Sidney, the fault in Spenser's language lay in the fact that it was not only old but "rustic" as well.

Readers of the *Shepheardes Calender* throughout the seventeenth and eighteenth centuries continued to cite the peculiarities of Spenser's language as a flaw that qualified the poet's achievement. These early modern Spenserians, however, believed they had hit upon the source of the problem: Spenser had combined archaisms with dialect words in a conscious imitation of Theocritus, who had composed his *Idylls* in an artificial dialect that came to be associated with rustic literature. John Dryden was able to write with confidence that "Spenser, being master of our northern dialect, and skilled in Chaucer's English, has so exactly imitated the Doric of Theocritus." Alexander Pope compared Spenser's "Doric" unfavorably with his supposed original:

> Notwithstanding all the care he [Spenser] has taken, he is certainly inferior in his Dialect: For the Doric had its beauty and

> propriety in the time of Theocritus; it was used in part of Greece, and frequent in the mouths of many of the greatest persons, whereas the old English and country phrases of Spenser were either entirely obsolete, or spoken only by people of the lowest condition.

Samuel Johnson, citing both the "obsolete terms" and "rustick words" of the *Calender,* called Spenser's Doric "a mangled dialect, which no human being ever could have spoken."[6] Whether he wrote "no language" at all, or the language of those of the "lowest condition," these men agreed, Spenser had recklessly alienated himself from his lettered audiences.

It is very unlikely, in fact, that Spenser was attempting to recreate the Doric of Theocritus, although this theory has survived into our own century. Spenser and his contemporaries generally knew Theocritus, if they knew him at all, through Latin translations, and few, if any, would have experienced Theocritus' Doric dialect firsthand.[7] Sidney censured the diction of the *Calender,* in fact, precisely because he believed it had no precedent in the Greek or Latin classics: He cannot allow Spenser's "old rustic language," he says "sith neither Theocritus in Greek, [nor] Virgil in Latin, . . . did affect it."[8] And surely E. K., who cited the archaisms of Sallust and Livy, would have mentioned Theocritus if he had believed Spenser was drawing on Greek practice.[9]

As early as 1754, Thomas Warton heralded a radical reassessment of the language of the *Calender,* one which foreclosed on the need to account for its strangeness altogether. Warton overturned the censure of Jonson, arguing that Spenser's diction was much more familiar than critics had allowed. Far from being "no language" at all, Warton argued, "the ground-work and substance of his [Spenser's] style is the language of his age."[10] While Warton's view was unusual in his own day, it would eventually come to dominate criticism of the modern period.

The strangeness of Spenser's language, we are now told, is an assumption that does not bear the weight of historical evidence, despite what E. K. led so many to believe. Bruce McElderry, using the O.E D. to search for other contemporary examples of the words E. K. glossed, has provided us with a statistical version of Warton's ground-breaking approach to the language of the poem. McElderry tackles all of Spenser's linguistic "innovations," including dialect words, archaisms, and neologisms. E. K. provided glosses for three hundred words that he deemed unusual enough to warrant explanation, but McElderry establishes that forty-five of these were probably familiar enough to Spenser's readers. Of the remaining words, between forty and fifty are dialect forms "apparently chosen by Spenser with a conscious effort to suggest rusticity." Approximately 165 are archaisms, and the rest are divided among invented words, borrowings, and variant forms. He is able to deduce from these totals, as Warton had done anecdotally, that Spenser's language is "largely the English of his day, enriched from legitimate sources and by legitimate methods." (One wonders, incidentally, what sources and methods McElderry did not consider legitimate for poets). Dialect, in parcular, is "almost neglible in Spenser after the *Shepheardes Calender* and indeed not imposing even in the early poem." McElderry concludes that E. K., in a frenzy of "overzealous editing not unlike the bristling annotations of many a modern text . . . at times explained the obvious or the near-obvious."[11]

McElderry, it should be noted, partly misled his readers about the paucity of unusual words in the *Shepheardes Calender.* Although he made both calculations, McElderry emphasized the number of different archaic or dialect forms Spenser employed, rather than the total number of times he employed them. The forty-five distinct dialect words he cites often appear multiple times in the eclogues; Spenser's readers, in fact, would encounter over a hundred provincial forms in the course of the work. There may be only 165 archaic words in the poem, but the number of actual occurrences is nearly twice that number. All told, Spenser's contemporaries would have continually come across "strange" words as they made their way through the poem.

Nevertheless, by the middle of this century McElderry and others had successfully established the view that E. K.'s concern about the unfamiliarity of Spenser's language in the *Shepheardes Calender* had been illplaced. Apparently, E. K. had nothing to "apologize" for at all. Archaisms, especially, flourished in English poetry of the sixteenth century, and it is unlikely that Spenser's sophisticated readers would have troubled over the meanings of his "antique" words.[12] As for dialect, Spenser was probably adapting ideas current in sixteenth-century French literary theory. The circle of poets known collectively as the Pleiade set forth a program for enriching and expanding the language that made provision for dialect. Du Bellay's *Deffence de la Langue Francoyse* (1549) and Ronsard's expanded version, the *Abrege de l'Art Poetique François* (1565) encouraged poets to search out new sources of diction in order to promote the vernacular. To this end, Du Bellay championed archaisms and neologisms, but Ronsard proposed a more radical poetic language that would draw on the technical fields, like founding and metallurgy, and the provincial dialects. Spenser was familiar with Du Bellay's poetry (Spenser's earliest literary endeavors were translations of Du Bellay) and the literary theory espoused in the *Tears of the Muses* suggests he knew Du Bellay's theoretical writings as well. There is no evidence that Spenser had read the *Abrege* of Ronsard, but Puttenham's writings, among others', seem to bear traces of Ronsard's treatise.[13] And if he did not discover the Pleiade's theories for himself, Spenser may have gleaned something from his teacher at the Merchant Taylor's School, Richard Mulcaster, whose rather unusual linguistic views have been traced directly to Du Bellay.[14]

This seems like a reasonable hypothesis, but it has its own share of problems. First of all, none of Ronsard's English enthusiasts, including Mulcaster, mentioned his ideas conceding dialect—let alone put them into practice. Proponents of this view, moreover, assume that Spenser's linguistic experiments were, like Du Bellay's, attempts to enrich the vernacular.[15] Mulcaster was indeed a vocal champion of introducing new words into the standard idiom, by a process he names "enfranchisement." Strange and foreign words, he wrote, must "becom bond to the rules of our writing . . . as the stranger denisons be to the lawes of our cuntre. . . . If we mean to make them ours, then let them take an oath to be trew to our tung, and the ordinances thereof."[16] But if Spenser was inspired by the theories of the Pleiade, either directly or indirectly through Mulcaster's teachings, his motives for using unusual words widely diverged from his masters'. Spenser's interest in variant forms seems to have nothing to do with expanding the English vocabulary according to the procedure outlined by Mulcaster, for he made not the slightest effort to accommodate his "strange" words to the "ordinances" of standard language. He did not, for example, adapt older spellings to the orthographic conventions of his day; on the contrary, Spenser deliberately manipulated orthography to give his diction an antique look.[17] Had Spenser been concerned that the provincial diction of the *Calender* gain general currency, he surely would have continued to use dialect in the same proportions in the *Faerie Queene,* or, at least, in his later pastoral poetry. As all of Spenser's critics have observed, however, Spenser concentrated dialect in the *Shepheardes Calender,* and largely abandoned it thereafter.[18]

Contemporary efforts to demystify Spenser's language, in general, fail to explain why E. K. insisted on its unfamiliarity, both in his letter to Harvey and in his glosses which, after all, are predicated on the idea that Spenser's diction required translation. If E. K. explicated only "the obvious or near obvious," why would Spenser's own contemporaries have objected so strenuously to his language, just as E.K. said they would? The early reception of the *Calender,* alone, compels us to take E. K. at his word.

The presence of archaism, perhaps, was not enough to produce the impression of unfamiliarity in a sixteenth-century pastoral poem, but the addition of dialect was something else entirely. The question of dialect in the *Shepheardes Calender,* in fact, has provoked some renewed speculation, despite so many efforts to put the matter to rest. Most recently, Patricia Ingham has helped to reopen the controversy. Ingham cites earlier critics who explained how Spenser might have acquired his knowledge of northern English but, she observes, their findings beg the larger issue: "Even if Spenser's North-country connections and residence were proved beyond possibility of doubt, the use of Northern forms by a court poet still presents a problem."[19] The decision to include provincial words in a courtly work, Ingham maintains, was very strange indeed.

McElderry had suggested that Spenser used dialect as an attempt to establish the rusticity of his shepherds. Ingham disagrees. Spenser's contemporaries, she reminds us, did not share modern ideas concerning linguistic verisimilitude. Sixteenth-centry pastoral poets, such as George Turberville, prescribed common diction for the language of shepherds: "For as the conference betwixt shephierds is familiar stuffe and homely: so have I shapt my stile and tempred it with suche common and ordinarie phrase of speach as Countreymen do use in their affaires. . . ." In the sixteenth century, however, "common and ordinarie" speech referred to plain or unadorned language, but never to dialect. McElderry's reading, in other words, pertains to Burns or Hardy, but not to Spenser.[20] Ingham forgets, however, that E. K., Spenser's contemporary, is the ultimate source of the view that the poet set out to create the effect of rusticity.

Nevertheless, Ingham finds other grounds for understanding the anomalous presence of dialect in Spenser's pastoral. Sixteenth-century grammarians generally deemed the English dialects "barbarous" or "rough." Ingram notes that Spenser clustered dialect in three eclogues, May, July, and September, which, in her estimate, contain thirteen, fifteen, and nineteen dialect forms respectively. These eclogues also share a thematic tie: Each belongs to E.K.'s "moral" group, and deals, specifically, with the evils of a bad clergy. From this evidence, Ingham suggests that Spenser sought to create an especially "rough" style for these eclogues, in order to fulfill the generic requirements of satire.[21]

But even if dialect appears with somewhat greater frequency in these eclogues, there is surely no statistical significance in the fact that while there are thirteen dialect forms in May, for example, there are seven in October, six each in August and November, and so forth. Ingham's attempt to understand Spenser's use of dialect according to the specific placement of northern words throughout the *Calender* is based, moreover, on the questionable assumption that dialect words lead an independent life in the poem. By isolating dialect in this way, Ingham brackets the most difficult and interesting issue of all—the relationship between Spenser's dialect words and his archaisms.[22] Ingham was right to alert us to the contradictions of a courtly pastoral that incorporated provincial forms; in a sense, she was picking up where E. K. had left off, four hundred years before. It is time, now, to look once again at the problems generated by the presence of dialect in the *Calender,* and its effect on the nature of Spenser's project as a whole.

Whether or not Spenser derived the idea to incorporate dialect in his eclogues from other writers, the poet was treading on new, even forbidden territory as far as his English contemporaries were concerned. While the literary use of archaisms had a long-standing tradition, the very idea of dialect—the speech of the provincial or the poor[23]—had just arrived on the Renaissance intellectual scene. The Renaissance interest in dialect was a by-product of the more immediate concerns of early modern language reformers, the men who compiled the first English dictionaries, grammars, and spelling reform treatises. Such works established the first guidelines of proper usage, based on the speech of upper-class Londoners, an elite version of the vernacular already known as the "King's English." Often enough, Renaissance language reformers isolated dialect as the source of the many linguistic ills plaguing the vernacular. Edmund Coote, author of one of the most influential treatises on orthography, blamed the vagaries of Renaissance spelling on the persistence of dialect: "I know not what can easily deceive you in writing, unless it bee imitating the barbarous speech of your country people." Richard Verstegan shared his view: "Differences in one same language do commonly grow among the common people; . . . of il pronunciation lastly ensueth il writing." John Hart, another spelling reformer, warned his countrymen of the influence of those of "the farre West, or North Countryes, which use differing termes from those of the Court, and London, where the flower of the English tongue is used. If some such one come to any good learning . . . and putteth some worke in print, his authoritie maketh many a rude English worde to be printed."[24] Apparently, these men were most concerned that dialect be excluded from writing, and kept out of print.

George Puttenham, in his *Arte of English Poesie,* applied the new dialectology to literature, prescribing the regional bounds of literary English. In the well-known passage, Puttenham decreed that

> neither shall [the poet] take the termes of Northern-men, such as they use in dayly talke, whether they be noble men or gentlemen or of their best clarkes, all is a matter; nor in effect any speach used beyond the river of Trent, though no man can deny that theirs is the purer English Saxon at this day, yet it is not so Courtly nor so currant as our Southerne English is; no more is the far Westerne mans speach. Ye shall therefor take the usuall speach of the Court, and that of London and the shires lying about London within lx. myles, and not much above . . . But herein we are already ruled by th'English Dictionaries and other bookes written by learned men.[25]

While Puttenham categorically excludes the dialects from the borders of poetic language, he wavers for a moment over the northern variety. In 1565 Lawrence Nowell began to compile the first Old English dictionary, the *Vocabularium Saxiconum.* Observing a resemblance between Anglo-Saxon vocabulary and terms that occurred exclusively in northern speech, Nowell included in his dictionary 173 words from his home county, Lancashire, as well as a handful from other shires. He noted northern survivals of older words as follows:

> Adreogan. To endure, to suffer, to abide. Lanc. to dree.
> Aetwitan. To blame, to reproache, to laye the fawte on.
> Lanc. to wite.
> Derian, To hurt, to harm. Lanc. to deere, etc.[26]

The pioneering work of men like Nowell generated the idea, evident in Puttenham's treatise, that the rubble of northern English could be mined for fossils of the older language. For these men, northern English satisfied a nationalistic desire to recover the nation's original linguistic purity.[27]

But the alliance Nowell forged between archaisms and northern words was an uneasy one at best. Despite recent advances in the field of linguistic history, and the new claims of northern English, traditional theories of poetic diction simply made no provision for provincial speech. Renaissance proponents of old words generally relied on Quintilian, an early champion of literary archaism. Yet Quintilian himself specifically denounced the use of dialect words, as well as other, "foreign" forms, in poetry.[28] Few critics, it seems, were willing to abandon Quintilian in the light of recent findings.

Nevertheless, a few radical thinkers struggled to integrate northern English into an orthodox poetics. Alexander Gill, for example, insisted that proper poetic language "will have to conform not to the pronunciation of ploughmen, working girls, and river-men, but to that used by learned and refined men." After describing the pronunciation of ploughmen, including that of northern ploughmen, he cements the alliance between poetic language and the King's English by reminding his readers,

> What I say here concerning the dialects, you must realise, refers only to country people, since among persons of genteel character and cultured upbringing, there is but one universal speech.

Poets, he continues, should therefore draw their materials from the "universal" speech of the genteel. But Gill qualifies the universality of standard poetic language with one exception:

> Unless they [poets] use the Northern dialect, quite frequently for the purpose of rhythm or attractiveness, since that dialect is the most delightful, the most ancient, the purest, and approximates most nearly to the speech of our ancestors.

To illustrate the point, Gill cites Spenser as a northern dialect poet, and concludes with a fragment of a popular northern ballad: "And so that we may not always quote the Sidneys and Spensers, note the epilogue of a story written in the Northern dialect entitled "Machiavelli the Villain:"

> Machil is hanged
> And brened is his buks.
> Thogh Machil is hanged
> Yet he is not wranged.[29]

The difficulty here is that Gill never denies that northern English, like the other regional dialects, is the language of ploughmen and working girls. At the same time, he hails the northern dialect for its poetic qualities, its "rhythms" and its "attractiveness." The integrity of his logic, finally, compels him to equate Spenser's experiment with the works of provincial balladeers.

George Puttenham, on the other hand, had managed to avoid this situation by adhering to a consistent appraisal of the English dialects. Puttenham simply refused to make an exception for the language of northerners, despite its purity, on the grounds that the dialect was not as "courtly" as upper-class London speech. Puttenham, of course, disapproved of old words as well. He decreed that the poet "shall not follow Piers Plowman no Lydgate nor yet Chaucer, for their language is now out of use with us."[30] By avoiding the entangled relations of archaisms and northern words, Puttenham's promotion of London English as the exclusive medium of literature remained relatively free of equivocation. But once both archaisms and northern words were admitted into poetry, contradiction followed right behind.

This contradiction was intensified by the fact that literary authors, alongside the grammarians, were drawing their own conclusions about the provincial dialects. Most Renaissance authors who choose to represent northern English were unaware, or unimpressed, by the work of men like Nowell.[31] English jest books from the early part of the sixteenth century often poked fun at the speech of country yokels. In the *Merie Tales of Master Skelton,* the author describes his travels to London with a foolish "Kendalman" whose language confirms his northern origins: "Ise wrang; I bus [must] goe tyll bed . . . In gewd faith, Ise bay your skott [charge] to London." Skeleton tricks the Kendalman into believing he has the sweating sickness by placing a stick of butter under his hat, and magically "cures" him by drying it off. The Kendalman, in effect, owes his infirmity to a Londoner, on whom all hope of advancement to the capital depends. Richard Verstegan tells an anecdote about a London courtier who orders a northern man to "equippe" his horse. The northerner, confounded by a standard pronunciation, believes that the courtier desires him to "whip" the animal.[32] The Renaissance virtually invented the genre of dialect comedy, and, from this time forwards, juxtaposing a peasant dialect with the King's English could always be played for laughs.

Later authors followed the lead of the jest boks, and northern provincials appear in plays and narrative poems dating from the 1580s.[33] In general, literary portraits of northerners were far from flattering. Thomas Heywood and Richard Brome, in *The Late Lancashire Witches,* show their contemporaries how funny it would be—and how dangerous—if northern speakers came to power. Basing their material on a scandal that was said to have occurred in contemporary Lancashire, the playwrights tell of a northern village in which the proper order of things has been rendered "topsie turvy" by a bevy of malevolent witches, disguised as ordinary housewives. In this bewitched English region, children command their parents and servants lord it over their masters. Two peasants named Lawrence and Parnell, the only dialect speakers of the play, usurp the role of their bourgeois employers. Lawrence describes his new-found authority:

> Heres sick an a din. . . . He mainteynes me to rule him, and i'le deu't, or ma' the hear weary o' the weambe on him. . . A fine world when a man cannot be whyet at heame.

Parnell, his fiancee, settles their plans to marry and seize full control of the household:

> Here's all as true as booke, here's both our Masters have consented and concloyded, and our Mistresses mun yield toyt, to put aw house and lond and aw they have into our hands. . . . And we mun marry and be master and dame of aw.[34]

This preposterous state of affairs is made all the more outrageous by the rustic language of the reigning servants.

Although the witches themselves do not speak in dialect, the social promotion of dialect speakers, the authors imply, can only be the work of the devil. Fortunately, the witches' sorcery is readily contained by the application of ordinary Lancashire law: "Witches apprehended under hands of lawful authority, doe loose their power; / And all their spells are instantly dissolv'd." Sure enough, the apprehension of the witches restores Lawrence and Parnell to their working class status, and their commitment to servitude: "Yie han pit on your working geere, to swinke and serve our Master and Maistresse like intill painfull servants agaone, as we shudden."[35] The ascendancy of dialect, we are led to believe, can and must be stopped by the authorities.

Ingham had taken issue with McElderry's claim that Spenser intended verisimilitude when he chose to include dialect in his eclogues, on the grounds that other pastoral poets had never done so before. But there is no reason to assume that Spenser's literary horizons weren't rather broader than that. Spenser may not have intended "realism" in the modern sense of the word, yet the provincial origins of the northern terms he used were real enough to him. Indeed, as soon as E. K. glossed the northern elements of his diction, Spenser could not avoid the assignation of rusticity. Northern English may have enjoyed historical ties to the ancient language, but no one, not even Nowell, attempted to deny its contemporary association with peasants.

It would be easy to assume that the *Shepheardes Calender,* with its open concern for patronage and its praise of the monarch, incorporated northern English as a display of the author's nationalistic zeal. But such a reading ignores the more prohibitive aspects of Renaissance English dialectology, and the testimony of numerous other authors who turned to northern English as an example of rude speech. By including northern English in his pastoral diction, the new poet, making his literary debut, was taking a considerable professional risk: his critics, rather than hailing his patriotism, might rank him as a dialect poet, akin to the common balladeers, far removed from the literary establishment in London. Some of his first critics, such as Pope and Johnson, did just that.

Indeed, Spenser invited such a reading as soon as he set foot in the provinces. The author of the *Shepheardes Calender* understood the contradictions he generated by incorporating dialect in a courtly work, and he deliberately let those contradictions stand. Spenser's language, as E. K. hinted again and again, was designed to disturb and provoke his readers, by forcing a confrontation between the provinces and the court. Spenser's language, to be sure, was not as quite as strange as E. K. implied, for the poet had to balance the effect of strangeness against the dangers of obscurity—the possibility that he would not be understood. But E. K., despite the modern consensus concerning his commentary, cannot be dismissed so easily. He was trying to tell us that the difficulties presented by Spenser's language represent the interpretive crux of the poem, and he merits a hearing.

North and South: "O pierlesse Poesye, where is then thy Place?"

In *The Northern Lass,* the early seventeenth-century playwright Richard Brome took provincial language beyond the realm of dialect comedy. Brome's heroine is a peasant girl named Constance who journeys south to many the prodigal Sir Philip Luckless, to whom she has been promised. When her prudish governess asks how often she has seen

Sir Philip, Constance answers in her northern dialect: "Feath but that bare eance nother, and you seln were by too. Trow yee that Ide not tell yee and twere maer. Buy my Conscience Mrs. Trainewell I lee not." The Londoners await the arrival of their northern guest and the language she will bring to them with great anticipation: "You said, she spoke and sung Northernly. I have a great many Southern Songs already; but Northern Ayres nips it dead. York, York, for my money" exclaims one of her enthusiasts. The northern dialect, it seems has become a saleable commodity, more attractive, and more highly valued, than southern speech.[36]

Brome's *Northern Lass* attempts to sell the novelty of "northernness" to its audience, exploiting the fact that the dialect, despite its casual appearance in a variety of works throughout the period, was "foreign" in the eyes of most London readers. In a dedicatory letter affixed to the play, Brome describes his protagonist: "A Countrey Lass I present you . . . Shee came out of the cold North, thinly clad, but wit had pity on her, Action apparrell'd her . . . She is honest, and modest, though she speake broad; And though Art never strung her tongue; yet once it yeelded a delightful sound." Without warning, Brome 's description of the northern girl's journey south becomes an account of his own literary odyssey. Constance's northern dialect, he writes,

> gain'd her many Lovers and Friends, by whose goodliking she prosperously lived, until her late long Silence and Discontinuance (to which she was compell'd). . . . Wherefore she, now, desirous to settle herself in some worthy service and no way willing . . .to return from this Southern Sun-shine, back to her native Air; I thought it might become my care (having first brought and estrang'd her from her Countrey) to sue, with her, for Your noble Patronage . . . Northern spirits wil soon wax bold. If you be pleased to accept of her, shee will travaile no further.[37]

The northern lass, it is clear, has much in common with the man who has authored her: Constance's enforced "long Silence" apparently refers to Brome's own frustrated attempts to write or produce his works. The northern girl, Brome claims, desires nothing more than to remain in the south; the author has "estrang'd her from her Countrey" to sue for a southern patron. Whether or not Brome literally made a trip to the capital at this time is not as important as the fact that he figures himself as a northerner yielding a new "delightful sound" to the southern literary market. If Brome's scheme succeeds, his patron will recognize the value of northern commodities. "York, York, for my money."

Brome's play was written fifty years after Spenser composed his eclogues, and the suit of the *Northern Lass* did not concern him. But it is not impossible that Brome borrowed the idea of exploiting linguistic novelty, and northern "boldness," from his predecessor. Assuming the status of a northerner, an outsider speaking a new language, Brome, in his own account, "estranges" his work in an effort to attract a patron. It was Spenser, I suggest, who invented such a strategy.

The author of the *Shepheardes Calender,* in his own account, is an outsider, and he identifies himself only by a cryptic, foreign title, "Immerito." Spenser made much of the idea that he was unknown to his readers, more, surely, than was actually necessary. He must have known that he was not fooling anyone by pretending that the authorship of his poem was a mystery. Nevertheless, in the dedicatory verses to the *Calender,* Spenser goes further, describing his work as a child "whose parent is unkent" ("To His Booke," 2). E. K. reinforces the poet's gestures of self-effacement at the start of his letter to Harvey, presenting the author as "uncouthe, unkiste", a phrase attributed to "the olde famous poete Chaucer" (2).

The archaic words "uncouthe" (unfamiliar, unknown), and unkiste" (literally, "unkissed," hence, untried or unknown) resonate with Spenser's self-identifying epithet "unkent" (also, unknown). "Unkent" is a northern dialect term, and since Spenser's dedicatory verses to the *Shepheardes Calender* mark one of its first appearances in print,[38] it is unlikely that the word would have been widely familiar to a courtly audience. These three terms, foregrounded at the onset of our reading of the poem, at once denote the meaning "unknown" and embody it linguistically, bringing the mystery surrounding the author to bear directly on his language. Spenser's refusal to name himself, then, is not an act of self-effacement, a plea for anonymity. When he called himself "unkent," he was trumpeting his arrival as the new poet by means of a bold new language.

In the first eclogue, the winter lament of "January," Colin sings, as other literary shepherds had before him, of the anguish of unrequited love. The earth, he explains, had once been full of hope: "Whilome thy fresh spring flowrd, and after hasted/Thy sommer prowde with Daffadillies dight" (*daffadilies* is northern, *dight* is both archaic and northern, and *whilome* is archaic; [21–22]). But now that Rosalind has rebuffed his amorous advances, the frost has destroyed the summer flowers and Colin, in turn, breaks his pipes—apparently out of despair. Louis Montrose has shown how the pastoral suit for love may represent other forms of desire ("Amorous motives displace or subsume forms of desire, frustration, and resentment other than the merely sexual"), including the desire for professional advancement.[39] In the opening eclogue, as many have suggested, Spenser establishes Colin's broken pipe as an emblem of the poet's thwarted hopes and ambitions.

Critics have often remarked on the way that Colin's opening performance in "January" finds its parallel in the final act of "December": Colin breaks his pipes at the end of the first eclogue, and hangs up his pipes at the end of the poem. The two certainly appear to be analogous gestures.[40] But while Colin's hanging up his pipes in the "December" eclogue represents a gesture of farewell, that is not where he begins: The broken pipes of the "January" eclogue characterize the peculiar nature of Colin's song—replete with "broken" English forms—and not its suppression. After all, Colin continues to sing in the "June," "November," and "December" eclogues, after he has allegedly destroyed the instrument of his music; although we never see or hear that he has mended them, Colin's pipes play on. Implicitly, Colin composes his "rurall musick" on pipes he has purposefully broken, not as an act of futility or resignation, but as a deliberate poetic strategy. Colin's breaking his pipes is not an act of destruction or a demonstration of impotence, but the enabling act of the eclogues as a whole.

That Colin seems to break his pipes out of despair, because he is suffering for love of Rosalind, is no more than a ploy, although it is easy to take the poet's self-characterization at face value. The poet represents himself as a victim, even a fool, according to Hobbinol: "Sicker I hold him, for a greater fon,/ That loves the thing, he cannot purchase" (158–59). But Spenser's Colin is no fool, and his suffering is disingenuous. If what Colin desires is out of reach, if what separates the poet from the realization of his ambitions is some form of distance—whether geographical or social, political or psychological—the poet makes a virtue out of the distance stretching across the divide. By insisting that his language is strange, too difficult for readers to understand without E. K.'s glosses, Spenser displaces the experience of desire onto his audience, who must translate Spenser's words.

Even the glosses, in fact, do not serve the reader fully in this regard, for E. K. is often deliberately coy about imparting information. E. K. declares that "as touching the generall dryft and purpose of his

Aeglogues, I mind not to say much, him self labouring to conceale it" (22). E. K. came by his knowledge of the poem from the author himself: "By means of some familiar acquaintance, I was made privie to his counsell and secret meaning in them. . . which albeit I know he nothing so much hateth as to promulgate, yet thus much I have adventured upon his friendship, him selfe being for long time furre estraunged" (23–24). E. K. sets up a kind of good cop/bad cop routine that works something like this: The poet refuses to publish his "secret meanings," yet E. K. will let us in on some of them; the poet is in some remote, inaccessible place, "furre estraunged," but his editor, despite Spenser's wishes, will bring him just a little closer. We are told just enough to know that we do not know everything about the poem, and we become, in Colin's stead, unrequited suitors of a meaning that the poet will not completely divulge. We, and not Colin, are left to suffer the effects of the poet's estrangement.

E. K. does not tell us why Spenser is "furre estraunged," or where exactly he has gone, but we are told of the whereabouts of Colin. In the "June" eclogue, Spenser explicitly locates his protagonist, and his broken pipes, in the north country. "June" consists of a discussion between Hobbinol and Colin concerning whether Colin is better off in staying where he is, in the "hylls," or migrating to Hobbinol's "dales." Hobbinol describes the dales as a kind of paradise, "where shepheards ritch, / And fruictfull flocks bene everywhere to see" (21–2). He invites Colin to "forsake the soyle, that so doth thee bewitch" (18) and join his community of prosperous shepherds. E. K. fills in the eclogue's sketchy geography when he explains in the glosses that

> this is not poetical fiction, but unfeynedly spoke of the poete selfe, who for special occasion of private affayres (as I have bene partly of himselfe informed) and for his more preferment, removing out of the North parts, came into the South.

E. K. then glosses the "hylles" as "the North countrye" and the "dales" as the "Southpartes . . . whiche . . . in respecte of the Northpartes they be called dales. For indede the North is counted the higher countrye."

As the eclogue continues, the issue of height, the physical elevation of the North country with respect to the South, takes on a broader meaning. When Hobbinol praises the songs that Colin was "wont on wastfull hylls to singe" (50) he is still referring to the "wastful hylls" of the North. But suddenly the "hylls" become charged with professional significance: The poet's place (where he sings) and the poet's ambitions (why he sings) become deeply implicated as the eclogue evolves. Colin swears he has never ascended any hills: "I never lyst presume to Parnasse hyll, / But, pyping lowe in shade of lowly grove, / I play to please my selfe" (70–72). He identifies "pyping lowe" with having no political aspirations: "Nought weigh I, who my song doth prayse or blame, / Ne strive to winne renowne, or passe the rest: . . I wote my rymes bene rough, and rudely drest . . . " (73–74;79). As a poet, Colin avers, he has no ambition to climb; his rhymes, "rough and rudely drest," are not songs of self-promotion. But the glosses give Colin the lie: E. K. tells us outright that Colin, representing Spenser, travels south in search of preferment. Why does the poet deny his desire to gain professional advancement, even as he contemplates joining Hobbinol's southern paradise of "ritch" and "fruitfull" shepherds?

This is the central paradox that defines Spenser's professional strategy. Colin sings in the north to please himself (in the fiction of the *Calender,* he never actually migrates south) and yet he succeeds in pleasing his southern audiences. Colin's humility is only a pose, for his fame is a foregone conclusion among his southern peers: "O Colin, Colin, the shepheards joye, / How I admire ech turning of thy verse" (Perigot, "August" 190–91). For Spenser, there is no contradiction in the idea that the North country is "higher" than the South, and yet a wasteland for poets seeking fame. Like Richard Brome in *The Northerne Lass,* Spenser characterizes his protagonist as a northerner, an outsider attempting to gain entry to the south, but the key to that entry is his northern language. Like Brome, Spenser hints that the north country is really the higher poetic region, even as he presses his suit for southern patronage.

When Piers in "October" cries out "O pierlesse Poesye, where is then thy place?" (79) he opens the debate between Colin and Hobbinol once again: Should poetry be the art of "pyping low in lowly grove" or the art of scaling the poetic heights? It has generally been assumed that the answer lies in Spenser's self-conscious imitation of Virgil's career, in which the successful poet begins by piping low and ends with higher kinds. With the hindsight of Spenser's subsequent achievement, culminating in the epic *Faerie Queene,* it seems a reasonable solution to the problem. The "October" eclogue, in fact, appears to promise such a progression. Cuddie, Spenser's "perfect patterne of a poete," yearns to sing in the tragic or epic mode: "O if my temples were distained with wine, / And girt in girlonds of wild yvie twine, / How I could reare the Muse on stately stage, / And teache her tread aloft in buskin fine, / With queint Bellona in her equipage!" (110–14). E. K. censures this "poetical fury" on the grounds that Cuddie has abandoned decorum: "The numbers rise so ful, and the verse groweth so big, that it seemeth he hath forgot the meanesse of shepheards state and stile." Piers returns Cuddie to matters more appropriate to pastoral, and the ecologue ends in a humbler mode, replete with dialect: "And when my *Gates* shall *han* their bellies layd, / Cuddie shall have a Kidde to store his farme" (119–20, emphasis added).

But had there been no *Faerie Queene,* the *Calender* alone provides little evidence the poet is presenting his pastoral as a low form that will be superseded by a higher one. "October," which critics have relied on to support the Virgilian model, ends with Cuddie's retraction:

> ah! my corage cooles ere it be warme,
> For thy content us in thys humble shade:
> Where no such troublous tydes han us assayde,
> Here we our slender pipes may safely charme
>
> (115–18).

The effect of Cuddie's "poetical fury," and his references to tragedy and epic, is not to defer higher forms, but to incorporate them within the literary and linguistic space of pastoral.[41] Spenser dismantles the hierarchies ordering high and low diction, and high and low kinds, in order to present himself, impossibly enough, as an untried poet at the height of his literary powers. Spenser's first poem indeed plots the path of his literary career, but not in terms of future accomplishments. The *Shepheardes Calender* did not merely presage the arrival of an eminent poet, for that poet, according to Spenser's scheme, had already arrived.

Spenser transformed the lowly grove of pastoral into a hill, a hill, in fact, that his own readers could not easily climb. The presence of northern English in the *Shepheardes Calender* reveals how far the poet was willing to travel in order to create the impression of novelty, and difference, even at the risk of alienating his "southern" audiences. *The Shepheardes Calender*, in fact, exploits that risk, making estrangement the very condition of poetic achievement.

If it is an exaggeration to compare Edmund Spenser with a dialect poet such as Robert Burns, perhaps one can allow this much: both distinguished their poetic worlds by means of a marginalized variety of English, using linguistic difference as a way to set themselves apart from a dominant culture. Both implied that their works were only apparently "low"; in fact, they invited us to recognize the superior values, both aesthetic and ideological, that their poetic language embodied. Charles Gildon, writing sixty years before the publication of Burns's early poetry, remained uneasy about the presence of dialect in the *Shepheardes Calender*, although he allowed that the poetic use of northernisms represented a new departure for English literature:

> He give us a Northern Dialect, which renders his Pastorale unintelligible, without the help of Spelman, or some other Glossarist . . . No body before this extraordinary Poet ever writ in any of our own Country Dialects, whether Western or Northern.[42]

Perhaps it is time, once again, to credit Spenser with the innovation.

Harvard University

NOTES

This essay is adapted from a book, in preparation, on the uses of dialect in Renaissance English literature.

1. George Puttenham, *The Arte of English Poesie,* ed. Baxter Hathaway (Kent, Ohio: Kent State University Press, 1970), p. 53.
2. Louis Adrian Montrose, "Of Gentlemen and Shepherds: The Politics of Elizabethan Pastoral Form," *ELH*, 22 (1982), 415–53.
3. E. K., *Epistle to Gabriel Harvey,* in *The Works of Edmund Spenser, A Variorum Edition*, ed. E. A. Greenlaw et al., 11 vols. (Baltimore, MD: Johns Hopkins Press, 1932–57),I,3. All subsequent citations from the *Shepheardes Calender,* including E. K.'s commentary, refer to volume one of this edition and are given parenthetically in the text.
4. Many critics have argued that "E. K." was a mask behind which the poet attempted to manipulate our reception of the poem. For recent attempts to prove that E. K. and Spenser were one and the same person, see for example, Patsy Scherer Cornelius. *E. K.'s Commentary on* The Shepheardes Calender (Salzburg: Institut for Englische Sprache und Literatur, 1974) and Louise Schleiner, "Spenser's 'E. K.' as Edmund Kent (Kenned/Of Kent): Kyth (Couth) Kissed, and Kunning-Conning," *ELR*, 20.3 (1990), 374–407.
5. Ben Jonson, *Discoveries*, in *The Works of Ben Jonson*, ed. C. H. Herford and Percy Simpson, 11 vols. (London: Oxford University Press, 1966), VIII, 618. Sir Philip Sidney, *A Defence of Poetry*, in *Miscellaneous Prose of Philip Sidney*, ed. Katherine Duncan-Jones and Jan Van Dorsten (Oxford: Clarendon Press, 1973), p. 112.
6. John Dryden, *Dedication of the Pastorals*, cited in Greenlaw, VII, 577; Alexander Pope, *A Discourse on Pastoral Poetry*, in *The Selected Prose of Alexander Pope,* ed. Paul Hammond (Cambridge: Cambridge University Press, 1987), p. 155; Samuel Johnson, *Rambler* No. 37 (July 1750), cited in Greenlaw, VII, 575.
7. Merritt Y. Hughes, "Spenser and the Greek Pastoral Triad," *Studies in Philology.* 20 (1923), 190.

8. Sidney, p. 112.
9. Hughes, 188.
10. Thomas Warton, *Observations on the Faerie Queene of Spenser,* cited in Greenlaw, VII, 575.
11. Bruce Robert McElderry, Jr. "Archaism and Innovation in Spenser's Poetic Diction," *PMLA*, 47.1 (March 1932), 149, 153, 145, 150.
12. For a discussion of archaism in sixteenth century verse, see for example Vere L. Rubel, *Poetic Diction in the English Renaissance: From Skelton Through Spenser* (New York: Modern Language Association, 1941).
13. Anne Lake Prescott, *French Poets and the English Renaissance: Studies in Fame and Transformation* (New Haven, Connecticut: Yale University Press, 1978), 263n.
14. W. L. Renwick, "Mulcaster and DuBellay," Modern Language Review, 17.3 (1922), 283.
15. Renwick, for example, argued that Spenser's diction was "an artistic procedure, part of a design for the improvement of English." See "The Critical Origins of Spenser's Diction," *Modern Language Review,* 17.1 (1922), 4.
16. Richard Mulcaster, *The Elementarie*, ed. E. T. Campagnac (Oxford: Clarendon Press, 1925), p. 175.
17. Noel Osselton, "Archaism." in *The Spenser Encyclopedia,* eds. A. C. Hamilton et. al. (Toronto: University of Toronto Press, 1990), p. 52.
18. McElderry, 149.
19. Patricia Ingham, "Spenser's Use of Dialect," *English Language Notes*, 8.3 (March 1971), 164. The sources of Spenser's nothernisms are continually debated by critics of his diction. N. F. Blake contends that Spenser's knowledge of dialect came entirely from medieval authors like Malory *(Nonstandard Language in English Literature* [London: Andre Deutsche, 1981]). But others have noted that some of Spenser's northernisms, while unrecorded in medieval texts, do occur in contemporary English dialects. This suggests that regional speech provided a primary source of his linguistic material. See for example John Draper, "The Glosses to Spenser's *Shepheardes Calender,*" *Journal of English and Germanic Philology,* 18 (1919), 556–74. It seems likely that Spenser took his northernisms from written and "living" sources alike.

Spenser might have gained a familiarity with the spoken dialect during his school years, under the tutelage of northern-born teachers like Richard Mulcaster. A contemporary of Mulcaster's reported that the teachers there "being northern men born . . . had not taught the children to speak distinctly, or to pronounce their words as well as they ought." (C. Bowie Millican, "The Northern Dialect of the *Shepheardes Calender,*" *ELH*, 6 [1939], 211–13). There is some evidence, too, that Spenser's own family hailed from Lancashire; although it has never been demonstrated with any certainty, it may be that Colin's north country, where the poet allegedly spends an extended holiday, refers to the home of some of Spenser's relations.

20. Ingham, 165–66. See also Ingham's entry, "Dialect" in *The Spenser Encyclopedia*, p. 215.
21. Ingham, 166–67.
22. Noel Osselton has suggested that we cannot, on philological grounds, distinguish between Spenser's dialect words and his archaisms at all ("Archaism," in *The Spenser Encyclopedia*, p.52). Most linguists, however, agree on at least forty forms that are dialectal rather than archaic. What is really at stake here, however, has

little to do with what contemporary philologists now know about Spenser's diction. The important question is whether Spenser intended to invoke the difference between dialect words and archaisms, and whether his contemporaries felt their dual presence.

23. Technically, the word dialect may refer to any systematic variant of a national language, including standard or prestige varieties. For convenience, however, I am using the term dialect in reference to nonstandard varieties of English only.

24. Edmund Coote, *The English Schoolemaister,* cited in E. J. Dobson, *English Pronunciation 1500–1700* (Oxford: Clarendon Press, 1968), I, 34; Richard Verstegan, *A Restitution of Decayed Intelligence* (Ann Arbor, Michigan: University Microfilms), Bb2r; John Hart, *A Methode or Comfortable Beginning.* (Ann Arbor, Michigan: University Microfilms), *Preface.*

25. Puttenham, p. 157.

26. Lawrence Nowell, *Vocabularium Saxiconum,* ed. Albert H. Marckwardt (Ann Arbor, Michigan: University of Michigan Press, 1952), p. 22.

27. On the sixteenth— and seventeenth—century interest in "pure" language, see for example William A. Craigie, "The Critique of Pure English from Caxton to Smollett," *Society for Pure English.* 65 (Oxford: Clarendon Press, 1946).

28. Marcus Fabius Quintilius, *The Institutione Oratoria,* trans. Charles Edgar Little (Nashville, Tennessee: George Peabody College, 1951), 8:24; 8:13.

29. Alexander Gill, *Logonomia Anglica*, in *Stockholm Studies in English*, 26–27, ed. Bror Danielsson and Arvid Gabrielson, trans. Robin C. Alston (Stockholm: Almquist and Wiksell, 1972), pp. 87, 104, 104, 169.

30. Puttenham, p. 157.

31. From what is known about Renaissance dialects, most sixteenth and seventeenth century literary representations of northern English are fairly accurate. Some of the most common phonological markers of northern English in Renaissance literature include the use of *a* for *o* in words like *fra* (from), *ane* (one), and *wrang* (wrong); *ae* or *ea for o* in *frae* (from), *wae* (woe) and *heame* (home); *u* for *oo* in *gude* (good) or *buke* (book), and *k* for *ch* in *sic* (such) or *whilke* (which). Northern morphology is commonly represented by the forms of the first and second person singular verb to be, as in *I is* (or *I'se)* and *thou is* (or *thou'se*). The literary northern lexicon includes words such as *deft* (neat, trim), *derne* (dismal), *dight* (to prepare or arrange), *gang* (to go), *gar* (to make), *mickle* (much), *mun* (must), and *til* (to). Renaissance authors who employ northern English often confuse its forms with the Scots dialect, with which it shared many features. For a detailed description of this literary dialect, see Eduard Eckhardt, *Die Dialekt und Auslandertypen des alteren Englischen Dramas,* in *Materialen zur Kunde des alteren Englischen Dramas*, 32 (Louvain, 1910), 108–87.

32. John Skelton, *The Merie Tales of Master Skelton*, ed. W.C. Hazlitt (London: Willis and Sotheran, 1866), pp. 5–6; Verstegan, Ccr.

33. See for example Nathaniel Woodes, *The Conflict of Conscience* (1581), Malone Society Reprints (Oxford: Oxford University Press, 1952); William Warner, *Albion's England* (1586) in *The Works of the English Poets from Chaucer to Cowper,* ed. Alexander Chalmers, 21 vols. (London, 1810); and Ben Jonson, *Bartholomew Fair* (1614), in Herford and Simpson, VII.

34. Thomas Heywood and Richard Brome, *The Late Lancashire Witches* in *The*

Dramatic Works of Thomas Heywood, 6 vols. (New York: Russell & Russell, 1964), IV, 1.1. (no lines given in this edition).

35. Heywood and Brome, 5.1.

36. Richard Brome, *The Northern Lass,* in *The Dramatic Works of Richard Brome,* 3 vols. (New York: AMS Press, Inc., 1966), III, 2.2, 2.1. (no lines given in this edition).

37. Brome, "To Richard Holford."

38. *Oxford English Dictionary,* 2nd ed., s.v. "unkent."

39. Montrose, 440.

40. See for example Richard Mallette, *Spenser, Milton, and Renaissance Pastoral* (Lewisburg, PA: Bucknell University Press, 1981), p. 59; and Richard Helgerson, *Self-crowned Laureates: Spenser, Jonson, Milton and the Literary System* (Berkeley: University of California Press, 1983), pp. 67–82.

41. Sukanta Chaudhuri makes this point in his *Renaissance Pastoral and its English Developments* (Oxford: Clarendon Press, 1989). As Chaudhuri writes, "Spenser is seeking to reflect the entire range of poetic concerns . . . in his shepherd world. He avoids the rejection of the pastoral that is the common concomitant to treating lofty themes in eclogue form, and with which he himself has sometimes been credited" (p. 144).

42. Charles Gildon, *Complete Art of Poetry,* cited in Greenlaw, VII, 575.

ELIZABETH HARRIS SAGASER

Gathered in Time: Form, Meter (and Parentheses) in *The Shepheardes Calender*

SPENSER'S FORMAL PATTERNS seem to generate the very momentum of his poems. His work contrasts markedly with those poems that fuel our debates on early modern subjectivity—poems by Wyatt, Sidney, Shakespeare, and Donne, in which we experience the illusion of an individual voice and mind. Spenser is simply not interested in that counterpoint of abstract pattern and speech intonation that produces the dramatic Renaissance "I."[1]

When we encounter parentheses in the midst of the bold forms and meters of *The Shepheardes Calender*, however, we do experience intermittent moments of tension between formal patterns and the rhythms of speech. Nothing like the sustained counterpoint that produces the voice of a Shakespeare or a Donne, but moments of this tension. Parentheses by their nature signal a shift in tone; they signal the shift necessary to make plain that what is now being read is an interruption, explanation, qualification, or digression. Parentheses therefore effect a fresh—if fleeting—focus on language as speech: they suggest a voice, and so, for a moment, the mind and person that produces that voice. Questions also work this way in the *Calender:* they signal a shift of tone, suggesting a submissive protest to a matter that is proceeding along unprotested. These brief illusions of voice suggest that the measuring of time (what meter is) is not ultimately a controlling of time, but merely a foregrounding of time: it makes time apparent. Once one has said, "All is vanity, and a seeking after wind," one has made a gesture that suggests *all* may not be vanity; this gesture may not be vanity. Yet the paradox of the gesture is this: what constitutes the gesture, and what makes it possible, is the recognition that all is indeed vanity. Such gestures could be characterized as defensive strategies of tolerance and deferral, the making of temporary meaning *out of* an apprehension of oblivion. In short, there is a strategic and compensatory authority in the voice that is born of its lack of authority, that makes plain its utter vulnerability, its origin and destiny in forces much greater than itself. Yet for all its foresight and acknowledgement, this authority of no authority is self-destructive: it complies with vanishing. But it *can* point to itself as it vanishes: it can show, and showing is always a kind of deferral—it accosts the minds of others, romances memory, postpones oblivion.

In the *Calender*, parentheses generate fleeting illusions of reference to persons making such gestures: persons swept up in a purposeless whole—generic mortals in the midst of coercive time. Some of these parenthetical phrases figure complicity with time by serving as repetitious filler: they waver between making a "voice" and pointing up a phrase's artificial, necessary role in rounding out a metrical line (and making sure it rhymes according to the scheme) as in some of Piers's lines in "Maye": "Thilke same Kidde (as I can well devise)/Was too very foolish and unwise" (174–75), or Diggon in "September": "My seely sheepe (ah seely sheepe)/That here by there I whilome usd to keepe," in "September" (62–63).[2] More distinctly figuring such complicity are the parenthetical phrases that comment on the narrative, often instructively. There are examples in every season:

> A Shepeheards boye (no better doe him call)
>
> "Januarye," 1

> With painted words tho gan this proude weede,
> (As most usen Ambitious folke:)
> His colowred crime with craft to cloke.
>
> "Februarie," 160–62

> His harmefull Hatchet he hent in hand,
> (Alas, that it so ready should stand)

And to the field alone he speedeth.
(Ay little helpe to harme there needeth)
"Februarie," 195–98

Sike mens follie I cannot compare
Better, then to the Apes foolish care
That is so enamoured of her young one,
(And yet God wote, such cause hath she none)
"Maye," 95–100

The time was once, and may againe retorne,
(For ought may happen, that hath bene beforne)
"Maye," 103–4

Thy father (that word she spake with payne:
For a sigh had nigh rent her heart in twaine)
"Maye," 193–94

And they that con of Muses skill,
sayne most what, that they dwell
(As goteheards wont) upon a hill
"Julye," 45–47

Such one he was, (as I have heard
old Algrind often sayne)
"Julye," 125–26

But tell me shepherds, should it not yshend
Your roundels fresh, to heare a doolefull verse
Of Rosalend (Who knowes not Rosalend?)[3]
That Colin made, ylke can I you rehearse.
"August," 139–42

At end the shepheard his practise spyed,
(For Roffy is wise, and as Argus eyed)
"September," 202–3

In these instances the "narrator" calls attention to "himself" and his knowledge, sometimes matter-of-factly, sometimes with humor, thereby advising the reader how to read (the poem, and in turn, the world). Yet the "narrator" is never quite in control of "his" narrative:

no parenthetical remark changes the formal patterns of the poem; we could argue that the remarks instead constitute them. In the lines above from "Maye" (193–94), the narrator's hushed descriptive comment is not "free" of the poem, nor does it even try to be: it breaks where the poem's lineation requires it to; it offers a couplet in keeping with the rhyme scheme; and it fits itself to the four beats per line necessary to maintain an abstract metrical structure. The poem itself sets the pace, and the speaker must play by *its* rules—its meter, line breaks, and rhyme scheme, *its limited time*—if "he" wants to remark at all.

I quote only the immediate contexts of these phrases here, but my reference is to the complete poems, and to the *Calender* as a whole. It is within sustained metrical patterns and rhyme schemes that we experience the parentheses, and within poems that are explicitly concerned with the year's progress, the passing of time. We find, indeed, that when E. K. says in the "generall argument of the whole book" that "these xij AEglogues [are] every where answering to the seasons of the twelve months," he means it quite literally; the "answering" is to the months and seasons as they happen physically in the world, the world that human bodies—not Christian souls—apprehend.[4] These stanzas from "Januarye" typify the way time is figured and implicated throughout the *Calender.*

> You naked trees, whose shady leaves are lost,
> Wherein the byrds were wont to build their bowre:
> And now are clothd with mosse and hoary frost
> Instede of bloosmes, wherwith your buds did flowre:
> I see your teares, that from your boughes doe raine,
> Whose drops in drery ysicles remaine.
>
> All so my lustfull leafe is drye and sere,
> My timely buds with wayling all are wasted:
> The blossome, which my braunch of youth did beare,
> With breathed sighes is blowne away, and blasted
> And from mine eyes the drizling teares descend,
> As on your boughes the ysicles depend. (31–42)

Although in dignified iambic pentameter, and in one of the most popular sixteenth-century forms, a quatrain and couplet, ababcc, these stanzas are a bit disconcerting for 1579.[5] Made up of "olde and obsolete" words which are "of most men unused," the stanzas boldly—and strangely—maintain regular meter and rhyme, alliteration, and line integrity.[6] It is a style unabashedly dependent on "poeticall" adjectives—"shady," "hoary," "drye" *and* "sere," compound verbs—"did flower," "doe raine," "did beare," abundant "and"s, inverted syntax, split infinitives, and prominent prepositional phrases as in line 38: "My timely buds with wayling all are wasted." The resulting "grace" and "auctoritie" of the verse undermine the words and sentences as spoken language.[7]

The effect of these stanzas is therefore quite contrary to the effect of another Renaissance poem where an aging man is compared to a winter tree, Shakespeare's sonnet 73. The very form of the sonnet is indicative of the reasoning power of the human mind: traditionally, it is the form of inwardness; the Shakespearean version of course enables three stages of logical development and then a short conclusion or reaction to that argument. Further, as Anthony Easthope has shown, sonnet 73's counterpoint between speech intonation and iambic pentameter effects the illusion of an individual voice—not an everyday voice, granted, but a dramatic voice, the voice of an individual performing his or her thoughts.[8] The conceit is controlled by this argumentative structure and this illusion of voice. The sonnet begins with an "I" prompting a "thou" to understand him and their relationship metaphorically: "That time of year thou mayst in me behold." In the "Januarye" stanzas, that time of year is *in* the world, outside of the man literally, and only in turn within him metaphorically: the world, not an "I" and a "thou," initiates the comparison between tree and man, and the comparison itself is not logically or socially accounted for: "all so" is the only connection between the two descriptions. Instead of testifying to the mind's power to make "sense" of time and the world—to order or organize it in some way, these lines testify to time's power, and meter's power, to inform—and subsume—the mind.[9]

In a poem so deferent to the forces of time, the most intense of the parenthetical phrases are almost Kafkaesque. The brief, fraught illusions of coherent consciousness punctuate the poem with warning and doubt, then vanish, so to speak. Cuddie describes the effect best: " . . . prayse is smoke, that sheddeth in the skye, / . . . words bene wynd, and wasten soone in vayne" ("October," 35–36).The meter and rhyme make it clear that there is barely time for asking questions or making observations, never mind time for answering them: the questions and observations in turn work as a kind of "reference" to the answerlessness of our existence and our inevitable surrender to that answerlessness.

I love thilke lasse, (alas why doe I love?)
And am forlorne, (alas why am I lorne?)
Shee deigns not my good will, but doth reprove
And of my rurall musick holdeth scorne.
"Januarye," 62–65

Nowe dead he is, and lyeth wrapt in lead,
(O why should death on hym such outrage showe?)
And all hys passing skil with him is fledde,
The fame whereof doth dayly greater growe.
"June," 89–92

But who rewards him ere the more for thy?
Or feedes him once the fuller by a graine?
Sike prayse is smoke, that sheddeth in the skye,
Sike words bene wynd, and wasten soone in vayne.
"October," 33–36

O pierlesse Poesye, where is then thy place?
"October," 79

Why doe we longer live, (ah why live we so long)
Whose better dayes death hath shut up in woe?
"November," 73–74

She while she was, (that was, a woful word to sayne)
"November," 93

Dido is gone afore (whose turne shall be the next?)
"November," 193

Why livest thou stil, and yet hast thy deathes wound?
Why dyest thou stil, and yet alive art founde?
"December," 95–96

As the "November" lines above intimate, the disquieting effect of the parenthetical phrase—the image of time and its henchman, death—is most potent of all in "November," the poem E. K. suggests is best of the twelve. Particularly because it is an elegy, its dwindling stanzas, refrain, and other unrelenting formal repetitions have a heightened ability to frustrate the poet's and readers' desire for a redeeming order and proportion, for a poet to be a "maker" in the transcendent sense of the term.[10] The beat goes on before, within, and after the observations and questions: the "carefull verse" simply becomes fuller and fuller of "care," always to no avail.

> Why doe we longer live, (ah why live we so long)
> Whose better dayes death hath shut up in woe?
> The fayrest floure our gyrlond all emong,
> Is faded quite and into dust ygoe.
> Sing now ye shepheards daughters, sing no moe
>   The songs that *Colin* made in her prayse
>   But into weeping turne your wanton layes,
>   O heavie herse,
> Now is time to dye. Nay time was long ygoe,
>   O carefull verse. (73–82)

By "November" we are as aware of the formal patterns that initiate and ultimately possess the poem as we are aware of the physical conditions of the world that always already possess the body. In "November"'s climactic stanza we find Spenser (ourselves?) conflating the two; the "carefull verse" is nearly at one with the herse that carries Dido's corpse; the parenthetical remark suggests the shock of recognizing the absence that herse and verse render intelligible.

> O trustlesse state of earthly things, and slipper hope
> Of mortal men, that swincke and sweate for nought,
> And shooting wide, doe misse the marked scope:
> Nowe have I learnd (a lesson derely bought)
> That nys on earth assuraunce to be sought:
>   For what might be in earthlie mould,
>   That did her buried body hould,
>   O heavie herse,
> Yet saw I on the beare when it was brought
>   O carefull verse. (153–62)

It is not words that accommodate meter, but meter that accommodates, indifferently, words, as the cycle of seasons, *the passing of time* accommodates the voices, and deaths, of individuals. Or we could say: so many individual deaths measure the passing of time, as the remarkable line 81 suggests, with its "parting of the breath"—its disconcerting caesura: "Now is time to die. Nay time was long ygoe."[11]

The post-climactic stanza of "November," which claims "She hath the bonds broke of eternall night," struggles rhetorically against the poem's fundamental knowledge, but it is, I believe, a gratuitous struggle. Colin's new claims are absorbed within the same coercive, funeral-procession meter that laments Dido's absence. And they are constituted by mere language, which has been devalued through every month of the poem and has no chance at this late date of mustering some unworldly authority. Replacing "happye herse" for "heavie herse" and "joyfull verse" for "carefull verse" will not do the trick: nothing new has been witnessed. In short, we have no means by which to receive these lines, or the ensuing stanzas, with their description of Dido reigning as a goddess in the Elysian Fields, as anything but testimony to passing time and the absences that measure it. As John Guillory observes, "time is hidden in our word for the not sacred. If the poet cannot escape the temporality of his medium, there cannot be sacred poetry."[12] Line 181 rings tinny, the parenthesis suggesting more doubt and longing than assurance: "Might I once come to thee (O that I might)." And the question in line 193 is far more haunting than it is hopeful: "*Dido* is gone afore (whose turne shall be the next?)."

Many have noted that Spenser had a problem with endings; impelled by the romance tradition, his poems merely begin, again and again. Indeed, the *Calender* may have no end if not proportioned to the twelve months of the year, and for that same reason, it does not end: the year begins again. But in the context of Spenser's metrical practice it is more productive to understand this poem, among others, as unable to begin; it is constituted by—even driven by—individual end after individual end, continually thwarting the possibility of a whole beginning. These lines from "Daphnaida," probably written within three years of the *Calender*, articulate this obsession with progress being driven by individual loss:

> So all the world, and all in it I hate,
> Because it changeth ever too and fro,
> And never standeth in one certaine state,
> But still unstedfast round about doth goe,
> Like a Mill wheele, in midst of miserie,
> Driven with streames of wretchednesse and woe
> That dying lives, and living still does dye.
>
> (428–34)

Life, time, and meter are all fetters in "Daphnaida": material, oppressive, earthly, plodding, and unrelenting as the loss and grief they make manifest. This is merely the untrustworthy Alcyon speaking, of course, not Spenser, who has also testified to the necessity and delight of perpetual change (in the "unperfite" canto at the end of *The Faerie Queene*, to name only the most obvious of many examples.) But in all of Spenser's poems there is this anxiety that endings are beginnings and beginnings endings; time is not our own. Guillory argues that two "models of tradition and change" inform the *Mutability Cantos*:

> one of which, in order to maintain the authority of tradition, forgets the violence of change; the other of which forgets the fact of continuity in its vision of history as a discontinuous series of violent moments. Mutabilitie is the poet of the latter view, and she does produce a beautiful poem on temporal change; discontinuity is her song: death, chance, and time. But she forgets that the seasons return.[13]

The Shepheardes Calender is also a poem "by Mutability"; the form, meter and parenthesis ensure that "the violence of change" will not be forgotten. But the poem does not achieve this remembrance by forgetting "the fact of continuity": its very premise and structure is that the seasons return. It achieves this remembrance by critiquing what we hope to mean by "continuity" and "return," by confronting the nature of repetition in the world of the individual. Dido, referred to in "November" as "the fayrest May she was that ever went" has passed away, as all particular months, and flowers, and people, must pass away. What returns (or continues, or repeats) is only a likeness of what has been (which is the very essence of repetition in meter and rhyme).[14] It is only the time of year we call May that repeats itself, not a particular May, a particular person. As Colin complains and questions in "November":

> Whence is it, that the flouret of the field doth fade,
> And lyeth buryed long in Winters bale:
> Yet soone as spring his mantle doth displaye,
> It floureth fresh, as it should never fayle?
> But thing on earth that is of most availe,
>   As vertues braunch and beauties budde,
>   Reliven not for any good. (83–89)

I. A. Richards's offers this metaphor for meter, a seemingly ideal one for the poet who emphasizes the strangeness of his "framing of words" and the "might" of setting "thy notes in frame": "Through its very appearance of artificiality, metre produces in the highest degree the 'frame' effect, isolating the poetic experience from the accidents and irrelevancies of everyday existence."[15] But Spenser is stranger than this. Quite contrary to being isolated from the accidents and irrelevancies of everyday existence, poems like *The Shepheardes Calender* and, as well, *The Faerie Queene,* are figuratively constituted by these things. The thousands of seductive, polished Spenserian stanzas in the latter are made up of, and made possible by, so many syntactical tricks, filler phrases, little contortions of language, great sighs and exclamations, forced rhymes, arguably silly elaborations and ornate descriptions; along these lines, Bridges remarks: "if you observe the rimes to *knight* in Spenser's *Faerie Queene*, you will find the poem considerably damaged thereby."[16] But as we ride on canto after canto through the strangely framed words of Book I, then Book II and III and IV, et cetera, punctuated as the *Calender* is with parenthetical observations and questions, but unflinchingly "graceful" and "authoritative" in style, we participate in, and surrender to, all the useless, silly, accidental and ordinary ways time is filled, the violent ways time twists, abbreviates or absorbs what we value, and, most horrible, the beauty and delight of this ruthless coercion. Spenserian form and meter do not finally allegorize divine order, but quotidian order, the order that is linear time, the long line of loss that is history. *The Shepheardes Calender*, and the greater poem it prepared Spenser to write, attest to the absence of everything that might—in the real world—challenge mutability's sway.

Brandeis University

Notes

1. See John Thompson, *The Founding of English Meter* (New York: Columbia University Press, 1961), pp. 88–127. Although I disagree with Thompson's conclusions, I am indebted to his detailed study of Spenser's metrical practice in the *Calender.* In "*The Shepheardes Calender*, Dialogue, and Periphrasis," *Spenser Studies* VIII, ed. Patrick Cullen and Thomas P. Roche, Jr. (New York: AMS Press, 1987), pp. 1–33, Roland Greene observes Spenser's disinterest in "the self" from a generic perspective, examining "Spenser's undermining of the criterion of lyric individuality," and noting how "everyone can stand in for nearly everyone else" in the world of the *Calender* (pp. 11–12). Compare also David Miller, "Spenser's Vocation, Spenser's Career," *ELH* 50 (1983), p. 225. "His ideal is not the individual voice, however striking its rhetoric," Miller writes, "but the communal tones of a poet whose identity coincides with that of his society."

2. *The Poetical works of Edmund Spenser,* eds. J.C. Smith and E. De Selincourt (London: Oxford University Press, 1960). All quotations of Spenser's poetry are from this edition. I have regularized i/j and u/v.

3. We hear echoes of this question in *The Fairie Queen:* "(Who knowes not *Colin Clout*?)" (VI.x.16) and "(Who knowes not *Arlo-hill*?)" (VII.vi.36). See John Hollander's mention of these two echoes in his discussion of Miltonic echo and the "memories" poems seem to have of themselves. *The Figure of Echo* (Berkeley: University of California Press, 1981), p. 51n.

4. Furthermore, despite E.K.'s inclusion of Christian as well as classical reasons for beginning the *Calender* with January instead of March, the poem does not explicitly valorize the seasons as part of God's order and proportion as *Epithalamion* does, nor are the months in the *Calender* contained within a larger progress and structure, as the anthropomorphized triumph of months in *Two Cantos of Mutabilitie* are contained within that poem's plot (as evidence at a trial) and contained within an already established stanzaic pattern. Instead the months of the *Calender* constitute the very structure and "narrative" impulse of the poem. Joel Fineman argues that "the description of months and seasons is a long established convention immediately evocative of, and convenient to, cosmological and metaphysical invention, a way of alluding through allegorical structure to the mysterious order of the cosmos and the position of God as unmoved mover within it." See "The Structure of Allegorical Desire," *Allegory and Representation,* ed. Stephen Greenblatt (Baltimore: John Hopkins University Press, 1981). But because the very structure of the *Calender* is a "description of" ("proportioning to") months and seasons, the poem is particularly good for demonstrating that any allusion to "the mysterious order of the cosmos" is undermined by the very medium with which (and because of which) one makes that allusion: language and meter.

My reading therefore challenges A. C. Hamilton's suggestion that the structure of the *Calender* is informed by Christianity. See "The Argument of Spenser's *Shepheardes Calender,*" *Spenser: a Collection of Critical Essays,* Harry Berger, Jr., ed. (Englewood Cliffs, N.J.: Prentice-Hall, 1968), p.32. Hamilton points out that E. K. justifies the poem's beginning with January because of its associations with the incarnation of Christ, but he neglects to acknowledge that this reason does not seem to be enough for E.K., who supplements it with Roman authority, explaining how it was Numa Pompilius who decided the year should begin with January, and how the month was named after the god Janus. It also seems important to note that even while arguing for Christian associations in the *Calender,* Hamilton finds himself allowing that it is notuntil "November" that "for the first time the pagan mood of despair is supplanted by the full Christian assurance of man's resurrection out of Nature" (p. 33). Not only does this claim testify to a "mood of despair" through most of the *Calender,* but it also necessitates reading the elegy for Dido as offering "full Christian assurance." In this essay I argue that it is in "November" that Spenser's testimony to loss is least reassuring and most poetically powerful.

5. Of course the form and meter vary from eclogue to eclogue; variety is the new poet's forte. But in all the eclogues, the formal patterns are highly wrought and privileged at the expense of speech intonation. See Thompson, and also O. B. Hardison, *Prosody and Purpose in the English Renaissance* (Baltimore: Johns Hopkins University Press, 1989), pp.212–14. Hardison argues importantly that the *Calender* is a rejection of quantitative meter. It is a "realistic pastoral" using "forms that are archaic or

associated with folk literature or both" (213), ". . . the tradition of the *Calender* is that of medieval, not classical, prosody" (214).

6. E.K. introduces these terms in his dedicatory letter.

7. Much recent scholarship documents the fundamental role Spenser's literary and career ambitions played in his choice of the pastoral mode, rustic language, and native forms, as well as his elaborate apparatus and design for his book. In addition to Hardison and Miller, see Ruth Samson Luborsky, "The Allusive Presentation of *The Shepheardes Calender*," *Spenser Studies* I, eds. Patrick Cullen and Thomas P. Roche, Jr. (Pittsburgh, PA: University of Pittsburgh Press, 1980), pp. 29–67; Richard Helgerson, "The Elizabethan Laureate: Self-Presentation and the Literary System," *ELH* 46 (1979), pp. 193–220; Helgerson, "The New Poet Presents Himself: Spenser and the Idea of a Literary Career, *PMLA* 93 (1978), pp.893–911; and Louis Adrian Montrose, "'The perfecte paterne of a Poete': The Poetics of Courtship in *The Shepheardes Calender*," *TSLL* 21 (1979), pp.34–67. My look at parentheses in the *Calender* is something of a complement to these studies; in the midst of new perspectives on Spenser's career strategies and literary-political milieu, it urges continued reading of the *Calender* as a poem.

8. See Anthony Easthope, *Poetry as Discourse* (London: Methuen, 1983), particularly pp. 97–103, for a detailed account of how this sonnet produces so powerful an illusion of mind, voice, and subjectivity. Easthope's theory of pentameter, which essentially argues that all pentameter "gives space to the 'natural' intonation and so to a single voice in the closure of its own coherence," is productive in analyzing much pentameter, but it does not explain Spenser's metrical practice. Spenser's pentameter poems, not peripheral Renaissance works, rarely aim "to deny [their] production as . . . poem[s]," nor do they exploit the counterpoint potential of pentameter to provide space for a "transcendental ego" (one reason no one wants to read Spenser in class). It is part and parcel of my observations here that Spenser's pentameter does not simply have "what might be called a constitutionalist significance," corresponding "to the ideological opposition between the 'social' and the 'individual,' an opposition which envisages society as a 'necessity' against and within which the individual finds his or her 'freedom.'" In the *Calender* and other poems, the abstract pattern does not suggest *social* demands and restrictions, but a more comprehensive one: the passing of time itself. In these poems, Spenser does not provide an "absolute position" for the subject, but a "relative" one. Quotations from pp. 67–74 and 28–29.

9. Compare Greene's reading of "Januarye," p. 5: "It is no matter simply that Colin is in love, as commentators sometimes assume, but that his account of love is dictated . . . by external circumstances." Spenser shows "a poet who has lost his referential priority to his world and has become, in fact, its object."

10. The belief that the poet had divine associations and attendant moral responsibilities was standard poetic theory of the day; my reference here is to Puttenham's first statement, in which he calls the poet a "maker": "such as (by way of resemblance and reverently) we may say of God." *The Arte of English Poesie. The English Experience,* number 342. (Amsterdam and New York: Da Capo Press, 1971). Spenser's formal practice has been understood in this vein—as an intended mirroring of cosmic and Tudor order and proportion. See A. Kent Hieatt, *Short Time's Endless Monument; the Symbolism of the Numbers in Edmund Spenser's Epithalamion* (New York: Columbia University Press, 1960), Alastair Fowler, *Spenser and the Numbers of Time* (New York:

Barnes & Noble, 1964), and, importantly, Miller. Miller argues that "Spenser conceived of his 'laureate enterprise' as both a visionary participation in the spiritual shaping of the material world and a rhetorical effort to extend that process in the making of community" (p.198). I do not challenge Miller's perception of Spenser's early work as a tension between Spenser's "ideal of the poetic vocation" and "the dynamics of his self-presentation," and his perception of tensions in the later work as "generated by his dual commitment to a poetics of vision and one of persuasion" (p. 198–99); however, as I argue in this essay, I believe Spenser's ultimate "commitment" is to time itself, and that even here at the start of his career, the most productive tensions in his work derive from his sense of poetry's testimony to the absence rather than the presence of selves and communities, and to meter's Janus-faced staging and mocking of "visions" and "persuasions" alike. See also note 4, above, on the overall structure of the *Calender.*

11. The description of Death in *Two Cantos of Mutabilitie* includes this line: "Yet he is nought but parting of the breath" (VII.46.3). For an important argument about the caesura and issues of time in the *Faerie Queene,* see Debra Fried, "Spenser's Caesura," *English Literary Renaissance* 11 (1981), 261–80.

12. John Guillory, *Poetic Authority: Spenser, Milton, and Literary History* (New York: Columbia University Press, 1983), p. 65. The word is "secular."

13. Guillory, pp. 63–64.

14. The discourse that returns with the inevitable end of a parenthetical phrase is also but a continuation, and likeness of, what has gone before: engendered by it, but new and distinct. What "returns" is ultimately part of a linear, not a circular, progression.

15. I. A. Richards, *Principles of Literary Criticism* (London, 1925), p. 145, quoted by John Hollander, "The Metrical Frame," in *The Structure of Verse,* ed. Harvey Gross (New York: The Ecco Press, 1979), p. 78. The Spenser quotes are from the dedicatory letter and "October," 25, respectively.

16. Robert Bridges, "A Letter to a Musician on English Prosody," Gross, p. 67n.

LISA M. KLEIN

"Let us love, deare love, lyke as we ought": Protestant Marriage and the Revision of Petrarchan Loving in Spenser's *Amoretti*

IN *THE FAERIE QUEENE,* Spenser often draws attention to the abuses wrought by lovers (and poets) in the Petrarchan tradition. Mirabella is the classic cruel mistress who

> Did boast her beautie had such soveraigne might,
> That with the onely twinckle of her eye,
> She could or save, or spill, whom she would hight.
> (VI.vii.31)[1]

Her punishment is to wander the world in the company of Scorn and Disdain, "'Till she had sav'd so many loves, as she did lose" (37), a vain endeavor. Spenser's women are not always the perpetrators of love's cruelty; often they are its victims, as Petrarchan poets and lovers oppress them with metaphors or by force. In a parody of the blazon poem so popular with sonnet writers, the cannibals subject the naked Serena to their lust (VI.viii.41–43). They would rape her, but their priest restrains them, and Spenser's narrator laconically remarks that "religion held even theeves in measure" (43). Busyrane, torturing Amoret, is a type of the poet-lover who would compel his lady's love:

> With living bloud he those characters wrate,
> Dreadfully dropping from her dying hart,

Seeming transfixed with a cruell dart,
And all perforce to make her him to love.
(III.xii.31)

Spenser's narrator also dissociates himself from Busyrane's force: "Ah who can love the worker of her smart?" (31). Over and against these tableaux of lustful cruelty and compulsion, Spenser's representations of true love are associated with freedom, life, marriage, and fruitfulness. Charissa, an allegory of Christian love, is married, unlike her sisters Fidelia and Speranza; when Redcrosse meets her, her breasts are exposed and she is nursing some of the several children who hang about her, a sign of her "bountie rare." She is "Full of great love, but *Cupids* wanton snare / As hell she hated, chast in worke and will" (I.x.30). As an image of love, she is as remote as can be from the courtly Petrarchan lady, who is anything but bountiful. Spenser's fullest expression of chaste married love is, of course, Britomart, whose quest is devoted to finding her destined husband, Artegall, and submitting to him in marriage. She also frees Amoret from the abusive Busyrane, and Artegall from the tyranny of Radigund.[2] Her first words, an allusion to Chaucer's *Franklin's Tale,* condemn mastery in love:

Ne may love be compeld by maisterie:
For soone as maisterie comes, sweet love anone
Taketh his nimble wings, and soone away is gone.
(III.i.25)

In *The Faerie Queene,* Spenser makes it clear that male and female lovers alike can exercise—and overcome—the mastery which threatens the establishment of virtuous love.

This concern also underlies the *Amoretti,* a sequence of sonnets that reveals Spenser's dual allegiance to the traditions of Petrarchan and Christian loving.[3] The clash of these (for Spenser) irreconcilable ethics—love as domination versus love as freely chosen submission—provides the main conflict in Spenser's poetic tribute to his lady and wife, Elizabeth Boyle. Because mastery destroys love itself, it poses a threat both urgent and personal for a poet contemplating his own marriage in poetry addressed to, or intended for, his wife-to-be. Spenser's response to the threat of mastery in love is to renounce Petrarchanism in favor of the Christian ethic of love as mutual submission within a divinely ordained hierarchy. Deeply imbued with his culture's views on marriage,

Spenser undertakes in the *Amoretti* no less than a reformation of Petrarchan loving. His revision of convention, which proceeds throughout the sonnets and culminates in the *Epithalamion,* is particularly evident in the roles he envisions for the lover and his lady. These roles accord with ideal behavior expected of Christian husbands and wives and expressed time and again by sixteenth- and seventeenth-century writers on marriage.[4] The lady of the *Amoretti* (like Britomart) is encouraged to overcome her pride and her desire for mastery and submit to love and to her husband, while her poet-lover abandons both abject submission and forceful desiring and prepares to assume the role of benevolent ruler and teacher, or husband. Elizabethan conventional wisdom about marriage, in tension with conventional Petrarchan attitudes, shapes Spenser's *Amoretti* sonnets.

Though many critics acknowledge that Spenser diverges from Petrarchan practice in his *Amoretti,* few acknowledge the extent to which he rewrites Petrarchan convention or explore his poetic means to that end. Joseph Loewenstein makes the perceptive observation (in passing) that "the *Amoretti* attempts a dialectical transformation of Petrarchanism . . . passing from subversion to conversion and, sadly, on to some slight reversion," demonstrating how difficult it is to "provide an enduring alternative to the Petrarchanism of Busyrane."[5] Leigh DeNeef explores Spenser's recasting of certain Petrarchan metaphors but does not see him as seriously differing with the tradition: "The conventional vocabularies of Petrarchan or neo-Platonic love need not . . . be denied or even satirized, only opened to metaphoric status."[6] Reed Way Dasenbrock, in a recent article, sees Spenser situating his sonnets firmly in the Petrarchan tradition, then turning that tradition inside out, "transforming it . . . and subjecting it to a searching critique." For Spenser, the self finds peace and stability in the marriage union, while Petrarch locates such peace in union with the beloved in heaven. Despite making this substantial distinction between the two poets, Dasenbrock sees the *Amoretti* as "an attempt to transform the [Petrarchan] tradition in order to redeem its seriousness" and insists that Spenser is truer to Petrarch than any Petrarchan before him."[7]

I would argue, rather, that Spenser's revision and critique of Petrarchanism is more thoroughgoing than Dasenbrock allows, more urgent than DeNeef recognizes, and more successful than Loewenstein believes. The poet consistently attempts to reform Petrarchan poetics and sexual politics, sometimes by representing and renouncing exaggerated Petrarchan ideas (discussed below), elsewhere by assimilating elements of the Petrarchan tradition to a Christian ethic. Ultimately he replaces Petrarchanism with a poetics expressive of the mutuality and concord which ought to characterize a loving marriage. From the opening sonnet he reinvests typical sonnet metaphors, such as the lover's captivity, with a Christian meaning, heralding the redemption of his poetry and his loving. He refers to his leaves of poetry as his life being held in his lady's hands "lyke captives trembling at the victor's sight" (1:4). On one level a conventional reference to an enthralled and powerless lover-poet, these lines also prefigure the promise of redemption offered by the "Most glorious Lord of lyfe" who "didst bring away/captivity thence captive us to win" (68:1,4). Christ's example teaches perfect love—one characteristic of which is reciprocity, or mutuality (68:9–12)—and thus the poet instructs his beloved in turn: "So let us love, deare love, lyke as we ought,/love is the lesson which the Lord us taught" (68:13–14). By this point in the sequence, the lady has in fact submitted to her lover, freely, like Christ—an unprecedented development for a sonnet sequence.[8] The poet's expectation that his love will be redeemed and rewarded is implicit in the entire sequence of sonnets. Indeed, marriage is explicitly signalled as early as sonnet 6, when he expects "to knit the knot, that ever shall remaine." The captivity in which Petrarchan lovers found themselves, by contrast, absolutely precluded the possibility of love's fulfillment in any form, let alone marriage.[9]

In *The Faerie Queene,* Spenser can intrude in the narrative to express ironic disdain for the cannibals and sympathy for the tortured Amoret. In *Amoretti,* he uses various and indirect poetic strategies to undermine Petrarchanism. One is simply to defuse the tension inherent in its conventional paradoxes, thus subverting the expectations raised by his use of Petrarchan conceits and the sonnet form. Sidney, in *Astrophil and Stella,* is the best practitioner of the oxymoronic couplet expressive of the poet-lover's insoluble dilemma and his perpetual frustration. Astrophil wails that Stella "So sweets my paines that my paines me rejoice" (57:14); he begs "Deare, love me not, that you may love me more" (62:14)[10]. Spenser, by contrast, often builds up to such a Sidneian conclusion but neatly evades its seemingly inescapable contradiction. In sonnet 14, for example, the poet invokes the metaphor of courtship as a siege of the lady's castle, but in the final couplet he simply gives over the battle:

> Bring therefore all the forces that ye may.
> and lay incessant battery to her heart;

playnts, prayers, vowes, ruth, sorrow, and dismay,
those engins can the proudest love convert.
And if those fayle fall downe and dy before her,
So dying live, and living do adore her.
(9–14)

Now, Spenser is certainly able to sustain the idea of love as an assault, but he rejects it in favor of an image of submissive love, reinforced by the "feminine" end-rhyme of lines 13–14. His references to converting the proud mistress and to the paradox of dying in order to live point to the promise of redemption offered by the "Easter" sonnet, cited above. The lover who gives up the siege also prefigures the hunter who gives up the chase in sonnet 67; it is the renunciation of force which enables the act of submission. The ease with which Spenser abandons the siege metaphor in sonnet 14 can be interpreted as a rejection of the love-as-war trope. The paradox in the couplet has a Christian, rather than a Petrarchan, flavor; with it Spenser simultaneously fulfills and circumvents the rhetorical demands of the sonnet form.

As he revised the notion of captivity, Spenser rewrites other Petrarchan conceits in order to praise his lady and to distinguish her from the bevy of literary cruel mistresses. One obvious example of such revision is his treatment of the related motifs of his lady's eyes and love's inception. Traditionally, the lady's glance unleashes Cupid's arrows which wound the poet's heart.[11] The wound is ultimately deadly, for the woman never bestows her love which would heal it. Spenser at first invokes this convention, addressing his mistress's "Fayre eyes" in sonnet 7: "both lyfe and death forth from you dart/into the object of your mighty view" (3–4). He then begs her not to destroy him but to "kindle living fire within my brest" (12). In the next sonnet, this living fire has a heavenly origin. The lady's eyes, "full of the living fire,/Kindled above unto the maker neere" (8:1–2), are elevated to membership in a divine trinity, mediating the heavenly fire to the poet-lover. Their divine function corrects and supersedes their function as bearers of Cupid's darts:

Thrugh your bright beams doth not the blinded guest
shoot out his darts to base affections wound:
but Angels come to lead fraile mindes to rest
in chast desires on heavenly beauty bound.
(8:5–8)

The mistress is even likened to the creator, bringing order out of chaos, forming the poet and his speech:

> You frame my thoughts and fashion me within,
> you stop my toung, and teach my hart to speake,
> you calme the storme that passion did begin. . . .
> Dark is the world, where your light shined never;
> well is he borne, that may behold you ever.
> (9–14)

Beholding the mistress is like being in the sight of God. This point is also made in the succeeding sonnet, as the poet rejects all comparisons between her eyes and things of the earth, concluding "Then to the Maker selfe they likest be,/whose light doth lighten all that here we see" (9:13–14). This final line could modify either "the Maker selfe" or the mistress' eyes. The ambiguity contributes to Spenser's analogy between his mistress and his God, both of whom sustain his life with their light.

This comparison of his lady to God is intended to be neither irreverent nor fanciful; rather it distinguishes his lady and his love from profane Petrarchanism. And yet Spenser's elevated praise of his mistress never allows her to become, like Petrarch's Laura, supra-human and unattainable; instead, the comparison of her to heaven is used to persuade her to return the poet's love: "Then sith to heaven ye lykened are the best,/be lyke in mercy as in all the rest" (55:13–14). Similarly, sonnet 53 concludes, "But mercy doth with beautie best agree,/as in theyr maker ye them best may see" (13–14). These are not the pleas of a captivated and disdained lover, but of a confident poet instructing his lady to "love . . . lyke as we ought," to heed Christ's example and exhibit mercy, love, and submission to the will of heaven.

Spenser also draws on Neoplatonism to revise Petrarchan poetic practice, but he ultimately rejects that tradition as inadequate. By idealizing the mistress, the poet escapes from the convention of the cruel, dominating tyranness, but encounters problems in the representation of married love. Neoplatonism proves useful for establishing the lady's divine resemblance, as when the poet makes her eyes bearers of heavenly light, kindling living fire in his breast. Taken to its philosophical extreme, however, a fully spiritualized Neoplatonic love is incompatible with consummated marital love.[12] Accordingly, Spenser does not allow his beloved to become an idealized, semi-divine abstraction, available only for worship and contemplation. While the early sonnets are more likely to elevate and idealize the lady, several later sonnets repudiate Neoplatonic love in favor of an earthly and physical expression of love. In sonnet 72, the poet's spirit, attempting to "mount up to the purest sky," sees the lady "resembling heaven's glory in her light/ [and] drawne with sweet pleasures bayt, it back doth fly,/and unto heaven forgets her former flight" (2.6–8). The poet opts for "none other happinesse,/but here on earth to have such hevens blisse" (13–14). In sonnets 76 and 77, too, the poet's idealizing impulses are countered by the strong pull of the flesh; he likens his lady's breast to a table richly spread with fruits of paradise, "Exceeding sweet, yet voyd of sinfull vice." (77:9) and his thoughts to the "guests, which would thereon have fedd" (14). This lover climbs no ladder of love; he does not progress from enjoyment of his mistress to communion with God. As Ellrodt sums it up, for Spenser "love is of heavenly nature, but its consummation is earthly" (146).[13]

In Spenser's syncretism of Neoplatonism and Christianity, the former is subsumed into the latter, for spiritualized love is not itself the goal; rather, it is a precondition for Christian married love.[14] In this view, Spenser accords more with contemporary writers on marriage, for whom love based on spiritual rather than material gifts is the only firm basis for marriage. Writers on marriage concur that virtue in a woman is more important than her gifts of fortune or nature. Henry Smith, in *A Preparative to Marriage,* advises that "the goods of the world are good, and the goods of the bodie are good, but the goods of the mind are better" (30). Edmund Tilney advises that women's "vertues . . . ought to be accounted [their] chiefest dowrie" (B2^{v}.). Early in the sequence, Spenser establishes that his beloved is virtuous, a fit partner for marriage. Sonnet 15, a conventional blazon, invokes "the goods of the world"—treasures of the Indies, rubies, ivory, and gold—only to renounce them in favor of the intangible and invisible "goods of the mind." Though his "love doth in her selfe containe/all this worlds riches that may farre be found" (15:5–6), her virtue caps all her beauties: "that which fairest is, but few behold,/her mind adornd with vertues manifold" (13–14).[15] Likewise, in sonnet 79, he affirms that though she is beautiful, "the trew fayre, that is the gentle wit,/and vertuous mind, is much more praysd of me" (3–4). He admits that her physical beauties are subject to "frayle corruption," but her true beauty is eternal; it

> . . . doth argue you
> to be divine and borne of heavenly seed:
> deriv'd from that fayre Spirit, from whom al true

and perfect beauty did at first proceed.
He onely fayre, and what he fayre hath made,
all other fayre lyke flowres untymely fade.
(79:9–14)

That his love is grounded on spiritual rather than material virtue makes him an ideal Christian husband-to-be. Juan Luis Vives, in *The Office and Duetie of a Husband* (1553), distinguishes husbands "that love the beautye, or the ryches of their wives, [who] are blynde and subjects to that earthly love" from those "true husbandes, [who] love the soule and vertue" of their wives and are "inspired wyth the strengthe and spirite of that celestiall love" (M4ʳ). Spenser, along with contemporary writers on marriage, drew on Neoplatonic ideals to promote the necessary spiritual element in the necessarily un-platonic relationship of marriage.

Spenser's syncretism of Neoplatonism and Christianity has a multiple function in the *Amoretti:* to promote an ideal of virtuous spiritual love leading to marriage, to elevate the argument of the entire sonnet sequence, and to assist his rewriting of Petrarchanism. In his *Defence of Poesy,* Sidney, premier Petrarchan though he was, had envisioned an exalted moral purpose for "that lyrical kind of songs and sonnets":

> . . . how well [they] might be employed, and with how heavenly fruit, both private and public, in singing the praises of the immortal beauty: the immortal goodness of that God who giveth us hands to write and wits to conceive.

Sidney implicitly opposes mortal beauty (Stella) to immortal beauty and goodness (God), and while his own sonnets praise his mortal mistress, they ultimately censure that earthly love "which reachest but to dust" (*Certaine Sonnets* 32:1). Spenser seems to have taken the sonnet sequence as seriously as Sidney urges, seeking to restore its high moral purpose and to reform its conventions of false loving.[17] But unlike Sidney, Spenser *conflates* his "immortal beauty" (Elizabeth Boyle) and the "immortal goodness" of God, undoing the opposition between earthly love and heavenly love that grounds Petrarch's sonnets and still prevails in Sidney's sequence. Spenser's sonnets instead affirm the highest form of earthly love, marriage. He situates the courtship in the famework of the Christian liturgical year, a structuring device Petrarch also used, but to a different purpose;[18] Spenser's lovers imitate Christ's immortal love not in order to transcend carnality (Petrarch's goal), but in order to bring their own earthly love to fruition in marriage. A further difference is that in Petrarch's *Canzoniere,* the anniversary poems recapitulate time and again the poet's first sighting of Laura and thus underscore the stasis of their relationship, while Spenser's calendrical and liturgical references establish progress in the relationship as well as movement towards spiritual redemption.

Given my depiction of a Spenser resolutely and consistently reforming Petrarchan poetics and Petrarchan loving, how does one account for the many sonnets in which Spenser "reverts," as Loewenstein would say, to stereotypical and often exaggerated Petrarchan attitudes? Why is Spenser's lady in one sonnet a woman of heavenly virtue, and in the next sonnet a "Tyrannesse [who] doth joy to see/the huge massacres which her eyes do make" (10:5–6) or a beast "more cruell and more salvage wylde" than a lion, who "taketh glory in her cruelnesse" (20:9, 12)? O. B. Hardison explains these clashing motifs of the *donna angelicata* and the "cruel fair" as the legacy of the Italian *stil nuovo* tradition; they embody the conflict between the claims of the spirit and those of the flesh which Spenser reconciles by affirming that human love fulfills the divine plan.[19] Louis Martz, rightly noting Spenser's sense of humor, sees elements of parody or even comedy in the exaggerated sonnets, as the lovers knowingly and mockingly strike the conventional poses for each other.[20] But the laws of the "unrighteous Lord of love" and the behavior of lady who "lordeth in licentious blisse" (10:1, 3) do seriously transgress God's law (as Spenser's puns on "lord" suggest) and cannot simply be laughed off.[21] An alternative way to apprehend Spenser's seemingly erratic relationship to Petrarchan conventions is to see him engaged in a process of presentation, renunciation, and re-presentation of the mistress. David Lee Miller, in his discussion of *The Faerie Queene,* theorizes that the "negative moment" that summons the poem's ideal form into representation is something intrinsic to Spenser's poetics.[22] Of Una he writes:

> Like the truth of the heavenly hymns, [which depends on the presence of the earthly hymns and on their renunciation], Una emerges into representation only through a differential repetition that sets her apart from herself and so makes her dependent on what she is not—dividing Truth to assert its self-resemblance in a phrase that echoes, as it opposes, Duessa's counterepiphany.[23]

A similar process can be seen operating in the *Amoretti*. Spenser's beloved, Elizabeth Boyle, "emerges into representation" only through the presence of, and the rejection of, the archetypal Petrarchan mistress whose qualities pervert the ideal of a Christian wife. A humble companion of a wife is formed from and supplants a proud tyrant of a mistress, and the concord of marriage is ensured only after the possibility of discord is eliminated. The lovers' union in marriage depends on the successful renunciation of Petrarchan loving—that is, love based on mastery—and the reformation and re-presentation of the Petrarchan mistress as a humble, virtuous wife and the Petrarchan poet-lover as an authoritative and loving husband.

The presentation of a "negative image" through which an ideal form is summoned into being is not solely a feature of Spenser poetics. It is evident as a persuasive and instructive tactic in two prominent wedding sermons of the period, the Elizabethan sermon "Of the State of Matrimony" in the Elizabethan *Book of Homilies* (1562) (hereafter cited as *Homily*) and William Whately's *A Bride-Bush* (1617), works alike enough in their attitudes and advice to be considered compendia of conventional wisdom regarding marriage. In the following passage from the *Homily*, the specter of a domineering wife is raised, horror is invoked, the example is rejected, and a vignette of ideal wifely behavior is substituted:

> Now as concerning the Wives duty. What shall become her? Shall she abuse the gentleness and humanity of her husband? and, at her pleasure, turn all things upside down? No surely. For that is far repugnant against GODS Commandment, for thus doth St. *Peter* preach to them, ye Wives, be ye in subjection to obey your own husbands. To obey, is another thing than to controle or command, which yet they may do, to their Children, and to their Family: But as for their Husbands, them must they obey, and cease from commanding, and perform subjection. For this surely doth nourish concord very much, when the Wife is ready at hand at her husbands commandment, when she will apply her self to his will, when she endeavoureth her self to seek his contentation, and to do him pleasure, when she will eschew all things that might offend him.
>
> (*Homily*, 311)[24]

Writers on marriage agree without question that pride is most unfitting for a Christian wife, who was enjoined to be humble, chaste, and silent, an obedient subordinate to her husband. Because woman's pride upsets the divine and natural orders, it is denounced in the strongest language; William Gouge, in his handbook *Of Domesticall Duties* (1622), writes that for a wife "to imagine that she her selfe is not inferior to her husband, ariseth from monstrous self-conceit, and intolerable arrogancy, as if she her selfe were above her owne sex, and more then a woman" (273). He deems pride the most "pestilent vice for an inferiour . . . it is the cause of all rebellion, disobedience, & disloyalty" (331). Spenser's representation of Radigund in *The Faerie Queene* confirms the view that women's pride imperils the proper order which ought to exist between men and women in the private realm of marriage and in the public realm of governance.[25] Radigund's prison, in which Artegall languishes in women's weeds, is a worst-case scenario for marriage to a proud wife as well as an image of a topsy-turvy political order. After Britomart defeats Radigund and restores women to men's subjection, Spenser in an editorial aside juxtaposes the negative image and the positive ideal. He condemns

> . . . the crueltie of womenkynd,
> When they have shaken off the shamefast band,
> With which wise Nature did them strongly bynd,
> T'obay the heasts of mans well ruling hand,
> That then all rule and reason they withstand,
> To purchase a licentious libertie.
> But vertuous women wisely understand,
> That they were borne to base humilitie,
> Unless the heavens them lift to lawfull soveraintie.
>
> (V.v.25)

Radigund exemplifies what Gouge describes as the "ambitious and proud humour in women, who must needs rule." Such women "thwart Gods ordinance, pervert the order of nature, deface the image of Christ, [and] overthrow the ground of all dutie" (287).

Pride, that vice most disruptive to Christian marriage, is also the most notable characteristic of the Petrarchan mistress. Hence the *Amoretti* poet's pervasive concern with his lady's pride—over half the poems before sonnet 62 treat the lady's pride or cruelty.[26] Gouge's charge that a proud woman possesses a degraded and disruptive nature could justly be levelled against a falsely proud mistress. Spenser agrees that pride and cruelty destroy the lady's divine likeness, the "fayre Idea of [her] celestiall hew" (45:7). In sonnet 31, he complains that her "pryde depraves each other better part, / and all those pretious ornaments deface" (3–4). He then likens the lady to a cruel or proud beast about to kill her prey, the poet. Pride, manifested in her destructive power, is associated with a descent in the scale of being, a perversion of nature's order like that Gouge decries. In sonnet 47, the lady is a deceptive enchantress whose pride, represented as rampant, animal sexuality, threatens the poet's very life:

> So she with flattring smyles weake harts doth guyde
> unto her love and tempte to theyr decay,
> whome being caught she kills with cruell pryde,
> and feeds at pleasure on the wretched pray. . . .
> O mighty charm which makes men love theyr bane,
> and thinck they dy with pleasure, live with payne.
> (47:5–8, 13–14)

The sexual overtones of pride and dying in this sonnet cannot be overlooked. A woman who uses her sexuality to master and devour her lover, Spenser warns, upsets the divine order and debases her own humanity.[27] But this expression of pride as insatiable lust is a long way from the simple moral failing which obscures his lady's beauty. Spenser extrapolates from the personal failing to which she seems prone to its most dire manifestation, unchastity, representing in progressive stages pride's potential threat to the order of their relationship and to the natural order established by God. This exaggerated Petrarchan lady who deceives and destroys her prey, is, to borrow Miller's terms again, the "negative moment" which summons the poems' ideal into existence, an ideal represented in the virtuous (yet human) Elizabeth Boyle. (In the same way, Britomart's virtue depends on its counter-representation in the powerful and lusty Radigund.) Extreme inversions of virtue are represented in order to be renounced, that the woman who embodies ideal virtue may spring into clear relief.

Spenser does counter his negative image of the proud enchantress by representing his mistress as a woman who possesses an abundance of proper pride:

> Such pride is praise, such portliness is honor,
> that boldned innocence beares in hir eies:

and her faire countenance like a goodly banner,
spreds in defiaunce of all enemies.
Was never in this world ought worthy tride
without some spark of such self-pleasing pride.
(5:9–14)

This virtuous pride is informed by a consciousness of what is befitting one's position: it prevents one from behaving unworthily. Such is the pride Artegall has lost while captive to Radigund. As Britomart mourns, looking upon her emasculated lover, "Could so great courage stouped have to ought?/Then farewell fleshly force; I see thy pride is nought" (V.vii.40). The pride of Spenser's mistress is also a mark of her well-tempered nature, in which "myld humblesse [is] mixt with awfull majesty":

for looking on the earth whence she was borne,
her minde remembreth her mortalitie:
what so is fayrest shall to earth returne.
But that same lofty countenance seemes to scorne
base thing, and thinke how she to heaven may clime:
treading downe earth as lothsome and forlorne,
that hinders heavenly thoughts with drossy slime.
Yet lowly still vouchsafe to looke on me,
such lowliness shall make you lofty be.
(13:6–14)

This sonnet also warns the mistress that by scorning earth as "loathsome" and "drossy slime," she risks tipping the virtuous balance on the side of false pride. It ends with a reminder that, ultimately, the mistress/wife attains her exalted position by humbling herself to her lover/husband. The scales of pride tip back and forth again in sonnet 58, which condemns her self-assurance as vanity, and sonnet 59, which praises it as a sign of steadfastness. In the latter, the mistress is a paragon of controlled, chaste sexuality, "well assured/Unto her selfe and setled so in hart" (1–2); she is like a "steddy ship" (5), firm "in the stay of her own stedfast might" (11).[28] Such pride and self-control make her eminently suitable for marriage, but the emergence of false pride remains an ever-present possibility. Near the end of the sequence, as the expectation of their union becomes assured, Spenser praises his love as "fayre when that cloude of pryde, which oft doth dark/her goodly light with smiles she drives away" (81:7–8). In the *Amoretti,* renunciation of false pride is not a once-and-for-all event, but a process requiring continual vigilance and self-control. Not until the *Epithalamion* does the lady achieve the proper synthesis of pride and humility that befits a virtuous wife.[29]

In his attempt to discourage false pride and inculcate wifely virtue in his beloved, the speaker of the *Amoretti* assumes a tone of gentle authority, in effect rehearsing his own role of husband. Conduct writers agree that one duty of the husband is gently and lovingly to reform his wife's faults (Tilney, Biiii5r), Henry Smith, in *A Preparative to Marriage,* reminds the husband that in taking a wife, he takes on a vineyard that he must nurture before it will bear fruit: "So hee must not looke to finde a wife without a faulte, but thinke that she is committed to him to reclaime her from her faults" (69). The poet assumes this role when he praises his lady's virtuous pride while gently warning her not to succumb to the temptations to master her beloved. A tone of gentle authority characterizes many of the sonnets, especially the imperative and epigrammatic concluding couplet:

> Then you faire flowre, in whom fresh youth doth raine,
> prepare your selfe new love to entertaine.
> (4:13–14)

> Faire be no lenger proud of that shall perish,
> but that which shal you make immortall, cherish.
> (27:13–14)

> Then fly no more fayre love from Phebus chace,
> but in your brest his leafe and love embrace.[30]
> (28:13–14)

This poet-lover, addressing gentle admonitions to his beloved, is unlike the conventional sonnet speaker who wallows in his own despair and sometimes chafes at his bonds of servitude. Nor is he like Sidney's Astrophil, who practices a poetics of force; when his verbal strategies for conquering Stella fail, he steals a kiss from her—an act of aggressive desire for which he suffers Stella's wrath, loss of her favor, and shame. Such tactics Spenser has wittily renounced in sonnet 14 (see pages 112–13 above), and in sonnet 32 he presents a stronger negative image of the self-destruction wrought by forceful desire. The lover is likened to a "paynefull smith" beating unsuccessfully "with his heavy sledge" to "fashion to what he . . . list" the hard iron of the lady's wit (1, 3–4):

But still the more she fervent sees my fit:
the more she frieseth in her wilfull pryde;
and harder growes the harder she is smit,
with all the playnts which to her be applyde.
(9–12)

Courtship is depicted as the forceful attempt to "fashion" the lady to his will with the result that his over-fervent, violent plaints only harden her "willful pride." The sonnet's concluding couplet appropriately expresses a dilemma familiar to a frustrated Petrarchan lover but completely unacceptable to a lover anticipating marriage: "What then remaines but I to ashes burne,/and she to stones at length all frosen turne?" This impulse to dehumanize the other (and destroy himself) through forceful desire is what the poet himself must renounce, for his task is to establish the order and loving harmony proper to marriage.

For all its metaphoric excess, sonnet 32 expresses a truism that applies to marriage as well. Men who use force, according to Vives, are responsible for turning love into hate in their wives; he further advises that "Love is gotten by love; by honestie and fidelities, and not by violence" (Cv2^{v}). Likewise, the Elizabethan marriage homily counsels that "frowardness and sharpness is [sic] not amended with frowardness, but with softness and gentleness" (316). Writers on marriage consistently reject the use of force to compel a wife's obedience and advocate alternatives such as setting a good example for her to follow, acceding to her in trivial matters, and using indirection and even dissembling to win her will. The duty of a husband, says Vives, is to set an example "the which to informe and fashion the womens life" (Q4^{r}). Such a process occurs in Spenser's sonnet 43, a response to something like a domestic quarrel:

Shall I then silent be or shall I speake?
And if I speake, her wrath renew I shall:
and if I silent be, my hart will breake,
or choked be with overflowing gall.
What tyranny is this both my hart to thrall,
and eke my toung with proud restraint to tie?
(1–6)

The poet-lover is angry that her pride and tyranny force him into a submissive silence, but he tempers his initial anger, which would break out in harsh words. Instead of condemning or attacking the mistress, he recommends silence and submission through his own example and even manages a compliment to her "deep wit":

> Yet I my hart with silence secretly
> will teach to speak, and my just cause to plead:
> and eke mine eies with meeke humility,
> love learned letters to her eyes to read.
> Which her deep wit, that true harts thought can spel,
> wil soone conceive, and learne to construe well.
> (91–14)

Such a strategy befits a good husband, who maintains authority

> by being an ensample in love, gravitie, pietie, honesty, &c. The fruits of these and other like graces shewed forth by husbands before their wives and family, cannot but worke a reverend and dutifull respect in their wives . . . for by this means they shall more cleerely discerne the image of God shine forth in their faces. (Gouge 354)

A good husband, says Whately, asserts authority not by "big looks, & great words, & cruel behavior . . . but by a milder & more artificiall course" (19). In correcting a wife's fault, he continues, a husband should never speak in anger, always be gentle, and mingle praise and reproof, thus enticing obedience. He should

> neither shew himselfe rigorous in every thing, but bee content to gratifie his wife in some things, that she may less unwillingly, yea with more cheerefulnesse bee subject in other things. (27)

In this advice, Whately echoes his predecessors; Tilney also recommends that a husband sometimes dissemble, consent to his wife in "trifling matters," and "deale with his wife, rather by subtiltie, than by crueltie" (Ciiii4^{r}). This advice the speaker of sonnet 43 follows to the letter: he swallows his anger and speaks no harsh words, but teaches virtuous humility by his own example and compliments her virtuous wisdom. Again in sonnet 51, Spenser opts for a more subtle strategy of indirection:

> Ne ought so hard, but he that would attend,
> mote soften it and to his will allure:
> so doe I hope her stubborne hart to bend,
> and that it then more stedfast will endure.
> (9–12)

The word "attend" implies both attention and waiting, suggesting a paradoxical attitude of patient persistence. This sonnet also echoes and softens the harsh blacksmith conceit of sonnet 32, as if to stress that the eventual concord of hearts will be achieved not by force, but by indirection, by allurement, and it will take some time.

In advocating indirection and dissembling, conduct writers raise to the status of Christian virtue those arts cultivated by courtiers, lovers, and allegorical poets alike.[31] Vives advises that husbands who love spiritually will use gentle persuasion, not force, "for pure and holye love . . . prudentelye doth both guyde, and conduct the gently perswaded to the place they would go unto" (M4^{r-v}).[32] Spenser's sonnet 67 enacts this process of persuasion which preserves the will of the guided. The huntsman forsakes the chase and reclines in a shady place, whereupon the "gentle deare" returns in search of water and submits to him voluntarily:

> There she beholding me with mylder looke,
> sought not to fly, but fearelesse still did bide:
> till I in hand her yet halfe trembling tooke,
> and with her owne goodwill hir fyrmely tyde.
> Strange thing me seemd to see a beast so wyld,
> so goodly wonne with her owne will beguyld.
> (67:9–14)

In this sonnet, mutual "beguiling" occurs; the hounds are "beguiled of their pray" (4) by the escaping deer, who gains the freedom to set the terms of her own surrender. Then the woman/deer is ambiguously "with her owne will beguiled" (14), suggesting both that she has been deceived of "her owne goodwill" and that she has exercised it. The best gloss on this sonnet is Whately's advice to husbands: "Obedience would be inticed and allured, and as it were by committing it to it [sic] own disposing. . . . So carry thy selfe to thy wife, that she may perceive herselfe to have entred, not into servile thraldome, but loving subjection" (28). Spenser, as the huntsman, indirectly entices the obedience of the lady/deer; he does not compel it, and she subjects herself willingly, but only *after* he abandons the chase.[33] The husband-lover, importantly, does not compromise his authority by granting the lady her will. David Lee Miller perceptively notes the replacement of the tremors of line 11 with masculine firmness of line 12 and the "quiet reassertion of masculine authority in the active voice, as the speaker muses on what he has 'wonne.'"[34]

In sonnet 65, Spenser addresses a mistress who has apparently shown a reluctance to marry and seeks to assuage her doubts about forfeiting her freedom. The metaphors of this sonnet, like those of sonnet 67, touch on what Prescott calls his sense of a "feminine fear of imprisonment and wounding that must be put aside when it is timely to do so."[35] Here is Spenser's most thorough affirmation of a marriage in which both partners submit willingly to a bondage that is paradoxically liberating:

> The doubt which ye misdeeme, fayre love, is vaine,
> That fondly feare to loose your liberty;
> when loosing one, two liberties ye gayne,
> and make him bond that bondage erst dyd fly.
> Sweet be the bands, the which true love doth tye,
> without constraynt or dread of any ill:
> the gentle birde feeles no captivity
> within her cage, but singes and feeds her fill.
> There pride dare not approch, nor discord spill
> the league twixt them, that loyal love hath bound:
> but simple truth and mutuall good will
> seekes with sweet peace to salve each others wound.
> There fayth doth fearlesse dwell in brasen towre,
> and spotlesse pleasure builds her sacred bowre.

He characterizes marriage as a liberating captivity, but recognizes that without loving harmony—the bird singing in its cage—it can become a prison. As Vives counsels, "ther shalbe in wedlocke a certayne swete and pleasaunt conversation, without the which it is no maryage but a prysone, a hatred and a perpetual torment of the mynde" (Nv3^{r}). In short, spouses must also be friends. Marriage is considered the highest form of friendship, as the title of Tilney's discourse on marriage, *The Flower of Friendship,* suggests. Vives also describes matrimony as the perfection of friendship; marriage is "the supreme and most excellent part of all amitie" that "farre differeth from tiranny. . . ." There can be no marriage, he says, where the husband and wife "agree not in wyll and minde" (K4r). The association of marriage and friendship is natural to Spenser, too, for the meeting, courtship, and engagement of Artegall and Britomart occur in Book IV, the Legend of Friendship.

Though sonnet 65 seeks to assuage the lady's fears of marriage, it also betrays some of the speaker's own fears as well, as the metaphors for marriage oscillate between negative and positive meanings. Marriage is first characterized as "bondage" from which the poet himself has admittedly fled; then these bonds become sweet bands. The "brasen towre" of line 13 connotes not only strong faith, but the kind of tower in which maidens or offenders are often immured. Finally, marriage is affirmed to be a "sacred bowre," a place of sinless pleasure, an enclosed and fruitful garden—an image which replaces the unsettling metaphor of the caged bird. The tower and bower both prefigure the description of the bride in *Epithalamion;* her

> Snowie necke [is] lyke to a marble towre,
> And all her body like a pallace fayre,
> Ascending uppe with many a stately stayre,
> To honors seat and chastities sweet bowre.
> (177–80)

Though a Spenserian bower can also be a place of sensual and sexual excess, these bowers and towers are firmly associated with a lady chaste in body and mind.[36]

Sonnet 65 also affirms the responsibility of spouses with "mutuall good will" to seek "with sweet peace to salve each others wound." Though the poet staves off discord and pride, there are still wounds to heal; perhaps the wounds of Cupid's arrow, perhaps a gash like Amoret's bleeding heart, the legacy of Petrarchan loving, perhaps sinfulness in general. Writers on marriage agree that husband and wife share the duty to provide solace, to reform each other's vices and to foster each other's virtues. Smith advises spouses in his wedding sermon:

> To begin this concord well, it is necessarie to learne one anothers nature, and one anothers afflictions, and one anothers infirmities . . . therefore they must learne of *Paule,* to fashion themselves one to the other, if they would win one another. . . .(59)

In sonnet 62, Spenser invites the mistress, "let us . . .

> chaunge eeke our mynds and former lives amend,
> the old yeares sinnes forepast let us eschew,
> and fly the faults with which we did offend.
> (5–8)

A New Year's resolution of sorts, this appeal also signals a rejection of stormy Petrarchan courtship for serene married love in which "all these stormes . . . shall turne to caulmes" (11–12). In sonnet 8, the activity of fostering virtue is given to the lady:

> You frame my thoughts and fashion me within,
> you stop my toung, and teach my hart to speake,
> you calme the storme that passion did begin,
> strong thrugh your cause, but by your vertue weak.
> (9–12)

In sonnet 45, Spencer invokes a long instructive tradition with his use of the looking glass motif:

> Leave lady in your glasse of christall clene,
> Your goodly selfe for evermore to vew:
> and in my selfe, my inward selfe I meane,
> most lively lyke behold your semblant trew.
> (1–4)

Because her "goodly ymage" is dimmed by her cruelty, he urges her: "if your selfe in me ye playne will see, / remove the cause by which your fayre beames darkned be" (13–14). The mirror image suits the poems' Christian context and conveys good advice for a wife, who ought to look to her husband as the image of Christ. There she will see her own divine nature mirrored.[37] The point is that in the *Amoretti,* mutual fashioning occurs; the poet is drawn to goodness by his mistress' virtue, and he in turn seeks to amend her faults by frequent moral exhortations and by his own example of patience and love.[38]

It is hardly surprising that Spenser's sonnets should be so concerned with matters of conduct and self-fashioning. One aim of *The Faerie Queene,* which Spenser interrupted to complete his sonnet sequence (see *Amoretti* 33, 80), was "to fashion a gentleman or noble person in vertuous and gentle discipline" ("A Letter of the Authors"); similarly one purpose of the *Amoretti* is to fashion a pair of virtuous married lovers. The process of fashioning identity in the *Amoretti,* however, contradicts the recent new historicist paradigm. Stephen Greenblatt argues that for Spenser the self is constituted by an act of power exemplified in Guyon's destruction of the Bower of Bliss, a representation of the not-self that threatens identity and thus triggers violence. Greenblatt's Spenser is the preeminent poet of empire for whom "civilization . . . is achieved only through renunciation and the constant exercise of power."[39] It should be immediately obvious that the poet of the *Amoretti* is hardly such a power-hungry figure practicing masculine domination over the feminine Other. Nor is he, as Miller cautions, a protofeminist, despite his "ethical concern for tempering masculine aggressiveness . . . [and his] sympathetic exploration of feminine sexual ambivalence" in *The Faerie Queene.* Miller continues:

> Male desire seeks restlessly to cross the threshold of the feminine "Other"; like allegory itself, it mingles the impulse to seek out what is mysterious with a need to domesticate it, to make otherness a medium through which sameness reconstitutes itself.

For Miller, Spenser's allegory always assimilates the feminine to the masculine in a subordinate role.[40] Common to Greenblatt and Miller's analyses is the assumption that the self establishes itself by overpowering, controlling, or assimilating the "Other," represented as female. This is, essentially, the new historicist paradigm of Renaissance self-fashioning.

At first glance, the *Epithalamion* celebrates the poet-lover's achievement of such control by his attainment of a wife who fulfills the ideal of a virtuous wife and who bears little trace of her former self—the lively, sexually powerful mistress of the *Amoretti.* Her appearance evokes that of Amoret in the Temple of Venus, sitting in the lap of Womanhood, arrayed in white and shining like the morning sun (IV.x.52):

> Loe where she comes along with portly pace,
> Lyke Phoebe from her chamber of the East,
> Arysing forth to run her mighty race,
> Clad all in white, that seemes a virgin best.
> So well it her beseemes that ye would weene
> Some angell she had beene. . . .
> Her modest eyes abashed to behold

So many gazers, as on her do stare,
Upon the lowly ground affixed are.
Ne dare lift up her countenance too bold,
But blush to heare her prayses sung so loud,
So farre from being proud.
(*Epithalamion* 148–53; 159–64)

Her virginal white dress and her portly pace befit her. They are badges of a pride appropriate to her noble position, a loftiness which inheres, without paradox, in her very lowliness. First she is likened to the sun, then to an angel, then to a "mayden Queen" (158); finally she is simply a blushing bride who exemplifies all her culture's prescriptions for wifehood: "a modest countenance, and womanly shamefastnesse, do commend a chaste wife" (Smith 37).

As in the *Amoretti,* Spenser makes clear that the bride's physical beauty is surpassed by the "inward beauty of her lively spright, / Garnisht with heavenly guifts of high degree" (186–87). Among these gifts are virtues which befit a wife: "constant chastity, / Unspotted fayth and comely womanhood, / Regard of honour and mild modesty" (191–93). She is the epitome of the well-ordered body, in which "vertue raynes as Queene in royal throne, / And giveth lawes alone" (194–95). In this well-tempered body/state, "regard of honour," synonymous with pride,[41] and "mild modesty" co-exist without contradiction. Her "regard of honour" could suggest several things: that she regards her own honor, or the honor bestowed on her by marriage and its requisite mildness and modesty, or her husband's honor, which implies her own modest subordination.[42] Moreover, "mild modesty" is a virtue which lends honor to a wife. Mildness and modesty, says Gouge, are marks of a wife's reverence for her husband (277–78). Yet a measure of self-regard is appropriate for the wife, who ranks just blow her husband in the hierarchy of the family. Humility involves an acknowledgment of this proper place; it is "that grace that keepes one from thinking highly of himself *above that which is meet*" (Gouge 331; emphasis mine); it will also make a wife "thinke better of her husband than of her selfe, and . . . make her more willing to yeeld all subjection unto him" (331). "Regard of honour" and "mild modesty" are thus not only not contradictory, but essentially related. By praising his bride's virtues of chastity, modesty, and honor, Spenser continues to promote his culture's ideal of a godly wife.[43]

Spenser's final words on pride and humility present an apparent conundrum, an oxymoron which resolves itself into an affirmation of the bride's honorable virtue. Entering the bridal bower, the speaker exclaims, "Behold how goodly my faire love does ly/In proud humility" (305–6). "Proud humility" is not really the contradiction it seems, for Spenser and writers on marriage agree that it is possible to be simultaneously humble and proud, though not "above that which is meet." (Sonnet 13 describes such a coexistence of humility and pride, "mild humblesse" and "awfull majesty," [5] and promises that "such lowlinesse shall make you lofty be" [14].) The emphasis of the phrase rests on "humility," which is modified and qualified by a pride as "goodly" as the fair bride herself. Good pride, for a wife, involves the consciousness that humility befits her, indeed, that it exalts her. Good pride also describes the virtuous sexuality of the wife humbled before her husband, her lord. Reclining in "proud humility," the bride exhibits (and awakens) a sexual desire which now occurs in its proper context of marriage. Heather Dubrow observes that the bride is strikingly (even disturbingly) passive, like "Maia, when as Jove her tooke,/In Tempe, lying on the flowry gras,/Twixt sleepe and wake, after she weary was. . ." (307–9); she is drained of all threatening sexual aggressiveness.[44] Her sexuality is now contained and controlled by the loving bonds of marriage and by the husband's (and poet's) authority. The phrase "proud humility" also suggests that her qualities of modesty, humility, temperance, and chaste desire for her husband are virtues of which the bride can justly be proud. Finally, this oxymoron expresses the conflict of Petrarchanism with Christian loving and a redefinition of their conventional languages. The phrase echoes the lady's vain pride and the lover's humiliation while rewriting and reconciling them as a Christian paradox.

That Spenser wins his lady and marries her constitutes his final abrogation of Petrarchan conventions of loving and writing poetry. But as the phrase "proud humility" still resonates with Petrarchan conflicts, the poet-lover's success raises a nagging fear: perhaps he has not after all renounced the Petrarchan ethic, only effected a turnabout by loving a woman he can dominate by marrying.[45] The poet's public celebration of mastery over his chaste and submissive bride, who blushes inordinately but speaks not a word, is admittedly problematic.[46] Spenser may have had cause to celebrate the triumph of her "proud humility" over her residual false pride, or he may be enacting a cultural wish fulfillment, incarnating with his art the ideal of a shamefast and silent wife and parading himself as a masterful poet and husband. The mistress-as-bride does finally conform to an ideology in which women are subordinated to their husbands in marriage, and thus the *Epithalamion* can seem to fit the self-fashioning paradigm described above. But the intimate, mutual relationship represented in the *Amoretti* qualifies our view of the "finished products" presented to public view on the marriage day. Spenser does not merely substitute for the Petrarchan hierarchy a patriarchal one: he does not subordinate the mistress to fulfill a desire for male power. Of crucial significance is the fact that the poet-lover, too, is conformed to this ideology of marriage in which the husband exercises not absolute power but a benign authority. Throughout the *Amoretti,* Elizabeth Boyle is transformed into a godly wife, true, but Spenser also creates himself as the ideal husband; his affection for his wife, his reverence for her heavenly virtues, and his gentle authority in correcting her faults help to establish the peace and concord deemed necessary for marirage. Otherness is preserved, not eradicated or assimilated into the poet's identity, for the poet is concerned to conform himself and his mistress to an external, higher law, Christ's law of love. The *Amoretti,* then, can be considered Spenser's Legend of Humility; its protagonists are the mistress who must learn that her pride imperils the proper order which should exist between husband and wife and the poet-lover who wins her only after repudiating force. The *Amoretti* enact Spenser's self-fashioning as a Protestant—versus a Petrarchan—poet and lover. The conventions, metaphors, and paradoxes of Petrarchan poetry and loving are redeemed and overwritten by the ideals of sixteenth-century marriage, with its own unique paradox: that mutual love and responsibility can and ought to exist within the hierarchical relationship of marriage.

The Ohio State University

Notes

I wish to thank Judith H. Anderson, David O. Frantz, John N. King, and Anne Lake Prescott for their valuable comments on earlier versions of this essay.

1. Citations from *The Faerie Queene* are taken from the Variorum edition of *The Works of Edmund Spenser.* References to the *Amoretti* and *Epithalamion* are from the *Yale Edition of the Shorter Poems of Edmund Spenser,* ed. William Oram et al. (New Haven: Yale University Press, 1989). All future references to these works occur in the text.

Isabel G. Maccaffrey notes Spenser's witty allusions to Petrarch in Britomart's complaint to the sea (III.iv.9), which is recited on the shore, and the creation of False Florimell out of sonnet cliches (III.viii.6–7) (*Spenser's Allegory: The Anatomy of Imagination* [Princeton: Princeton University Press, 1976], 291–92).

2. See the analyses of Britomart's role by Thomas P. Roche, Jr. in the *Kindly Flame: A Study of the Third and Fourth Books of Spenser's* Faerie Queene (Princeton University Press, 1964) and A. Kent Hieatt, *Chaucer, Spenser, Milton: Mythopoeic Continuities and Transformation* (Montreal: McGill-Queens University Press, 1975).

3. While recognizing that Petrarch was profoundly Christian, I am distinguishing the "Petrarchan tradition" as a set of conventional attitudes popularized by practitioners of courtly poetry and loving (on the Continent and in England) who saw themselves as indebted to Petrarch.

4. I have drawn on the following works: Juan Luis Vives, *The Office and Duetie of a Husband* (London, 1553) and William Gouge, *Of Domesticall Duties* (London, 1622), both conduct manuals; *An Homily of the State of Matrimony,* in *Certain Sermons* (London, 1562), Henry Smith, *A Preparative to Marriage* (London 1591), and William Whately, *A Bride-Bush, or a Wedding Sermon* (London, 1617), all sermons; and Edmund Tilney, *A brief and pleasant discourse of duties in Mariage, called the Flower of Friendshippe* (London, 1568), a courtly discourse akin to Castiglione's *Book of the Courtier.* Citations from these works appear parenthetically in my text.

Literary critics and social historians disagree concerning the status of marriage in late Elizabethan times. Some point to the new Puritan ideal of marriage emphasizing love and domestic relations and find that it elevated a wife's position. Among them are William Haller, "Hail Wedded Love," *ELH* 13 [1946], 79–97; William and Malleville Haller, "The Puritan Art of Love," *HLQ* 5 (1942), 235–72; C. S. Lewis, *The Allegory of Love* (New York: Oxford University Press, 1958), and Juliet Dusinberre, *Shakespeare and the Nature of Woman* (London: 1975). Lawrence Stone, on the other hand, while acknowledging the new emphasis on domesticity, sees the period 1580–1640 as one of increasing patriarchal control over the wife and family. See *The Family, Sex and Marriage in England 1500–1800* (New York: Harper, Row, 1977), chapter 5. Margaret J. M. Ezell rejects Stone's idea of restrictive patriarchy as a bugbear in *The Patriarch's Wife: Literary Evidence and the History of the Family* (Chapel Hill: University of North Carolina Press, 1987). Kathleen M. Davies, in "Continuity and Change in Literary Advice on Marriage," *Marriage and Society: Studies in the Social History of Marriage,* ed. R. B. Outhwaite (London: 1981), 58–80, agrees with Stone but finds that attitudes expressed towards domestic relations changed very little from the mid-sixteenth to the mid-seventeenth century, despite changes in theological views about the status of marriage. Because my own reading of the above primary texts bears out Davies' conclusions, I refer to their advice and prescriptions regarding men's and women's roles in marriage as the "conventional wisdom" of Spenser's culture. Like Davies, Keith Wrightson emphasizes the continuity between pre- and post-Reformation tradition regarding marriage, in *English Society 1580–1680* (New Brunswick: Rutgers University Press, 1982), 91. Most recently, Heather Dubrow has refueled the debate, noting the inconsistencies and outright contradictions within and between conduct books on marriage. While finding agreement on some issues of marital conduct, she argues that there was not a single, coherent "Protestant discourse of marriage" in Tudor and Stuart England. See *A Happier Eden: The Politics of Marriage in the Stuart Epithalamium* (Ithaca: Cornell University Press, 1990), 4, 12–14.

5. "Echo's Ring: Orpheus and Spenser's Career," *ELR* 16 (1986): 294, 295.

6. *Spenser and the Motives of Metaphor* (Durham: Duke University Press, 1982), 73.

7. "The Petrarchan Context of Spenser's *Amoretti, PMLA* 100 (1985): 46, 47.

8. See Anne Lake Prescott's discussion of the deer of sonnet 67, its Christlike connotations and liturgical and biblical associations in "The Thirsty Deer and the Lord of Life: Some Contexts for *Amoretti* 67–70," *Spenser Studies* 7 (1986), 47ff. A. Leigh DeNeef finds that the Song of Songs, with its central metaphor of the *hortus conclusus,* affords Spenser's lover the means of transforming his previously literal understanding of captivity (70).

9. See John N. King, *Spenser's Poetry and the Reformation Tradition* (Princeton: Princeton University Press, 1990), chapter 4. King's treatment of *Amoretti* and *Epithalamion* is similar to mine. He argues that they feature "a distillation of Spenser's position concerning love and marriage and a *modification* of imported literary models in line with Protestant ideology" (182; emphasis mine). Though King's emphasis differs, his reading of the *Amoretti* complements and supports my own.

10. Sir Philip Sidney, *Astrophil and Stella, The Poems of Sir Philip Sidney,* ed. William A. Ringler (Oxford: Clarendon, 1962).

11. See for example Petrarch's *Rime sparse* 39 ("I so fear the assault of those lovely eyes where Love and my death dwell . . ."); 61 ("Blessed be the day . . . where I was struck by the two lovely eyes that have bound me; and blessed be . . . the bow and the arrows that pierced me, and the wounds that reach my heart!"); and 75 ("The lovely eyes that struck me in such a way that they themselves could heal the wound . . ."), *Petrarch's Lyric Poems,* trans. and ed. Robert M. Durling (Cambridge: Harvard University Press, 1976).

12. According to Robert Ellrodt, Louis LeRoy, whose commentary on the *Symposium* Spenser may have known second hand, is the only other Renaissance Platonist to agree with Spenser that the perfection of human love is generation. Most Renaissance Platonists (Castiglione, for example) separated the consideration of marriage from the platonic philosophy of love and even contrasted the two. See *Neoplatonism in the Poetry of Spenser* (Geneva: 1960), 105, 146.

13. Ibid, 146. See also William Nelson's discussion of Spenser's philosophy of love in *The Poetry of Edmund Spenser* (New York: Columbia University Press, 1963), 97–101. He also establishes that for Spenser, earthly love and heavenly love are comparable and not incompatible.

14. Ellrodt finds that Spenser is essentially conservative, that his Christian and medieval inheritance was rooted deeper than the "newer" Renaissance Platonism (129–30) and influences his very apprehension of the Neoplatonic philosophy of love and beauty (129). For Nelson, the question is academic, for Christianity itself had from its early centuries become saturated with Platonism (114).

15. Anne Lake Prescott believes this poem to be a paraphrase of Desportes' *Diane* I, xxxii, and comments on Spenser's turn from "the precious splendor of her body to the *invisibilia* of her mind" (*French Poets and the English Renaissance: Studies in Fame and Transformation* [New Haven: Yale University Press, 1978], 150–51). As she has noted, this turn is further evidence of Spenser's refashioning of his predecessors.

16. Sir Philip Sidney, *A Defence of Poetry,* ed. J. A. Van Dorsten (Oxford University Press, 1960), 69.

17. DeNeef sees Spenser consciously announcing himself as a "Sidneyan Right Poet" (13).
18. On the calendrical structure of Petrarch's *Canzoniere* see Thomas P. Roche, Jr., *Petrarch and the English Sonnet Sequences* (New York: AMS, 1989), 32–69. One entire vein of *Amoretti* criticism deals with its calendrical contexts. See for example Alexander Dunlop, "The Unity of Spenser's *Amoretti*," in *Silent Poetry: Essays in Numerological Analysis,* ed. Alastair Fowler (London, 1970): 153–69; G. K. Hunter, "'Unity' and Numbers in Spenser's *Amoretti*," *YES* 5 (1975): 39–45; A. Kent Hieatt, "A Numerical Key for Spenser's *Amoretti* and Guyon in the House of Mammon," *YES* 3 (1973): 14–27. More recently, Anne Lake Prescott's article expands the liturgical contexts of the sequence.
19. "*Amoretti* and the *Dolce Stil Nuovo*," *ELR* 2 (1972), 211, 216.
20. "The *Amoretti:* 'Most Goodly Temperature,'" *Form and Convention in the Poetry of Edmund Spenser,* ed. William Nelson. (New York: Columbia University Press, 1961): 146–68.
21. Like Martz, King prefers to read Spenser's exaggerated Petrarchanism as parodic; however, he perceptively notes that sonnet 10, in which the lady scorns her suitor "of her freewill," and sonnet 67, in which she surrenders out of "her owne goodwill," form a poetic diptych. Her acquiescence "accords with the right operation of that human faculty [free will] in accordance with divine grace, by contrast to the prideful state of *Am.* 10" (169).
22. "Spenser's Poetics: The Poem's Two Bodies," *PLMA* 101 (1986): 171, 175.
23. *The Poem's Two Bodies: The Poetics of the 1590* Faerie Queene (Princeton University Press, 1988), 81–82. This passage also occurs verbatim in the earlier *PMLA* article, 175.
24. The same rhetorical strategy is employed by Whately in a somewhat less concise passage of *A Bride-Bush,* 36–37.
25. Writers on marriage typically employ the husband-king analogy to justify a wife's obedience. In the divinely ordained hierarchy of the family, the husband is "king in his family: the woman [is] the Deputie subordinate" who, if not governed reasonably, will "breake out into open act of rebellion" (Whately, 16, 23).
26. Before sonnet 62, twenty poems refer to pride (2, 5, 6, 13, 14, 19, 21, 27, 28, 31–33, 38, 43, 47, 49, 56, 58, 59, 61). Sonnet 62 is the New Year's sonnet; shortly thereafter is the "engagement" sonnet (67), after which references to pride are scarce. In addition to the above twenty sonnets, several refer to the mistress as cruel, a tyrant, or a beast: 10, 11, 20, 25, 36, 41, 45, 53, 57. Five poems describe her as "hard" or "stubborn": 18, 29, 30, 51, 54. Spenser's preoccupation with his lady's pride and its manifestations, cruelty and hard-heartedness, is without precedent or match in his contemporaries.
27. See also sonnets 20, 31, 38, 47, 53, 56. For the definition of pride as sexual desire or excitement, see *OED,* s.v. *pride,* II. 11; *proud,* 8. Sexual pride is apparent in Shakespeare's Dark Lady, who "Tempteth my better angel from my side, / And would corrupt my saint to be a devil, / Wooing his purity with her foul pride" (144:6–8) (*Shakespeare's Sonnets,* ed. Stephen Booth [New Haven: Yale University Press, 1977]). In conduct books, the association of pride with sexuality is implicit in the endorsement of "shamefastness" as a primary virtue for women. (Its opposite, shamelessness, still connotes sexual looseness.) Writes Tilney, shamefastness is "the roote of godli-

ness" and the woman's only defense against unchastity and dishonor (D3). Vives inextricably links the two: "Chastitie is kept with shamefastnes, nor the one can not be without the other" (R3^{v}).

28. King discusses these two poems in terms of Protestant doctrine concerning grace and justification by faith. In sonnet 58, her spiritual autonomy suggests original sin and is an impediment to true faith, while in sonnet 59, "her apparent pride actually represents proper 'assurance,'" a term Protestants used to define election (166).

29. See the discussions of pride by William Nelson, 89–90; Louis Martz, 162–64; and Carol Kaske, in "Spenser's *Amoretti and Epithalamion* of 1595: Structure, Genre, and Numerology," *ELR* 8 (1978): 271–95. Kaske finds that sonnets 58, 59, and 61 fail to resolve the issue of pride or the "conflicts of sexual desire with virtue and virginal pride with wifely submission" (285), but she sees the debate settled with sonnet 67 (281).

30. See also sonnet 13, discussed above, sonnets 38, 41, 45, 49, 50, 53, 55, 57, 58, 68, 79, 82.

31. George Puttenham, in *The Arte of English Poesie* (1589) (Menston, England: Scolar Press, 1968), discusses allegory as an art of dissembling essential to courtiers and princes, as well as to poets (155–156).

32. In this advice to husbands, I am reminded of Peter Ramus's "prudential method," characterized by indirection and used to persuade an inattentive or unfriendly audience. John Webster, in "'The Methode of a Poete': An Inquiry Into Tudor Conceptions of Poetic Sequence," *ELR* 11 (1981): 22–43, claims both Sidney and Spenser use prudential strategies to control a reader's experience of their poetry (42).

33. For a related reading of this sonnet, see Anne Lake Prescott, especially her discussion of sonnet 68 as an anthology of scriptural quotations appropriate to the Easter season (42–47), the discussion of Biblical deer (48–52), and the analysis of the resemblances of certain sonnets to the Sarum liturgy.

34. Miller, *The Poem's Two Bodies,* 219–20. Incidentally, the courtship of Artegall and Britomart, like that of the *Amoretti* lovers, begins in a contest for mastery and ends with the establishment of loving concord. In IV.vi.12, Artegall greedily assails Britomart, like a hound cornering a hind. Her own "hart"-heart leaps with "sudden joy, and secret feare" (29) as she recognizes her mate. Glauce reconciles the battling lovers with a moral instruction regarding marriage (31), and Artegall proceeds to woo Britomart properly, "with meeke service and much suit" (40).

35. Prescott, 35.

36. See King's discussion of the Bower of Bliss as an anti-epithalamium, 179–80.

37. Another example of the mirror conceit used in an advice book for married Christians is Robert Snawsell's *A Looking Glasse for Married Folkes. Wherein they may plainly see their deformities: and also how to behave themselves one to another, and both of them towards God . . .* (1610).

38. Most critics are reluctant to see Spenser in the role of teacher, as if direct didacticism compromises Spenser's artistry. Instead, readers of sonnets are attached to the concept of persona, insisting on separating Spenser from his poet-lover and tracing the spiritual growth of the latter. See for example William C. Johnson, "Amor and Spenser's *Amoretti,*" *English Studies* 54 (1973): 217–26 and Peter M. Cummings, "Spenser's *Amoretti* as an Allegory of Love," *TSLL* 12 (1970): 163–79. DeNeef, too, though he notes the lover's role as teacher in sonnet 65, emphasizes that the lover progresses in

the sequence by learning "to perceive metaphorically . . . [and] to appropriate and approximate the voice of the poet" (69).

39. *Renaissance Self-Fashioning from More to Shakespeare* (Chicago: University of Chicago Press, 1980), chapter 4, 173–74.

40. Miller, *The Poem's Two Bodies,* 217.

41. *OED,* s.v. *proud,* 2.

42. Britomart exhibits such "regard of honour" at Artegall's departure. Though she grieves, she "wisely moderated her owne smart,/Seeing his honor, which she tendred chiefe,/Consisted much in that adventures priefe" (V.vii.44). Like a proper wife, she puts her husband's honor before her own desires and represses her own complaints; here she embodies humility, sincerity, cheerfulness, and constancy, the four virtues which "season a wives subjection" (Gouge 331).

43. Milton shares this ideal; his description of Eve exhibits a similar tension between "regard of honour" and "mild modesty": "Innocence and Virgin Modesty,/Her virtue and the conscience of her worth" (*Paradise Lost,* VIII: 501–2, in *John Milton: Complete Poems and Major Prose,* ed. Merritt Y. Hughes [Indianapolis: Odyssey Press, 1980], 374). In Spenser's praise of his lady's inward beauties, there is, however, a troublesome likeness to the power of "Medusaes mazeful hed" (190) to turn the viewer to stone. As the editors of the Yale edition note, Medusa is sometimes associated with chastity, but Nancy Vickers notes a less benign association of Medusa with unchastity. She cites Gerard Leigh's *Accedence of Armorie* (London, 1591) and its account of Medusa "openly fle[eing] the discipline of womanly shamefastness" for which she was punished with transformation into "a beastlie monster, horrible to mankinde, a mirror for Venus minions" ("'The blazon of sweet beauty's best': Shakespeare's *Lucrece,*" *Shakespeare and the Question of Theory,* ed. Patricia Parker and Geoffrey Hartman [New York: Methuen, 1985], 109). Vickers also discusses associations of Medusa with female violation and with artful eloquence (110–11). Perhaps the specter of the powerful mistress still haunts the bridegroom of the *Epithalamion;* in any case, Spenser's reference to Medusa invokes a vast and complex tradition of representation.

44. Dubrow, 37–38. Kaske's interpretation of the bride's "proud humility" differs somewhat from mine; the oxymoron expresses "mutuality of desire, the bride humble in her surrender to her husband, but the groom also now a servant to her awakened desire" (282). Dubrow and other critics of the *Epithalamion* see Spenser as expressing, containing, controlling, or resolving tensions and anxieties about marriage, variously personal and cultural. See Dubrow's Introduction for a good summary.

45. For this observation, I am indebted to Ann Prescott.

46. Carol Thomas Neely, in a paper delivered at the Ohio Shakespeare Conference in March 1989, discusses the discontinuity between a woman's roles of maid and wife in Renaissance drama. She also referred to the letters of Leonard Wheatcroft, which trace a mid-seventeenth century courtship after the manner of sonneteers; at the wedding, however, the woman disappears as a speaker ("Representing Women: Disjunctions, Divisions, Disappearances").

WAYNE ERICKSON

Spenser's Letter to Ralegh and the Literary Politics of *The Faerie Queene*'s 1590 Publication

Et quisuis placuisse Studet Heroibus altis,
Desipuisse studet, sic gratia crescit ineptis.
Denique Laurigeris quisquis sua tempora vittis
Insignire volet, Populoque placere fauenti,
Desipere insanus discit, turpemque pudendae
Stultitiae laudem quaerit.[1]

Edmund Spenser to Gabriel Harvey,
October, 1579

Representing a Publishing Event: Voices and Audiences

BENEATH THE SUPERFICIAL disguise of Latin verse and private correspondence, the epigraph exposes a Spenserian persona that remains, despite its active appearance throughout Spenser's career, a relative stranger to Spenser studies, even, remarkably, to most recent attempts at repoliticizing Spenser's personal and fictional strategies in response to contemporary critical theory. The persona presented here, in a letter to Harvey at about the time Spenser was readying *The Shepheardes Calender* for the press, reappears as one of several subtly revealed personae in another piece of personal and public correspondence, Spenser's Letter to his friend Walter Ralegh, dated 23 January 1589/90 and appended to the 1590 *Faerie Queene.*[2] Because of its intimate and intriguing relation to *The Faerie Queene,* Spenser's "Letter to Ralegh" elicits responses from most students of the poem it purportedly defends and explains. Yet despite the Letter's provenance as Spenser's most sustained literary critical statement, and despite its dynamic role in one of the most important publishing events in English literary history, it has not received the searching and comprehensive analysis it deserves. The mostly piecemeal critical attention given the Letter reflects, in part, critics' assumptions about its status as a written text: most critics treat the Letter as a secondary source, a stable, unified discourse with a transparent and unmediated relation to *The Faerie Queene*. Recent critical theory—structuralist, deconstructionist, and historicist alike—has convincingly demonstrated the distortions inherent in any interpretive procedure that privileges too radically one cultural text over another. But this is what has happened to the Letter: dwarfed by the massive complexities of *The Faerie Queene,* the Letter plays a subliterary explanatory role that helps legitimize the practice of critics who mine it as a straightforwardly authoritative source, extracting fragments to serve their immediate purposes. In this essay, I aim to provide some sustained analysis of the Letter, not primarily as a commentary on *The Faerie Queene,* but as an independent pluralist text born out of a matrix of personal and professional responsibilities: a complex politico-literary act of damage control, cultural criticism, and rhetorical play by an inspired and informed Renaissance intellectual.

Not all critics, of course, have been as ready as those alluded to above to embrace uncritically the Letter's authority; some, puzzled and even annoyed by portions of the Letter, have severely questioned its value and accuracy as a guide to the poem. Some of these have searched near and far for the elusive source of Spenser's "twelue priuate morall virtues, as Aristotle hath deuised,"[3] while others have created a minor critical industry out of speculations on a few narrative and structural discrepancies that seem to afflict the Letter's relation to the poem.[4] A brief review of a longstanding critical controversy involving the latter issue will provide an initial if limited entry into the problematics of the text. Among those who have taken part in the dispute, Josephine Waters Bennett and W. J. B. Owen are most comprehensive in citing apparent inconsistencies between the Letter and the poem, and within the Letter itself, as crucial pieces of evidence corroborating speculative reconstructions of the poem's composition. While both critics, enlarging on summary statements by Janet Spens and disputing claims by other critics, contend that the Letter outlines not an abandoned early (1580) plan but a late (1589) "omnibus scheme" that Spenser lacked sufficient time to incorporate into his poem,[5] their stated attitudes toward the value of the Letter differ radically. Bennett defends the Letter, despite inconsistencies, as an invaluable source of hints about Spenser's method of composition and a serious attempt on the poet's part "to systematize the product of ten years of experimentation";[6] in contrast, Owen ends up disparaging the Letter as "a curiosity of criticism, all but irrelevant to the poem it purports to describe."[7] Amid the chorus of contentious voices in essential agreement with Owen, we might hear C. S. Lewis branding Spenser's account of the poem "demonstrably untrue"[8] and Lawrence Blair, the first to outline in print the supposed inconsistencies, categorically asserting that "Spenser fails to follow his avowed plan" and does "not tell the truth about his plot."[9]

I mention this protracted controversy over the relative accuracy of the Letter not so much to indict the superficiality of its readings, which I imagine would have left Spenser more amused than incensed, as to emphasize the Letter's potentially problematical relation to the poem. And although I cannot agree with those who claim that Spenser mistakenly misrepresents his poem in the Letter, it is worth considering that the narrative and structural inconsistencies outlined by Blair (1932) and Spens (1934) stood substantially unchallenged for twenty-five years, until A. C. Hamilton all but silenced the skeptics and stalled the flow of commentary by stressing the power of the poet's allegory to redeem apparent inconsistencies.[10] Hamilton convincingly points out what should have been noted all along: that the beginnings of the quests outlined in the Letter are, according to Spenser, presented as they would "be told by an Historiographer," not by a "Poet historical." Thus, Hamilton concludes, since "Spenser is free to recreate the time and action as his allegory demands," "no divergencies" exist between the Letter and the poem: "The simple allegorical pageant in the *Letter* is quite properly displaced by the poem's pleasing analysis."[11] Although Hamilton's major contention here seems sensible and convincing, his implicit assumption concerning the Letter's absolute and unified coherence leads him to overstate his case, ignoring Spenser's often ambiguous rhetorical and terminological strategies.

Inspired, in part, by Hamilton's perspective, those who have not been perplexed by the Letter have been pleased to find in it a convenient, authoritative, and relatively tractable source of quotations to serve one or another interpretation of *The Faerie Queene* or to illustrate arguments concerning Spenser's avowed literary theory: his moral and nationalistic intentions, his place in the classic line, and his method of allegorical and fictional composition. The latter issue, particularly Spenser's stated attitude toward his allegorical fictions, is the textual focus of this essay, which analyzes a few familiar passages from the Letter in order, initially, to expose a widespread distortion of Spenser's text by critics who discuss—or, more likely, mention—his critical theory. This analysis illustrates my larger purpose: to view the Letter within its Elizabethan cultural context as an integral part of a carefully planned and executed publishing event of notable importance to literary history and unparalleled significance to Spenser's career. Thus, I will focus on a few literary critical and historiographical cruxes of the Letter as they illustrate Spenser's masterful manipulation of his cultural persona.

Recent historicist criticism, though relatively silent on the Letter, has deepened my conviction that Spenser uses the Letter to fashion *The Faerie Queene* in a composite image consistent with his various public duties and private intentions. The lack of sustained analysis of the Letter by historicist critics is particularly surprising in view of the document's dynamic textual and cultural position, situated both literally and figuratively between *The Faerie Queene* and its audiences. As such, the Letter occupies a politico-literary space where poem, poet, and audience intersect, a position that defines the poet's role as mediator between his work and his audiences and the Letter's role as mediator between the poet and the various forms of political and literary production that sustain, restrain, supply, and deny the power and meaning of the poet's language. The Letter, together with the Dedicatory Sonnets and, with some help from Spenser's friends, the Commendatory Verses, constitutes a consciously articulated act of self-presentation, self-fashioning, and social representation—though not quite the act that Richard Helgerson, Stephen Greenblatt, or Jonathan Goldberg would probably expect of Spenser.[12]

Although the Letter may well give "great light to the Reader" by providing a selective commentary on the poem, it includes few if any substantive details that could not be gleaned from a careful reading of the poem itself. More centrally, the Letter remakes the poem in accord with the expectations of particular audiences and in response to the conditions of Elizabethan literary production. Spenser writes the Letter, so he tells us, because Ralegh has "commanded" him to do so, and the possibilities of irony, private jokes, and serious business centered in the word are open for speculation. Ralegh would certainly be among the first to advise Spenser to write in defense of his work, anticipating "gealous opinions and misconstructions" and acting to stall them[13]—a stratagem well known to both of them. In fact, in the second of his Commendatory Verses, Ralegh hyperbolically commands Spenser to revise and rewrite his published poem in response to any hints of royal displeasure:

> If thou has beautie praysd, let her sole lookes diuine
> Iudge if ought therein be amis, and mend it by her eine.
> If Chastitie want ought, or Temperance her dew,
> Behold her Princely mind aright, and write thy Queene anew.[14]

In the Letter and in the Dedicatory Sonnets, Spenser does some preventive rewriting of the kind Ralegh suggests. In some of the Sonnets, playing the repentant prodigal,[15] the lowly suppliant, the earnest flatterer, Spenser solicits the undeserved patriarchal pardon, approbation, and kind favor of his betters. There, the same poem whose author, in the Commendatory Verses, is thought worthy to be accorded the "leaues of fame"[16] bestowed upon Virgil and Petrarch is explicitly disparaged in eleven of the seventeen Sonnets: "this Bryttane *Orpheus*,"[17] the English counterpart to Homer, Virgil, and Petrarch, is self-transformed into a rude rhymer, *The Faerie Queene* becoming "this base Poeme," "this rusticke Madrigale," "the fruit of barren field," and "unripe fruit of an unready wit"—in all, "these ydle rimes . . . The labor of lost time, and wit vnstayd."[18] In the Letter, Spenser defends his poem against those who might question its status or misconstrue the allegory while simultaneously apologizing for the fictional subject matter and the allegorical method. The public voice that produces these texts, alternately contrite, self-effacing, learned, obsequious, and reactionary, dominates the discourse of the Letter, re-presenting the product of the loyal subject's poetic labor to the queen, the court, the lords of power, and the epic poet's national audience.

Knowing better than most the risks and rewards attending his friend's situation, and for compelling personal reasons, Ralegh had sound motives for hoping Spenser accomplished a sterling performance. Ralegh's always visible and often precarious position at court had been mightily tested since Essex returned, knighted, from Zutphen to challenge the Captain of the Guard's favored place in Elizabeth's affections. Less than a year before Ralegh's reappearance at court with Spenser in fall, 1589, a duel between Ralegh and the new favorite had been halted by the Privy Council, and there were persistent rumors afoot that Ralegh "had left court in some slight disfavor"[19] when he traveled to Ireland in late spring, 1589, to inspect his vast domain and, fortuitously, spend some time with Spenser during the summer. Even if Ralegh's enemies exaggerated when they claimed that Essex had all but chased him out of England, evidence points to the rising prominence of the young earl and to the queen's typical manipulation of her rival favorites, frustrating and thereby aggravating ambition and envy by turning them against one another. Although Ralegh was not yet in deep trouble, he had no dearth of enemies and, like Spenser, must have been more than usually cognizant of the limitations imposed upon him by his relatively humble birth. Out of the savage country and into this complex and potentially dangerous scene of royal and courtly politics entered the expectant poet, along with the controversial friend who had apparently secured Spenser's audience with the queen. Ralegh and Spenser had every reason to affect the humility and caution figured in the material appended to the 1590 volume.[20]

But there is more going on in the Commendatory Verses than ardent praise and fatherly advice, more at issue in the Dedicatory Sonnets than servile apology and sycophantic fawning, and much more intended in the Letter than straightforward defense and selective commentary. To begin with, it is difficult to imagine, given what we know about Ralegh and Spenser, that either would be rendered impotent by the intimidation of the moment. No doubt they wisely respected and suspected the power that held them in subjection and granted them favor, but both had fiercely independent minds, neither feared controversy, and both saw in this important publishing event an opportunity for a provocative engagement with power. All of the ancillary texts to the 1590 *Faerie Queene,* particularly those that establish a dialogue between Ralegh and Spenser, display a studied complexity of implication and a deliberate pattern of interrelationship.

One might note, for instance, the potentially ironic and even subversive juxtaposition of Ralegh's two Commendatory Verses, the one a startling poetic vision placing Spenser preeminently in the classic line, the other a condescending nod to the national audience and a hard lesson in right relations with autocratic power. In the first, "A Vision vpon this conceipt of the *Faery Queene*" — upon, simultaneously, Spenser's originary idea and controlling image, Elizabeth, Gloriana, the "celestiall theife," and the poem itself—Ralegh envisions the sudden appearace at Laura's tomb of the "Faery Queene": "At whose approach the soule of *Petrarke* wept," the graces "loue" and "vertue" abandoned Laura to attend the new queen, and "*Homers* spright did tremble all for griefe." The Spenserian conceit displaces the Petrarchan and even gives Homer pause to consider the violently authoritative power of the new poet's creation, which makes "the hardest stones . . . bleed" and "buried ghostes" pierce "the heauens" with their "grones." In the second poem, "Another of [by or about] the same," Ralegh describes a more practical-minded approach to the judgment of literary value. He instructs Spenser to disregard the "prayse of meaner wits" because such praise to "this worke like profit brings, / As doth the Cuckoes song delight when *Philumena* sings." In fact, Spenser should listen only to the judgment of the queen, who, though she will probably "excuse and fauour [his] good will" because the poem flatters her sufficiently and because, in any case, her perfect "vertue can not be exprest, but by an Angels quill," is after all the ultimate and absolute arbiter of value. If anything about the poem displeases her, Spenser must "write [his] Queene anew." Ralegh ends the poem with his personal opinion that Spenser is his favorite English poet, prudently and ironically qualifying the authority of his initial vision.

The irony implicit in the juxtaposed pair of Verses rests upon the identity of the "Faery Queene" in the first. If the being that displaces Laura is Elizabeth and only Elizabeth, there is no problem because then any royal critique of *The Faerie Queene* issues from the sole source of and inspiration for the poem's power. If, however, the "conceipt" is Spenser's own idea and the poem that emerges from it, Ralegh's second poem sets up a potential scenario for playing the queen's power against itself, strenuously and audaciously challenging the queen's discernment of literary value. For although she is free to censure the poem for whatever reason she wishes, such censure would—given the validity of Ralegh's vision—expose very poor judgment since it would cancel a poetry that overgoes Petrarch's and challenges the preeminence of Homer's.[21] As one might expect, Ralegh's rhetorical strategy skillfully deflects the foregoing reading at every turn, neutralizing any hints of overt subversion; but while nothing as obviously counterproductive as open defiance is in evidence here, clever flirtations with dangerous play and covert intimations of hidden agendas are hardly inconceivable.

Such, I think, is also the case in the Letter, where, counterpointing the public discourse of apology and defense, Spenser writes a personal letter to a friend and patron with whom he had spent some time during the previous six months of his life—a fellow poet who perhaps knew more about *The Faerie Queene* in 1589 than anyone except the author. Ironically, given the latter probability, Spenser addresses his Letter to the person least in need of the information it claims to provide; in that case, if he writes for Ralegh's "better light in reading" the "booke"—offering whatever profit and delight his sophisticated, controversial, and powerful friend might draw from the text—the "light" revealed to the private audience would be relatively distinct from that offered to the larger public audiences. By asserting the existence of a private voice, I merely announce my recognition of the speaker's self-consciousness, naming the source of covert texts manipulated by various rhetorical roles; but I also admit that the private voice is more latent than manifest, for the person who speaks to Ralegh, Harvey, and others among Spenser's friends and associates is thoroughly embedded in the public address and all but lost to the passage of time. Yet perhaps by searching out and establishing a satisfactory control text of public performance, we might glimpse, coexistent with the various manifestations of the public voice, a witty, unsettling, and subtly ironic private voice that exploits the resources of language play afforded by the Letter's highly charged and potentially ambiguous critical terminology and examples. This voice, while sufficiently respectful of decorum, is also informal, generous, assertive, resentful, discontent, and even smug, the source of the play of language and convention that rewards a close reading of the Letter within the context of its various audiences. The Letter's private voice reflects the 1590 version of the person who, near the time of his anonymous yet portentous debut as incipient epic poet, writes the Latin verse epistle from which the epigraph to this essay comes. The 1579 persona views any seeking after public fame and popular approval as both counterproductive and dangerous to the poetic spirit, engendering madness and nonsense. The passage disdainfully dismisses the self-deceiving folly of ambition, which the Letter's public voices claim as their necessary though problematical territory. Still, while the Letter's private persona seems more overtly cautious, not to say jaded, than the writer of the poem to Harvey, some measure of the former perspective survives, particularly an abiding recognition of the poet's frustratingly paradoxical public position.[22]

Insofar as dualistic models can serve as useful (though always incomplete) explanatory analogies, the oppositional motives of defensive submission and assertive control that characterize the Letter are roughly analogous to the "opposing forces"[23] that define, for Greenblatt, Ralegh's "paradoxical" "self-fashioning," which both "reflects the world and creates its own world,"[24] accepting "the play metaphor as an image of life's limitations" while revealing a "self-assertive theatricality" with the "power to transform nature and fashion . . . identity."[25] In the Letter, Spenser justifies his subject matter and technique by, in essence, denying their originality, defending his poem by detailing its conformity to authoritative ancient and modern models: the poet becomes a mere player on the stage of literary history, acting a script that has been written for him. Simultaneously, Spenser subtly inverts expectation, mastering the power to which he submits and asserting his own imaginative potency by advertising a poem that undermines, dissects, and transforms some of the very qualities represented in the Letter as its own. These contrary strategies articulate Spenser's dialogue with his audiences and define the public and private voices of the "Letter to Ralegh." Now, to isolate the public voices.

ALLEGORICAL DEVICES

Spenser's apology for poetry—for fiction and for allegory—lies at the heart of his public address. In the first part of the Letter, Spenser examines the distinction between history and fiction, which he returns to later in distinguishing the historiographer from the poet historical. Next, after engaging the classic models, Spenser outlines his method of allegorical composition. This oft-quoted section serves as an illuminating entry into the complexities of the public voices. Having outlined the means by which "Poets historicall" — Homer, Virgil, Ariosto, and Tasso—"hath ensampled" in their heroes the ethical and political virtues, Spenser begins to explain what he creates out of "the historye of king Arthure": "By ensample of which exellente Poets, I labour to pourtraict in Arthure, before he was king, the image of a braue knight, perfected in the twelue priuate morall vertues . . . . "

> To some I know this Methode will seeme displeasaunt, which had rather haue good discipline deliuered plainly in way of precepts, or sermoned at large, as they vse, then thus clowdily enwrapped in Allegoricall deuises. But such, me seeme, should be satisfide with the use of these dayes, seeing all things accounted by their showes, and nothing esteemed of, that is not delightfull and pleasing to commune sence. For this cause is Xenophon preferred before Plato, for that the one in the exquisite depth of his iudgement, formed a commune welth such as it should be, but the other in the person of Cyrus and

> the Persians fashioned a gouernement such as might best be: So much more profitable and gratious is doctrine by ensample, then by rule. So have I laboured to doe in the person of Arthure. . . .

The issues and examples drawn into this passage reverberate self-consciously, ironically, and dead seriously with the critical theory in the English air as Spenser readied *The Faerie Queene* for the press. Spenser comments pointedly on the current scene, implicitly asking questions that bring literary theory face to face with the political actualities of publishing. Most intriguingly, Spenser makes his readers create for themselves the "some" who find his allegorical method "displeasaunt."[26] I hazard a guess, briefly and summarily: the lovers of "precepts" are humanist moral philosophers and theologians; those who would have "good discipline . . . sermoned at large" must include all those connected with the various forms of protestant populism. Additionally, those who find allegory (or fiction or poetry) both useless and dangerous also include those whose motive for disdaining or seeking to disarm Spenser's "Allegoricall deuises" is civic or, rather, political. They are species of Spenser's conception of "*Heroibus altis*" in his 1579 letter to Harvey; and their power haunts Spenser's works, issuing, finally, in the "venemous despite" of the Blatant Beast, sprung bodily out of the fiction at the end of Book 6 of *The Faerie Queene,* intent on curbing the poet's energy by making his "rimes keep better measure" (6.12.41). These are the masters of political and financial success. Yet Spenser boldly suggests in the "Letter to Ralegh" that they submit to or at least content themselves with the realities of contemporary life, where only ornamental "showes" attract attention and where most prefer Xenophon to Plato because "doctrine by ensample" is more "profitable and gratious" than "doctrine . . . by rule."

Critics of Renaissance poetry often mention portions of the quoted section in discussions of critical theory and in defense of one or another interpretation of Spenser's allegorical method, but all too often they pay inadequate attention to the subtleties of tone, emphasis, and context in the Letter itself. Anxious to find supporting evidence for larger arguments involving other texts, most critics see the text they expect to see, one that authorizes what they consider the Sidneian poetic enacted in *The Faerie Queene.* Almost twenty years ago, Anthony Low and Lawrence Sasek called upon the authority of the Letter to explain Milton's reference to "Plato and his equal, Xenophon" in the *Apology for Smectymnuus.* After noting Sidney's praise of Xenophon in the *Defence,*

Low cites and interprets Spenser's Letter to clinch his argument: "If Spenser . . . could say that Xenophon was to be 'preferred before Plato,' then it is possible that Milton could consider them to be, in a sense, equals . . . . "[27] Sasek offers a more precise interpretation of the Letter – "Spenser ranked Xenophon above Plato as a teacher" – as evidence that Milton could be equating the two ancients on their relative powers as teachers.[28] Both critics illustrate Spenser's supposed preference for Xenophon over Plato by quoting the sentence from the Letter beginning "For this cause is Xenophon preferred before Plato . . . ," ignoring the previous sentence – "But such, me seeme, should be satisfide with the vse of these dayes . . . . " – which severely qualifies Spenser's praise of Xenophon.

More recently, Leigh Deneef and David Norbrook quote the same sentence ("For this cause . . . by rule") to illustrate what they see as Sidney's and Spenser's comparable attitudes toward the exemplary value of poetry. Deneef finds in the Letter "specific evidence" of Spenser's knowledge of Sidney's *Defence:* "Discussing, like Sidney, the relation between poetry, history, and philosophy, Spenser repeats both Sidney's language and his meaning when he uses Xenophon as his literary example."[29] Deneef then quotes the sentence from the Letter. Norbrook does likewise, introducing the quotation by making essentially the same point that motivates Deneef's conjecture: "Like Sidney, Spenser argued that poetry could convey political ideas more memorably than abstract philosophy."[30] Apparently convinced by Spenser's choice of examples and by the general evidence of *The Faerie Queene* itself that Spenser must be aligning his view in the Letter with Sidney's in the *Defence,* these critics fulfill their expectations by quoting out of context. To be sure, Spenser chooses terms and examples that seem to invite direct comparison with Sidney, and he does accept – given his duty to engage a national audience – Xenophon's poetic method of teaching "doctrine by ensample" as an appropriate and convenient literary technique. However, the disdainful tone of the sentence introducing the Xenophon example reveals a speaker who esteems the philosopher Plato more highly than the poet Xenophon and adopts the poet's method under protest.

Several contemporary critics who mention this passage do pay some attention to context, acknowledging Spenser's pointedly qualified praise of the allegorical method and his condescending attitude toward the superficial pleasures of the allegorical poet's intended audience. Daniel Javitch notes Spenser's "misgivings"[31] about his method, Judith Dundas the "deprecatory tone" of his "apparent concession to the reading public,"[32] and Jan Karel Kouwenhoven his "less than grudging concession to 'the use of these days': the failure of most of his contemporaries (or, perhaps, of people generally . . .) to esteem anything but fictions 'delightfull and pleasing to commune sence.'"[33] In their own ways, however, they all capitulate; unwilling to believe that the author of *The Faerie Queene* could possibly be critical of his own method, they attribute Spenser's tone to momentary irritation or pass it off as fleeting loss of faith. Javitch begins his analysis of the section on firm ground: "Despite his misgivings, Spenser knows that the hedonism of a sophisticated public" allows the poetic method "to achieve ethical ends ineffectively sought by plain moral discourse." But within two sentences he has Spenser implicitly championing rather than conceding to the poet's method: "Spenser is saying, in effect, that the faith in the orator's (even the preacher's) ability to rouse virtue has to be replaced by a trust in the more subtle persuasiveness of the poet."[34] Misgivings are painlessly discarded, to be replaced by the poet's faith in a Sidneian poetic. Dundas, reading *The Faerie Queene* and Sidney into the Letter, assures us that Spenser's "deprecatory tone should not deceive us: behind the apparent concession to the reading public lies the artist with all the commitment to beauty implied in Colin Clout's vision of the Graces dancing. A sermon in plain terms was not his style. What was his style was a magical world of beauty realized in decorative form." By telling his readers that he offers them the "delightfull and pleasing" "showes" of things, Spenser has, according to Dundas, "explicitly endorsed" "Sidney's dictum" that "it is ornament which supplies beauty."[35] Kouwenhoven, in an original variation, celebrates Spenser's "concession" to "temporality" as "the most magnificent expression since *The Canterbury Tales* of Time as a pilgrimage to Eternity."[36] The self-consciously articulated public voice of the poet succumbs to the force of larger arguments: the poet's dilemma evaporates in the face of his brilliant poetic success.

Two critics who do take Spenser's tone seriously, though they come to opposite conclusions concerning its meaning, are A. C. Hamilton and D. M. Beach. Both note Spenser's disparaging attitude toward Xenophon, but while Beach—accurately, I think—sees Spenser giving in to the "vse of these dayes" and thereby agreeing "with Sidney that historical concreteness makes Xenophon's *Cyrus* a more effective speaking picture of virtue than abstract philosophy by itself,"[37] Hamilton shows Spenser out-Sidneying Sidney by embracing the poet in Plato, rejecting the *Cyropaedia* "on Sidney's own ground that the poet ranges only 'into the divine consideration of what may be and should be'" and following "Plato in offering 'doctrine by ensample.'"[38] The text of the Letter cannot, I am convinced, accommodate Hamilton's claim, because those to whom Spenser's "Methode will seeme displeasaunt" are the same ones who would prefer Plato to Xenophon. These, Spenser states, "should be satisfide with the vse of these dayes," when Xenophon is preferred and his and Spenser's method the more expedient to the poet's didactic purpose. This reading is also supported by Spenser's diction: just as Xenophon "fashioned a gouernement" "in the person of Cyrus and the Persians," so Spenser labors "to fashion" or "pourtraict" "good discipline" and "priuate morall vertues" "in the person of Arthure" and the "other knights."[39]

Hamilton's and Beach's views on Spenser's poetic as stated in the Letter are equally at odds. While both agree that at the foundation of Sidney's poetic lies the concept of the synthetic image, delivered whole and immediately without any separation between or priority given to precept or example, they diverge concerning Spenser's relation to this reading of Sidney's method. Hamilton contends that the methods outlined by Sidney and Spenser are entirely consistent: Spenser's "method . . . is to 'ensample' a virtuous man, that is, to deliver an image rather than to hide doctrine under the historical fiction . . . . "[40] This may well be Spenser's dominant method in *The Faerie Queene,* but it is not what he supports in the Letter. Significant consequences in meaning, intention, and tone attend the very different metaphors Spenser and Sidney use to describe the production of poetic examples and images. Spenser says that he has "coloured" history with "fiction," "shadow[ed]" Elizabeth in various ways, and "enwrapped" "precepts" in "Allegoricall deuises." These figures, particularly the latter two, accord well with Spenser's notice to Burghley in the Dedicatory Sonnets that his poem's "fairer parts are hid" beneath a "dim vele"; employing similar language, Spenser instructs the Earle of Oxenford that defending *The Faerie Queene* "may thee right well besit, / Sith th' antique glory of thine auncestry / Vnder a shady vele is therein writ"; and in the proem to Book II, Spenser requests Elizabeth's pardon for his having "to enfold / In couert vele, and wrap in shadowes light" (5) "thy face," "thine owne realmes," and "thy great auncestry" (4).

In contrast, Sidney's "right poets," in "feigning notable images," "coupleth the general notion with the particular example" and thereby "yieldeth to the powers of the mind an image," "delivering" or "figuring forth . . . a speaking picture."[41] Spenser's allegorical imagery suggests, among other things, an extrinsic relation between "precepts" and "Allegoricall deuises," a relation in which the hidden or veiled meaning takes priority over poetic ornaments that act as metaphoric clothing, enticing and pleasing the readers' "commune sence" while inhibiting, obscuring, and frustrating naked apprehension. Conversely, Sidney's language describes an intrinsic, dynamic relation between the "general" and the "particular," issuing in a synthetic image "which doth . . . strike, pierce, [and] possess the sight of the soul";[42] such a relation, and such a poetic creation, provokes, encourages, and nurtures unmediated apprehension of the poet's truth. Beach takes the contrast to its conclusion: "Sidney had eliminated scorn from true delight by insisting that it is the picture not the precept alone which speaks. But when [as with Spenser in the Letter] the ethical concept is . . . elevated and the image is distrusted . . . out of yearning for an absolute, then metaphysical contempt easily re-enters parabolic poetry." Spenser "yearns," Beach tells us, "for a philosophy untrammeled by fictions."[43] Although I would insist on drawing a distinction between the person who may or may not "yearn" and the speaker who fashions a role, Beach describes accurately the position articulated in the Letter by Spenser's public persona.

Writing the voice of the national poet's role, Spenser acknowledges, with Sidney and other defenders of poetry, the practical efficacy of fiction and allegory to move the will toward virtuous action by making bitter or bland subject matter sweet and palatable; fiction embellishes the bare facts of history as allegory softens the stern precepts of philosophy. But Spenser's tone and emphasis diverge considerably from Sidney's relatively unabashed celebration of poetic fiction. Sidney disparages the "thorny arguments" of the philosopher, "so hard of utterance and misty to be conceived," and exposes the limited usefulness of the historian's questionable facts.[44] In contrast, Spenser insists that the philosopher's "precepts" are "deliuered plainly" and that it is allegory that obscures or clouds the moral ideas; likewise, Spenser refuses to question the exemplary moral power of historical truth, stating that he introduces a "historicall fiction"—the story of Arthur "before he was king"—because most readers enjoy a fictionalized account of history, "rather for variety of matter, then for profite of the ensample." Moral and political "doctrine" may be more "delightfull and pleasing to commune sence" when "clowdily enwrapped in Allegoricall deuises," and history may be more "pleasing" to a larger audience when "coloured" by fiction, but in both cases the poetical adornments are mere "showes," superficial attractions and distractions, since the moral "ensample" inheres in the historical record as the doctrinal "rule" inheres in the philosophical discourse.

The voice of this speaker is at least relatively distinct from the voice of the poet whose *Faerie Queene* celebrates, usually without apology, the beauty and power of allegorical narrative in a fictional setting. It is a voice whose source and intentions become clear when we view the Letter within a wider context, as part of a literary event with significant extraliterary consequences. The tone and emphasis of the public voice serve to underscore Spenser's consciousness of his grave responsibility to portray truth for his age. Acutely aware of the authoritative public expectations and potentially hazardous political consequences that accompany the national poet's task, and mindful of the very real possibility that the Letter—written by a poet hailed as the English Virgil to one of the most controversial public figures of the day—would be more thoroughly scrutinized by more of his contemporaries than the poem itself, Spenser assumes the reactionary voice of ideological authority. He speaks the mostly unspoken assumptions of the guardians of discipline, powerful lords of church and empire and grave gentlemen of learning. Poised, we might say, between Ralegh and Burghley, between his poem and his audiences, in a precarious social place at a crucial moment in his career, Spenser gives voice to a "sage and serious"[45] public persona, furrowing a "rugged forhead" (*F.Q.* 4.Proem.1) of his own, speaking the words of paternal authority by chiding those who require the enticement of fiction and allegory—Sidney's "medicine of cherries"[46]—to inspire moral behavior and draw them toward virtuous civic duty. This voice guides its audience toward the desired conclusion: fictional events "clowdily enwrapped in Allegoricall deuises" are merely the pleasing surface of a national epic built upon the firm foundation of unadorned history, ethical philosophy, and true religion.

The poet's dilemma is not, however, as neatly resolved, his position not as secure as the foregoing analysis of the public voice implies; and his phrasing, full of reversals, concessions, and reservations, strongly suggests his full apprehension of the problem. For while his tone of paternal rebuke and his ambivalent attitude toward his own method apparently allow him to ally himself with those "prudent heads"[47] who would not hesitate to name more profitable activities than either writing or reading poetry, he is well aware that these same authorities demand his concession to a method that will move the national audience most expediently toward virtuous and obedient conduct; in other words, the same cultural powers that the public voice sets out to appease necessarily censure what they command.[48]

At the same time, Spenser's recognition of the contradictory obligations placed upon him hardly signals his defeat; rather, it ratifies the success of a rhetorical strategy that makes the best of an impossible situation, exposing the entire self-consciousness of the public voice and opening the way to play. To begin with, the theory of allegorical composition presented in the Letter is itself paradoxically playful, for although Spenser implies that the superficial "showes" constituted in the "Allegorical deuises" are supposed to make "discipline" accessible by delighting and pleasing "commune sence"—the vulgar and commonsensical audience that delights in that which titillates the senses—he dresses his statements about allegory in metaphors of darkness, disguise, and clouding that suggest hidden or esoteric meanings inaccessible to the audience he presumably seeks to attract and enlighten. Furthermore, the same agile speaker whose analysis of allegorical making maneuvers a paradox in the Letter advertises contrary theories and justifications of allegory in response to the demands of other audiences.

In the Proem to Book II, for example, Spenser tells Elizabeth why he must "enfold / In couert vele" her presence in the poem: "That feeble eyes your glory may behold, / Which else could not endure those beames bright, / But would be dazled with exceeding light." If he did not "wrap" her "light" in "shadowes," his reader's "eyes" would be so "dazled" that they could not see to read (5). Instead of competing with or obscuring truth, allegory here participates in truth as the vehicle by which it is disclosed. Rather than conflicting with and canceling one another, poetic imagination, political power, and popular audience engage and interact. In the Dedicatory Sonnet to Burghley, to take another example, Spenser is equally concerned with making his expression of theory consistent with his audience. In presenting his "ydle rimes" to the august lord, Spenser argues that the "dim vele" of allegory, to which Burghley would presumably object, hides the "fairer parts" of the poem from "comune vew." Here, Spenser presents the most esoteric and elitist theory of allegory, flattering the "mighty Peres" (*F.Q.* 6.12.41) potential ability to weigh the "deeper sence" of the "rimes."[49] If he is able to do this, "Perhaps not vaine they may appeare," though the obvious conditions and qualifications may subtly indicate Spenser's skepticism about Burghley's ability to read rightly. Spenser concludes the sonnet ambiguously, assertively, drawing on the resources of a private voice to play the disgruntled poet whose hand has been slapped but who yet marshals the power to command Burghley to "receaue" the "rimes" "Such as they be" "And wipe their faults out of

[his] censure graue" if he does not like what he reads—a rather different reaction to Ralegh's pressure to rewrite than that displayed by the public voice in the Letter.[50] These examples should demonstrate the inadequacy of any contention that Spenser promulgates or sustains a single view of allegorical composition, either one of Sidney's views or anyone else's. His public voice fits the theory to the occasion, and then the poet does whatever he wants in the poetry itself.

When, supposedly at the instigation of his theatrically inclined friend, Spenser performs his defensive and explanatory role in the Letter, he employs connotatively loaded language which, while successfully accomplishing its nominal purpose, also asserts the poet's power to make his meaning and method problematical in the face of contradictory demands. In his presentation of his allegorical method, Spenser finds himself defending a mode of composition that is both demanded by his duty as national poet and censured by the authority that would have "good discipline deliuered plainly." He offers no solution to this dilemma except to maintain the dutiful tone of learned condescension consistent with the expectations of the more powerful reactionaries among his public audience. At the same time, however, he offers his private audience—Ralegh and others among his friends and fellow travellers—the potential for an ironic perspective derived from the multiple significations of his critical terminology. The distinction I draw between public and private audiences is not meant to suggest any clear line between two stable interpretations tied to a dualistic model of the text; rather, the words should be conceived as the ends of a spectrum (or the points on a grid) constituted in the poet's language and the audiences' responses. The distinction rests upon the relative exclusivity of two kinds of interpretation, one that seeks more or less stable, unified meanings and another that responds to the instability and multiplicity of the language. This language allows Spenser's various public audiences to draw conclusions about meaning based on their own expectations, interpreting the Letter in ways consistent with their interpretations of *The Faerie Queene* and ignoring the potential for alternative readings. The private audiences, on the other hand, sensitive to the play of language and willing to risk the plunge into pluralism, participate in a literary critical linquistic game—serious though it may be. In the sections on literary critical theory, Spenser uses key terms such as *history, conceit, ensample,* and *fashioned* in contexts that exploit their flexibility; and he plays on phrases such as "plausible and pleasing," "profitable and gratious," and "delightfull and pleasing" to fulfill ironic potential.

Writing to the man who, in 1589, was, Greenblatt claims, "perhaps the supreme example in England of a gentleman not born but fashioned,"[51] Spenser outlines the "general intention and meaning" that he has "fashioned" in his poem:

> The general end therefore of all the booke is to fashion a gentleman or noble person in vertuous and gentle discipline: Which for that I conceiued should be most plausible and pleasing, being coloured with an historicall fiction, the which the most part of men delight to read, rather for variety of matter, then for profite of the ensample: I chose the historye of king Arthure, as most fitte for the excellency of his person, being made famous by many mens former workes, and also furthest from the daunger of enuy, and suspition of present time. In which I haue followed all the antique Poets historicall.

This passage on subject matter and fiction-making serves as a companion piece to the passage on allegorical composition quoted above and, similarly, often provides critics with an authorized foundation for discussions of Spenser's didactic methodology. In fact, the "fashion a gentleman" section of this passage is perhaps the most quoted phrase in Spenserian criticism, a sound reason in itself to continue analyzing the resources of Spenser's multivalent language by focusing on *fashion,* the operative word in the phrase. The word occupies a particularly significant place in recent historicist criticism, due in large part to its being the central concept in Greenblatt's seminal book, *Renaissance Self-Fashioning,* and, insofar as it defines self-conscious role formation, the controlling theme of his book on Ralegh. In both earlier and contemporary criticism, the phrase about fashioning a gentleman in discipline is tirelessly reiterated to establish Spenser's serious moral purpose. But seldom do critics before Greenblatt attempt any thorough definition of the word *fashion,* assuming, I suppose, that the term merely names the means by which moral education is imposed upon the malleable wills of *The Faerie Queene's* readers: reading the poem will mold readers in virtue and, if the effect becomes widespread, lead to cultural reformation. There is nothing particularly invalid about this kind of assumption, but it only scratches the surface of what Spenser is doing in the Letter.

Even when critics do attempt to define the term, they often end up either confusing the issue or limiting the word's connotations in order to emphasize meanings consistent with the immediate demands of their theses. Hamilton, for instance, in defending his view of Spenser as a maker of startling images rather than a conventional allegorist, argues that Spenser's intention to fashion a gentleman "means something more than that his work has a didactic bent."[52] This in itself is a step in the right direction, for it suggests a broadening of perspective that recent critics have made explicit: "This process of fashioning is at once the book's subject and its object";[53] that is, Spenser attempts to fashion a poem that fashions a gentleman who is "both character . . . and reader."[54] Hamilton's analysis, however, becomes too exclusive when he suggests that "'fashion' means to 'form' or 'create.'"[55] To begin with, Spenser himself draws a distinction in the Letter between the words *form* and *fashion* when he writes that while Plato "formed a commune welth such as it should be," Xenophon "fashioned a gouernement such as might best be." Plato's forming reflects "the exquisite depth of his iudgement" in establishing what ideally "should be" while Xenophon's fashioning remains tainted by the false artifice of "showes . . . delightfull and pleasing to commune sence" and by Spenser's grudging acceptance of the poet's allegorical method, which allows him to present only what "might best be." Furthermore, Hamilton's assertion that *fashion* and *create* are synonymous terms takes undue liberties with the vocabulary of the Letter and suggests, implicitly, Hamilton's assumption of identity between Spenser's poetic in the Letter and Sidney's in the *Defence.* Spenser avoids words such as *invention, creation, inspiration, imagination,* and even *fiction,* except when qualified by *historicall,* setting his making apart from that of the inspired, godlike Sidneian poet, who creates and bodies forth a golden world out of nothing but an erected wit. For Spenser in the Letter, fashioning does not suggest creation from nothing; rather, as Richard Waswo observes, "to 'fashion'(*facere*) is to do what a blacksmith does with iron,"[56] to mold, build, or fabricate something out of received raw materials, whether these be history, literary tradition, human beings, or everyday life. While this may serve as an initial, general definition, it only begins to tell the story that Ralegh would have found in the Letter.

In his introduction to *Renaissance Self-Fashioning,* Greenblatt provides a relatively inclusive definition of the concept: fashioning "describes the practice of parents and teachers; it is linked to manners or demeanor, particularly that of the elite; it may suggest hypocrisy or deception, an adherence to mere outward ceremony; it suggests representation of one's nature or intention in speech or actions." Additionally, fashioning "invariably crosses the boundaries between the creation of literary characters, the shaping of one's own identity, the experience of being molded by forces outside of one's control, the attempt to fashion other selves."[57] So, given this fairly exhaustive definition, which would surprise neither Spenser nor Ralegh (nor, probably, Burghley, which is why he might be concerned), what does Spenser mean by his stated intention "to fashion a gentleman or noble person in vertuous and gentle discipline"? First, and most obviously, Spenser sets out to fashion virtuous and potentially virtuous characters whose actions are meant to move the wills of readers to fashion themselves in imitation of the characters' virtues; these refashioned readers would, by their virtuous actions, move others to refashion themselves, and so on. From this perspective, Spenser assumes the role of teacher or parent, guiding students and children toward virtuous behavior. This all sounds perfectly legitimate, salutary, and commendable, but there is a subversive irony lurking in the program, for at least some of those students and children must be the gentlemen and noble persons (perhaps even the queen herself) who supposedly inspire the poet's characterizations in the first place. In a boldly humorous ploy, Spenser asserts his power by implicitly claiming to instruct his social betters in the aristocratic virtues they would already claim as their own. Moreover, others among Spenser's readers—courtiers and would-be courtiers—might learn from Spenser's "ensamples" not how to fashion themselves in virtue but, rather, how to fashion themselves in whatever ways might allow them to rise in the esteem of the courtly circle, dissembling aristocratic behavior and courtly grace as they reach for social and political favor and profit. These might dress themselves in exactly the kinds of potentially deceptive "showes" upon which Spenser claims to build his allegorical compositions.[58]

But whomever Spenser regards as the members of his audience, he treats them with some measure of condescension, for they demand a poetry that Spenser's public voice apparently disdains. Assuming that the only way to attract an audience is to make his subject both "plausible and pleasing," Spenser colors his poem with "an historicall fiction," the historical portion supplying the plausibility (and thus the applause of those who distrust fiction) and the fiction supplying the pleasure. This is the kind of subject matter "the most part of men delight to read," not because they seek "profite of the ensample" but merely because they enjoy "variety of matter," something "delightfull and pleasing to commune sence." Thus, by coloring history with fiction and enwrapping precepts in "Allegoricall deuises," Spenser offers his audience "doctrine by ensample," which is more "profitable and gratious" than "doctrine . . . by rule." The humorous or perhaps bitter irony inherent in this formulation derives in part from Spenser's attitude toward his audience, but it also depends upon the answers to two questions about the value of "doctrine by ensample": first, who is the recipient of the profit and graciousness and, second, what do those words connote? The conventional answer to these questions is that readers are more likely to reap moral benefit from a pleasing and courteously offered illustrative characterization or story than from a philosophical or historical treatise. But there are other possibilities. To begin with, "gratious" may connote a condescendingly kind attitude toward inferiors; in that case, depending on the audience, a "gratious" offering of ensamples would be either merely elitist or dangerously presumptuous. Another reading is also possible: if the recipient of the profit and graciousness is the poet rather than the audience, the words might be read as suggesting quite different meanings. Because the national poet is duty-bound to reach as large an audience as possible, and because allegorical and fictional ensamples would presumably be more widely read than sermons or historical chronicles, Spenser's offer of "doctrine by ensample" instead of "by rule" would, theoretically at least, secure him not only greater social favor among the powerful but also a larger pecuniary reward for his work. The possibility that Spenser might here be using the word *profitable* to mean financially gainful may at first seem unlikely or even preposterous, for such a reading suggests a willful impudence and darkly humorous irony inconsistent with the prudent, staid, and decorous Spenserian persona that continues to dominate critical perceptions of the poet, whether in its more conventional formulation as the Miltonic sage and serious moralist or in its recently fashionable manifestations as potentially ignorant pawn or worshipful servant of Elizabethan autocracy. But these descriptions of the poet are at best incomplete, for there are other parts of the persona that may here be playing on *profit.* And several pieces of evidence, textual and biographical, support the possibility. A close look at Ralegh's second Commendatory Sonnet, for instance, suggests that talk of financial reward may be part of an inside joke between Spenser and Ralegh: the sonnet begins and ends with possible allusions to money and presents the general argument that if Spenser surrenders his poem to the queen's judgment, she will probably be gracious and "fauour [his] good will." The poem begins, "The prayse of meaner wits this work like profit brings, / As doth the Cuckoes song delight when *Philumena* sings," where *profit* can hardly mean moral benefit.[59] And the poem concludes, "Of me no lines are lou'd, nor Letters are of price, / Of all which speake our English tongue, but those of your deuice." Spenser's "Letters" may have both literary and monetary value, not to mention their moral value in moving the national will toward virtuous renovation.

Of course, while Spenser and Ralegh may playfully exploit the connotations of the word *profit,* the issue of patronage was, for Spenser, no laughing matter, particularly in view of how events proceeded following the publication of *The Faerie Queene.* On the one hand, Spenser's expectations of remuneration for his work could be seen as falling within the legitimate system of literary patronage. But this is a very ticklish business, for receiving patronage is one thing, but in effect selling an epic poem as a lowly playwright sells a play is quite another matter, involving a profit motive held in contempt by many of Spenser's contemporaries. Whatever produces this contempt, whether a valiant but futile desire to preserve the purity of poetry from the pollution of filthy lucre, a statesmanlike disdain for the time-wasting profession of poet, fear of immorality or, as Helgerson convincingly argues, a prodigal sense of guilt—real or affected—on the part of poets themselves, it existed for the "new poet" to contend with as, in somewhat different guises, it remains to haunt artists today. And while I would warrant that Helgerson correctly identifies Spenser's self-assured and boldly provocative laureate ambitions,[60] these ambitions, even if or perhaps especially if realized, are not so much the solution to the poet's dilemma as the source of new problems. Not surprisingly, a paradox similar to the one Spenser outlines concerning his poetic method, which is simultaneously demanded and censured, is built into the situation: laureate ambitions, as Helgerson rightly argues, presuppose the necessity of taking poetry seriously, which, in turn, authorizes aspirations to, for Spenser, pre-Jonsonian professionalism. The paradox follows apace because serious poets are tainted by the very professionalism that defines their role; they cannot seek laureate status without giving up their amateur position, but to become professional—that is, to expect the same remuneration and respect accorded soldiers and civil servants—is to surrender their poetic freedom and to become the instruments and hirelings of at least some of those whom they set out to fashion. In a worst-case scenario, the poet becomes a manufacturer and merchant whose commodities are poems. In all, as Spenser and Ralegh well knew, poetry for profit is paradoxical and problematical.

Following the publication of *The Faerie Queene* in spring, 1590, Spenser waited most of a year before receiving the financial support the queen had apparently promised him. Whether or not we even consider the reports of Burghley's stalling that seem to have fascinated earlier readers of Spenser,[61] even Alexander Judson admits the difficulty of Spenser's situation and quotes the appropriate passages from *Mother Hubberds Tale* to illustrate Spenser's justifiable disdain for the insidious machinations of Burghley; these passages, which "may have been altered or expanded when the old poem was prepared for the press" during 1590, "must depict accurately the sort of exasperation that Spenser felt as days stretched into weeks and weeks into months without any sign of the patronage on which he had built high hopes."[62] After at least eight months of stalling, on 25 February 1590/91, Burghley did finally disburse the money Spenser had been promised, or at least part of it, in the form of a fifty-pound annual pension, though I am not so convinced as Judson is of Spenser's "enthusiasm" about the "'goodly meed' and 'bountie' that the queen had bestowed upon her shepherd Colin."[63] That Spenser had to bow low to receive even a portion of what was coming to him I assume as a matter of course in these affairs, but at least there was some profit to accompany the queen's apparent graciousness.

Historical Fiction

Spenser makes his comments on subject matter roughly analogous to those on allegorical method, and he plays on history in some of the same ways he plays on allegorical devices. He says he "chose" to focus his "historicall fiction" on "the historye of king Arthure, as most fitte for the excellency of his person, being made famous by many mens former workes, and also furthest from the daunger of enuy, and suspition of present time." In doing so, he has "followed all the antique Poets historicall"—Ariosto and Tasso in addition to Homer and Virgil. With a tempting dose of irony juxtaposed to the serious considerations of a thoughtful antiquary historian about the relation of historical inquiry to myth, fable, legend, and chronicle, Spenser enters boldly into the controversy surrounding the Arthurian question. The dizzying array of literary critical and historiographical issues condensed into Spenser's apparently straightforward expression of his subject provides a fairly exhaustive inventory of the poet's responses to some of the major intellectual currents of his time, which might most simply be stated as an analogous series of familiar Renaissance debates between fact and fiction, history and poetry, and epic and romance. The European Renaissance, much less its English component, holds no monopoly on the basic intellectual issues at the root of these analogous pairs, but late sixteenth- and early seventeenth-century experimentation and discussion involving the forms and concepts implied by these words were centrally important in producing modern historical discourse and fictional narrative.

In the portions of the Letter dealing with the Arthurian subject matter, Spenser's innovative participation in signal issues of his day includes a satisfactory display of the official view, some ironic play, and, most important, fascinating revisionist suggestions about the relation of poetry to history. To the Tudor leadership and its many chauvinistic partisans, who, finding in the Arthurian material—particularly the myth of Arthur's return—a valuable propagandistic tool, sought to preserve the unquestioned authority of Geoffrey of Monmouth's account,[64] Spenser offers a straight "historye of king Arthure" coupled with a narrative invention that brings Arthur into direct coordination (not to say intimate contact) with Elizabeth as Faery Queene. Additionally, in *The Faerie Queene* itself, Spenser presents chronicle accounts which, at least superficially, ratify Tudor legend. At the same time, Spenser plays on the alternate connotation of the word *history*, fashioning the Arthurian material as mere story or fable, for the "historye" turns out to be an entirely fabulous contrivance, the story of Arthur "before he was king," which even the most reactionary Tudor propagandists would be forced to scoff at as romantic fluff. As for the "former workes" by which Arthur had been "made famous," there is no sure means of knowing what Spenser may have had in mind, but he is likely to be once again playing on both words and contemporary options. In this case, *famous* might as easily mean controversial or even notorious as renowned; and *workes* could refer as readily to Geoffrey of Monmouth's *Historia* and the voluminous romance material that flowed in part from it, to Polydore Virgil's *Anglica Historia* (1534) and John Leland's dutifully reactionary *Assertio* (1544)[65] or, more generally, to all the polemical works that produced what Edwin Greenlaw named the "sixteenth century battle of the books."[66] Spenser was, at least in his public persona, probably one with William Camden in being "content to survey the prospect,"[67] though even such a mildly undogmatic stance could have appeared dangerous in some quarters; as Charles Bowie Millican judiciously observes after quoting an anonymous attack on Polydore Virgil concluding with the exhortation that the debunker be hanged, "when Ponsonby was printing *The Faerie Queene,* the Arthurian wing of the Ancients was in triumph over the Moderns, and without sweetness and light."[68] Whatever Spenser refers to as the source of Arthur's fame, and I would guess he takes the broad view, his choice of Arthurian subject matter is as startling as it is expected; for rather than choosing legendary material from the distant past that was indeed "furthest from the daunger of enuy, and suspition of present time," as epic poets since Virgil had apparently been wont to do, Spenser sets himself squarely in the heat of political and intellectual debate. In portraying the youthful Arthur, Spenser conceives an epic while embracing the radical fringe of romance writing, in effect suspending judgment on the historical Arthur while revaluating the whole situation in the light of a new generic classification, the allegorical historical fiction. Moreover, by consciously avoiding the terms *epic, heroic,* and *romance,* Spenser effectively thwarts criticism based on generic expectations and thereby preserves some measure of creative freedom.

Spenser's experimentation with genre and his sophisticated rethinking of the issues surrounding the Arthurian legends are intimately related to his active and seminal role in what, following F. Smith Fussner's ground breaking work, has come to be known as the English "historical revolution," the development of modern approaches to historical inquiry that began to accelerate during the last two decades of the sixteenth century, in spite of the stultifying effects of Tudor propaganda.[69] One way of assessing Spenser's historiographical perspective in the Letter is to call once again on Sidney in the *Defence* as a magisterial and eminently serviceable foil. When Sidney sets the poet's didactic value up against the philosopher's and the historian's, he presents two versions of historical methodology that show him to be fully conversant with the state of historiography in his time.[70] On the one hand, he depicts a whimsically sophisticated portrait of the humanist historian, who advertises an exemplar theory of history and beats the moralist philosopher at his own game by manipulating his "mouse-eaten records, authorizing himself (for the most part) upon other histories, whose greatest authorities are built upon the notable foundation of hearsay." This historian "denieth, in great chafe, that any man for teaching of virtue, and virtuous actions is comparable to him." On the other hand, Sidney presents a telling description of the new scientific or empirical historian, who, "being captived to the truth of a foolish world" and "wanting the precept, is so tied, not to what should be but to what is, to the particular truth of things and not to the general reason of things, that his example draweth no necessary consequence, and therefore a less fruitful doctrine."[71] The former fulfills his duty as teacher of virtue only by playing the poet's part while the latter abandons his didactic responsibility in the face of hard facts.

Writing sometime before 1580, Sidney exposes some very real limitations in contemporary historiography, limitations that become even more pronounced when political issues replace moral didacticism, when Arthur replaces ethics in Sidney's portraits.[72] In that case, we have either myopic and time-serving patriots whose nationalist frenzy or envious fear drives them to sacrifice their status as legitimate historians to preserve the mythical Arthur; or we have a few empiricist choniclers willing to breast the tide of political pressure by presenting a historical Arthur, a minor sixth-century Briton or Saxon chieftain whose story gives no indication of the massive cultural significance of this historical nobody. Spenser brought Arthur into his own revisionist literary historiography by outlining the perspective of a poet historical who merges and transcends Sidney's pair of historians. On the one hand, as an innovative participant in the new history, Spenser respects the authority of verifiable sources; Arthur B. Ferguson claims that when Spenser wrote *A View of the Present State of Ireland,* he proceeded "with an empirical treatment of evidence which bore developmental, even progressivist implications."[73] Long before Spenser composed *A View,* this methodology helped to shape his conception of *The Faerie Queene*'s Arthur. I do not think Spenser believed the Arthurian mythology to be a fact of political history, much less an adequate justification for the rage to imperial designs; "he was too good an antiquary to take the Arthurian legends at their face value."[74] However, this is only the initial step toward a revised historiography that truly, so to speak, puts Arthur in his place; to broadly based research and critical assessment of data must be added some room for educated guesswork that could yield a creative yet empirically grounded reconstruction of the past.[75] This methodology both inspired and was inspired by the beginnings of a recognition by Spenser and some of his fellow antiquaries that the frontier between history and myth was not so clearly defined as even the most enlightened chroniclers assumed, and that historical inquiry could yield other kinds of fruits besides narratives of political events. In the course of investigating, collecting, and recording all manner of cultural texts, these sixteenth-century antiquary historians were beginning to explore and interpret "that broad and ill-defined area of historical experience which stretched beyond *res gestae*"; in so doing, they exposed the domain of cultural myth and stumbled upon the theory of cultural change that became the foundation of modern historical thought.[76]

Spenser saw that the myth of Arthur was of far greater significance to the history of England than random political facts about a minor figure out of ancient history, for he understood that the unrealized potential of history often takes the form of cultural myths which, in turn, motivate historical events. In Spenser's "historye of king Arthure," empiricist historiography, cultural mythology, and poetic inspiration intersect and define one another in a maze of coordinated conflicts. Spenser portrays an invented youthful Arthur who, having been "rauished" "in a dream or vision" by the "excellent beauty" of "the Faery Queen," wanders Faeryland in search of her, never succeeding Uther to the throne of sixth-century Britain. Instead, at the crucial moment (*F.Q.* 2.10.68), Spenser excises the historical Arthur from his poem and from chronicle history; the historical Arthur ceases to exist except as an inference born of an absence in the minds of readers whose conscious or unconscious cognizance of cultural myth instinctively mends the gap that stands open at the end of *Briton moniments.* Spenser never closes this narrow but crucial breach in Tudor genealogy between Uther and Cador's son Constantius (*F.Q.* 3.3.27–29); Arthur's reign and, strictly speaking, everything that goes with it, disappears from British political history. And the usual bland and time-honored observation that Artegall replaces Arthur in *The Faerie Queene*'s chronicles simply cannot explain away either the Arthurian vacancy or Spenser's audacity in appropriating the power to manipulate history. Spenser creates an ellipsis in the British succession, obfuscates chronicle history by leaving Artegall's son nameless, and presumptuously supplies the Tudors with a newly fabricated (or fashioned) royal genealogy descending from the Cornish Artegall's "Image dead," the son of two pseudo-historical inventions (*F.Q.* 3.3.29).[77] Spenser, Ralegh, and, yes, Burghley, knew that these machinations illustrate perfectly why and how poets can be dangerous and useless; and they all probably also knew that the dangerous or fearful can be pacified by and absorbed into ideological myth, which is exactly what Spenser does in his poem. For despite his bold and perhaps ironic assertion of history-making potential, his poem serves the historical Arthur whose very absence engenders the almost sovereign power of myth as cultural determinant. According to Spenser's long-range plans for his poem, Arthur will be initiating Tudor apocalypse by serving and marrying Gloriana while Artegall (like Aeneas) is being "Too rathe cut off by practise criminall / Of secret foes" in sixth-century Britain (*F.Q.* 3.3.28), leaving his son to wrest the crown from Artegall's (and Arthur's) nephew Constantius.

Spenser's "historye of king Arthure" is a complex bag of tricks built to frustrate or compromise readers who seek from Spenser a neat, unified intention. Perhaps Spenser's Arthur was inspired by patriotic fervor, perhaps by objective historicist analysis, but probably by some of each in combination with the mind of a genius who harbors a touch of ironic humor and skepticism.

Before I close, it might be worth looking briefly at Spenser's penultimate sentence in the Letter, keeping in mind the kind of pluralist perspective hypothesized in this essay to be Spenser's own. In the sentence, Spenser summarizes the central argument he has "ouerronne" in the Letter, using terms—*understanding, History, intention, conceit,* and *discourse*—firmly rooted in literary, philosophical, and historical writing, words whose long history and varied uses in the Letter afford the multiple significations and potential for understatement that yield ironic play with serious issues:

> Thus much Sir, I haue briefly ouerronne to direct your vnderstanding to the wel-head of the History, that from thence gathering the whole intention of the conceit, ye may as in a handfull gripe al the discourse, which otherwise may happily seeme tedious and confused.

The "wel-head of the History," particularly insofar as it embodies the Arthurian mythology, explains the "intention of the conceit," while the "conceit" gives meaning to history. History and fiction empower each other, and the poet controls the interaction. Our understanding should be directed at Arthur, the source of the historical fiction and the organizational center of the moral allegorical dark conceit, whose whole intention is to fashion persons and celebrate the return of mythical Arthurian glory in the prophecy of Elizabeth the Tudor Faery Queen. Spenser "conceiue[s]" Arthur—the epic focus of the history and allegory—to seek in Faeryland his vision of the Faery Queen, who Spenser "conceiue[s]" as his "soueraine the Queene" and, alternately, "express[es]" as Belphoebe, a name "fashion[ed]" after Ralegh's "excellent conceipt of Cynthia." This is Spenser's bare bones working out of his "conceit," or Sidney's "fore-conceit."[78] We can gather this intention and "gripe" it all in a "handfull" of unified public discourse, which will help Spenser's story seem less "tedious and confused." But we are also invited by understated suggestion to enjoy what most anybody who reads Spenser more than once enjoys: the "particular purposes" and "by-accidents," the intricate plenitude of beauty and terror that reveals a profound representation of reality.

In another context, this accomplished but fairly ordinary sentence might easily be passed over. But here, at the end of Spenser's public/private Letter to Walter Ralegh appended to *The Faerie Queene* and animating the publishing event, the sentence, along with the rest of the 1590 volume's ancillary matter, fairly burns with the controlled intensity of Spenser's and Ralegh's dynamic seizure of the moment. In the Letter and in the Dedicatory Sonnets, Spenser engages Ralegh and the world with the full force of a Renaissance critical imagination.

Georgia State University

NOTES

1. From Spenser's first letter to Gabriel Harvey; *The Works of Edmund Spenser: A Variorum Edition,* ed. Edwin Greenlaw et al., 10 vols. (Baltimore: Johns Hopkins University Press, 1932–57), vol. 9, 10, lines 176–81. Cf. Rudolf Gottfried's translation, vol. 9, 257, lines 176–81:

> Whoever strives to tickle the fancy of mighty patricians
> Strives to be foolish, for follies ever multiply favor.
> Whoever wishes, in fine, to ennoble his forehead with bands
> Of laurel and, by pleasing the people, to win their applause,
> Learns to play mad and reaps the base praise which rewards
> Ignominious nonsense.

2. All references to Spenser's "Letter to Ralegh," to the Commendatory Verses and Dedicatory Sonnets to *The Faerie Queene,* and to *The Faerie Queene* itself are to A. C. Hamilton's annotated edition of *The Faerie Queene* (New York and London: Longman, 1977). Citations from *The Faerie Queene* will be given in the text; citations from the Letter, the Verses, and the Sonnets, for which, given their brevity, page numbers are not provided in the text, are from, respectively, 737–38, 739–40, and 741–43. On the Letter generally, see *Variorum,* vol. 1, 314–62.

3. On Spenser's twelve virtues, see J. J. Jusserand, "Spenser's Twelve Virtues," *Modern Philology* 3 (1906): 373–83; *Variorum,* vol. 1, 327–29.

4. Particularly in light of my summary and dismissive review of what became a thirty-year critical dialogue, a selective bibliography on the problem of inconsistencies between the Letter and *The Faerie Queene* deserves inclusion here, if only to suggest that the issues remain puzzling enough to warrant another hard look, which the present essay provides only implicitly and superficially. The point is that these references include significant scholarly speculations on Spenser's responses to the 1590 publication of his poem. Three major issues emerge: one, discrepancies between the plot outlines in the Letter for the beginnings of Books II and III and those incorporated into the poem; two, the questionable status of Arthur as central thematic and narrative focus of the poem; and three, problems involving the temporal dimension of the narrative considering Spenser's mention of the Faery Queen's annual feast as the source of the major quests.

For these topics and others, see, in chronological order by publication date: Lawrence Blair, "The Plot of the *Faerie Queene*," PMLA 47 (1932): 81–88; Richard H. Perkinson, "The Plot of the *Faerie Queene*," *PMLA* 48 (1933): 295–97 (reply to Blair); Blair's reply, 297–99; Perkinson's "Rejoiner," 299–301; Janet Spens, *Spenser's* Faerie Queene: *An Interpretation* (New York: Russell and Russell, 1934), 9–37; J. H. Walter, "*The Faerie Queene:* Alterations and Structure," *Modern Language Review* 36 (1941): 37–58; Josephine Waters Bennett, *The Evolution of* The Faerie Queene (Chicago: Univ. of Chicago Press, 1942), 24–52, 154, 163; J. H. Walter, "Further Notes on the Alterations to the *Faerie Queene*," *Modern Language Review* 43 (1948): 239–41; Janet Spens, "*The Faerie Queene:* A Reply," *Modern Language Review* 44 (1949): 87–88; W. J. B. Owen, "Spenser's Letter to Ralegh," *Modern Language Review* 45 (1950): 511–12; W. J. B. Owen, "'In these xii books seuerally handled and discoused,'" *ELH* 19 (1952): 165–72; W. J. B. Owen, "The Structure of *The Faerie Queene*," *PMLA* 68 (1953): 1079–1100; A. C. Hamilton, "Spenser's *Letter to Ralegh*," *Modern Language Notes* 73 (1958): 481–85; W. J. B. Owen, "Spenser's Letter to Ralegh: A Reply," *Modern Language Notes* 75 (1960): 195–97; Donald Baker, "The Accuracy of Spenser's *Letter to Ralegh*," *Modern Language Notes* 76 (1961): 103–4; A. C. Hamilton, *The Structure of Allegory in* The Faerie Queene (Oxford: Clarendon Press, 1961), 54–56; C. S. Lewis, *Spenser's Images of Life* (Cambridge: Cambridge Univ. Press, 1967), 140.

5. Quotation from Bennett, 245; see Owen, passim.
6. Bennett, 245
7. Owen, "'In these xii books,'" 172.
8. Lewis, 140
9. Blair, 85, 88.
10. See Hamilton, "Spenser's *Letter*," 484–85; Hamilton, *Structure of Allegory*, 54; cf. William Nelson, *The Poetry of Spenser: A Study* (New York: Columbia University Press, 1963), 116, 136–37. More recently, some of the same words from the Letter have been employed by Jonathan Goldberg (*Endlesse Worke: Spenser and the Structures of Discourse* [Baltimore: Johns Hopkins University Press, 1981]) as evidence of the endless textuality of *The Faerie Oueene* (25) and as sources of "the incitement to narrative pleasure" that draws both poet and reader toward the frustrations and deferrals embodied in the text (28–29). The same inconsistencies have been redeemed in a very different way by Jan Karel Kouwenhoven (*Apparent Narrative as Thematic Metaphor: The Organization of* The Faerie Queene [Oxford: Clarendon Press, 1983], 28–66 passim, especially 55–59), who sees them as partners in Spenser's conspiracy to seduce his readers into believing his poem tells a story.
11. Hamilton, "Spenser's *Letter*," 484, 485.
12. I have particularly in mind the poetic, political, and linguistic acts of representation put forward by these critics as Spenser's in: Richard Helgerson, "The New Poet Presents Himself: Spenser and the Idea of a Literary Career," *PMLA* 93 (1978): 893–911; Helgerson, *Self-Crowned Laureates: Spenser, Jonson, Milton, and the Literary System* (Berkeley: University of California Press, 1983), 1–100; Stephen Greenblatt, *Renaissance Self-Fashioning: From More to Shakespeare (*Chicago: University of Chicago Press, 1980), 19, 157–92; Goldberg, *Endlesse Worke,* passim, especially 122–74.
13. Compare Kenneth Gross, *Spenserian Poetics: Idolatry, Iconoclasm, and Magic (*Ithaca, NY: Cornell University Press, 1985), 17: the Letter may be "a partly retrospective attempt to contain and defend from violation the proliferating suggestions that the poem opens up."

14. Compare, among the Commendatory Verses, Hobynoll:

> But (iolly shepheard) though with pleasing style,
>   thou feast the humour of the Courtly traine:
> Let not conceipt thy settled sence beguile
>   ne daunted be through enuy or disdaine.
> Subiect thy dome to her Empyring spright,
> From whence thy Muse, and all the world takes light.

And note H.B.:

> Graue Muses march in triumph and with prayses,
> Our Goddesse here hath giuen you leaue to land:
> And biddes this rare dispenser of your graces
> Bow downe his brow vnto her sacred hand.

15. I use the word *prodigal* with Richard Helgerson's use in mind: *The Elizabethan Prodigals* (Berkeley: University of California Press, 1976).

16. Verse by H.B.

17. Verse by R.S.

18. Dedicatory Sonnets to, respectively, Essex, Ralegh, Ormond, Oxenford, and Burghley.

19. Stephen J. Greenblatt, *Sir Walter Ralegh: The Renaissance Man and His Roles* (New Haven and London: Yale University Press, 1973), 60. Compare "Colin Clouts Come Home Againe," lines 164–71.

20. For reconstructions of events in the lives of Ralegh and Spenser that brought them together in Ireland in summer, 1589, and led to the publication of *The Faerie Queene* in London less than a year later, see: Alexander C. Judson, *The Life of Edmund Spenser, Variorum,* vol. 8, 128–55; J. H. Adamson and H. F. Folland, *The Shepherd of the Ocean: An Account of Sir Walter Ralegh and His Times* (Boston: Gambit, 1969), 168–69, 178–88; Robert Lacey, *Sir Walter Ralegh* (New York: Atheneum, 1974), 141–43; Greenblatt, *Ralegh,* 164–71.

21. A similarly ironic paradox is implicit in Spenser's rhetorical strategy in the Dedicatory Sonnets, for the "ydle rymes" of his "base Poeme" are nonetheless sufficiently worthy to praise "Vnder a shade vele" some of those whose favor the poet seeks; in other words, the poem builds an "euerlasting monument" to those whose censure it deserves, immortalizing those who may well view poetry as, at best, a waste of time (quotations in note from sonnets to, respectively, Hatton, Essex, Oxenford, and Howard; see also sonnets to Hunsdon, Norris, and Walsingham).

22. Recent reappraisals of Stephen Greenblatt's version of Spenser's textual engagement with power lend independent support to the kind of implicit confrontational tactics and self-conscious social positioning I see at work in the Letter. These usually respectful critiques call attention to and question some of Greenblatt's more absolute pronouncements concerning Spenser's "worship" of power, autocracy, and imperialism (*Renaissance Self-Fashioning,* 174). Compare Gary Waller, *English Poetry of the Sixteenth Century* (London: Longman, 1986), 206. For critiques of Greenblatt's Spenser, see Jonathan Goldberg, *Endlesse Worke,* 148; Goldberg, "The Politics of Renaissance Literature: A Review Essay," *ELH* 49 (1982): 533; Goldberg, "The Poet's

Authority: Spenser, Jonson, and James VI and I," in *The Power of Forms in the English Renaissance,* ed. Stephen Greenblatt (Norman, OK: Pilgrim Books, 1982), 81; Louis Adrian Montrose, "The Elizabethan Subject and the Spenserian Text," in *Literary Theory/Renaissance Texts,* ed. Patricia Parker and David Quint (Baltimore: Johns Hopkins University Press, 1986) 330–31; Maureen Quilligan, *Milton's Spenser: The Politics of Reading* (Ithaca, NY: Cornell University Press, 1983) 67, n.54; Alan Sinfield, "Power and Ideology: An Outline Theory and Sidney's *Arcadia,*" *ELH* 52 (1985): 275.

I favor Sinfield and Montrose, who avoid, for the most part, both Greenblatt's and Goldberg's brands of ideological determinism. Sinfield claims "that the complexities of the power structure make it possible to envisage the literary text . . . as a site of contest" (275). Montrose sums up what appears to be the main point: "Every representation of power is also an appropriation of power" (331).

23. Greenblatt, *Ralegh,* 31.

24. Greenblatt, *Ralegh,* 59–60.

25. Greenblatt, *Ralegh,* 31; compare Thomas Greene, "The Flexibility of the Self in Renaissance Literature," in *The Disciplines of Criticism: Essays in Literary Theory, Interpretation, and History* (New Haven: Yale University Press, 1968), 252: "The fashioning of the pupil by the pedagogue was replaced by the reflexive fashioning of the individual's own mind and soul. Humanist formation first assisted in, then gave way to, metaphysical transformation."

26. After explaining and defending his "saucy . . . comparison" of "the highest point of man's wit with the efficacy of nature," Sir Philip Sidney says something whose sense may well have been ringing in Spenser's ears as he wrote the Letter: "But these arguments will by few be understood, and by fewer granted" (*Defence of Poetry,* in *Miscellaneous Prose of Sir Philip Sidney,* ed. Katherine Duncan-Jones and Jan van Dorsten [Oxford: Clarendon Press, 1973], 79).

27. Anthony Low, "'Plato, and His Equall Xenophon': A Note on Milton's Apology for Smectymnuus," *Milton Quarterly* 4 (1970): 22.

28. Lawrence A. Sasek, "'Plato, and his equall *Xenophon,*'" *English Language Notes* 7 (1969–70): 261. To digress, both Low and Sasek fail to notice that there may be no solid grounds for validating any comparison between Milton's and Spenser's references to Plato and Xenophon. First, they assume that Milton uses *equall* as a value term, neglecting to note, as Merritt Y. Hughes does in his edition of Milton (*Complete Poems and Major Prose* [New York: Bobbs-Merrill, 1957], 694, n. 32; all references to Milton are cited from this edition), that Milton may merely be equating the two authors as contemporaries. Second, while Milton may be treating both as philosophers, referring, as Hughes suggests (694, n. 32), to Xenophon's *Memorabilia,* Spenser, like Sidney, contrasts the poet Xenophon, author of the *Cyrus,* to the philosopher Plato, author of the *Republic.* Thus, Milton may not be equating them on the same grounds as Spenser, as examples illustrating the relative didactic value of poetry and philosophy.

29. A. Leigh Deneff, *Spenser and the Motives of Metaphor* (Durham, NC: Duke University Press, 1982), 181, no. 4.

30. David Norbrook, *Poetry and Politics in the English Renaissance* (London: Routledge and Kegan Paul, 1984), 109; compare Deneef, 30.

31. Daniel Javitch, *Poetry and Courtliness in Renaissance England* (Princeton, NJ: Princeton University Press, 1978), 101.
32. Judith Dundas, *The Spider and the Bee: The Artistry of Spenser's* Faerie Queene (Urbana, IL: University of Illinois Press, 1985), 93.
33. Kouwenhoven, 71.
34. Javitch, 101.
35. Dundas, 93–94.
36. Kouwenhoven, 71. Maureen Quilligan, to mention a final and fairly radical example, makes sweeping assumptions about the relationship between Sidney's *Defence* and Spenser's Letter, and then extends the comparison to Milton. Quilligan sets out to interpret the *Defence* in order "to flesh out the letter's assumptions" (32). From here she proposes a shaky assertion: "all that Sidney described in the Apology, Milton learned how to do by reading Spenser" (41).
37. D. M. Beach, "The Poetry of Idea: Sir Philip Sidney and the Theory of Allegory," *Texas Studies in Literature and Language* 13 (1972–72), 384; compare Nelson, *Poetry of Spenser,* 130.
38. Hamilton, *Structure,* 57, 56.
39. As James Nohrnberg succinctly points out in *The Analogy of* The Faerie Queene (Princeton, NJ: Princeton University Press, 1976), 28: "The superiority of Xenophon to Plato seems to have been an old chestnut"; Nohrnberg provides classical and Renaissance examples (28, n. 62). On this issue, Spenser is sparring with several contemporary commentators, involved in a literary critical dialogue with, at the very least, Sidney, Puttenham, and Harington. See Sidney, *Defence,* 75, 81, 86; George Puttenham, *The Arte of English Poesie,* in *Elizabethan Critical Essays,* 2 vols., ed. G. Gregory Smith (London: Oxford University Press, 1904), II, 42–43; Sir John Harington, *A Preface, or rather a Briefe Apologie of Poetrie,* in *Elizabethan Critical Essays,* II, 196.
40. Hamilton, *Structure,* 57; compare Richard Waswo, *Language and Meaning in the Renaissance* (Princeton, NJ: Princeton University Press, 1987), 230: "Spenser himself speaks of allegory, in the letter to Ralegh, as a 'method' for achieving the Sidneian delight that is instruction."
41. Sidney, 80, 85, 79, 80.
42. Sidney, 85.
43. Beach, 385, 382–87 passim; compare Norbrook, 109: for Spenser, "each image is inferior to the transcendent truth it images, and yet it also partakes of the dignity of its prototype . . . . " Beach's "yearning" Spenser has recently become a rather fashionable figure: "Spenser's art does not lead us to perceive ideology critically, but rather affirms the existence and inescapable moral power of ideology as the principle of truth toward which art forever yearns" (Greenblatt, *Self-Fashioning,* 192; compare Waller, 206: "What the poem attempts . . . is a denial of historical change. *The Faerie Queene* yearns for stasis, to project truth as unalterable, . . . natural, given, and unassailable."
44. Sidney, 85, 83–84. On issues concerning Sidney's *Defence* relevant to this essay see, for example: O. B. Hardison, Jr., "The Two Voices of Sidney's *Apology for Poetry,*" *English Literary Renaissance* 2 (1972), 98; Helgerson, *Elizabethan Prodigals,* 155; Ronald Levao, "Sidney's Feigned *Apology,*" *PMLA* 94 (1979): 953–55; A. Leigh Deneef, "Rereading Sidney's *Apology,*" *Journal of Medieval and Renaissance Studies* 10

(1980): 155–91; Deneef, *Motives of Metaphor,* 6–8; Martin N. Raitiere, "The Unity of Sidney's *Apology for Poetry,*" *Studies in English Literature* 21 (1981): 52, 56–57; John Guillory, *Poetric Authority: Spenser, Milton, and Literary History* (New York: Columbia University Press, 1983), 10–11; Margaret W. Ferguson, *Trials of Desire: Renaissance of Defenses of Poetry (New Haven: Yale University Press, 1983), 137–39*, 146, 159; Waswo, 229–30. On Puttenham see: Javitch, passim; Derek Attridge, "Puttenham's Perplexity: Nature, Art, and the Supplement in Renaissance Poetic Theory," in *Literary Theory,* Parker/Quint, eds., 265, 273–74.

45. Milton, *Areopagitica,* 728.

46. Sidney, 93.

47. Dedicatory Sonnet to Hatton.

48. Compare Goldberg, *Endlesse Worke,* 28: "For 'knowing how doubtfully all Allegories may be construed, 'Spenser goes on to justify the 'cloudily enwrapped' text as necessary to give pleasure to those who would be put off by simple and straightforward moralizing; yet this enwrapment, he admits, is also the likely source of the displeasure the text causes, giving rise to 'gelous opinions and misconstructions.' What gives pleasure give displeasure." And Gross, 17: the Letter "suggests that the necessary hiddenness of meaning in the poem is the very thing that leaves it open to the threat of violation by willful and slanderous misinterpreters."

49. As with the matter of Sidney criticism, and more so, this is no place to engage fully the theory of allegory, but since Spenser is in the thick of it in the Letter, I will at least take note of the most immediate issue from the perspective of two critics who teach us something about Spenser. Jacqueline T. Miller has recently observed *(Poetic License: Authority and Authorship in Medieval and Renaissance Contexts* [New York: Oxford University Press, 1986]: 196, n. 24), with the appropriate understatement, I hope, that "The question of the intended accessibility of allegory to its audience is a vexed issue among modern critics." And so it was, for pretty much the same reasons, among Spenser's contemporaries, because the issue goes to the heart of political and metaphysical questions about the nature of art and the art of nature. Miller proceeds: the "principle of clarity" and of "concealment" both emerge from Renaissance definitions of allegory, so "tension" is "inherent in the form" (197, n. 24). Spenser, of course, exploits them both, along with the territory in between. See Miller's provocative discussion of Boccaccio, Puttenham, and allegory (81–85, 110), rooted in a modern critical tradition I share (see 195–99, n. 16–29).

From another quarter comes Anthea Hume (*Edmund Spenser: Protestant Poet* [Cambridge: Cambridge University Press, 1984]), who, after a fascinating discussion of the "hide from common view" theory of allegory, boldly concludes that *The Faerie Queene* is not an esoteric text and that Spenser's "purpose [is] communication with the many" (171). The combination of populist poet and radical experimental pluralist suggests a proto-romantic Spenser (see Gross, 10, 16, 82) not unlike the one I see projected by part of Spenser's persona in the Letter.

50. Helgerson (*Self-Crowned,* 66) sees Spenser intimidated by Burghley: "Confronted with the statesmanlike gravity of Lord Burghley, Spenser forces himself back into the mold of the prodigal poet." Helgerson, I think, takes this ploy too seriously, for although I agree that Spenser recognizes and publicly acknowledges his laureate role, this hardly means that he cannot also be playfully ironic or even willfully subversive, as long as he is careful. Additionally, I do not think the guilt and contrition

Helgerson associates with the "prodigal poets" he so categorically distinguishes from Spenser is necessarily as heartfelt as Helgerson contends (*Elizabethan Prodigals,* passim; see also Helgerson, "The Elizabethan Laureate: Self-Presentation and the Literary System," *ELH* 46 (1979): 217; and Quilligan, 207–08).

The sonnet to Burghley is among the seven dedications added after a number of copies of the poem had already been bound. The conventional critical assumption about this matter is that Spenser had forgotton to include Burghley and the others and had to be reminded by Ralegh or someone else to write the appropriate dedications (see Judson, 141–43). Although there is no way of knowing the truth, I find it much more likely that the omission was a deliberately subtle act of social confrontation rather than an ignorant blunder of a naive courtier poet.

51. Greenblatt, *Self-Fashioning,* 285–86, n. 29.

52. Hamilton, *Structure,* 54.

53. Montrose, 318.

54. Waswo, 230; compare Greenblatt, *Self-Fashioning,* 3. Among earlier critics, Nelson (*Poetry of Spenser,* 121-22) tackles the same issue, only to retreat from plural connotations: "Spenser's use of 'fashion' echoes a long-established tradition which shows that he must intend by it not 'educate' or 'train' but 'represent,' 'delineate.'"

55. Hamilton, *Structure,* 54.

56. Waswo, 231.

57. Greenblatt, *Self-Fashioning,* 3.

58. See Javitch, 105, 112–15.

59. Ralegh, of course, according to Spenser's Dedicatory Sonnet to him, is "the sommers Nightingale," which might make Spenser the cuckoo who, in the Letter, courts the "commune sence" of the "meaner wits," from whom no material benefit is forthcoming.

Spenser's Sonnet to Ralegh is thick with ironic reverberations, one being its dominant theme. Spenser gives Ralegh the advice that Burghley and the rest of the "rugged forhead[s]" (4.Proem.1) would give Spenser: if you must write poetry, at least write about war rather than love, about death rather than sex; write our epic—cultural propaganda—instead of your hybrid romance. For we know about war and we control it, but love leaves us frightened, confused, anxious, defenseless; we're scared of women, including Elizabeth. So both Spenser and Ralegh write to Elizabeth about love, leaving the "thonder of martial stowre" (which Spenser finds "Fitter" to Ralegh's muse) for poetic histories unwritten. A further irony is implicit too, for the big audience of "meaner wits" that Spenser's allegorical method in the Letter seeks to please would probably be more likely to buy and read broadsides, sermons, and Italian novels than *The Faerie Queene.*

60. See Helgerson, *Self-Crowned,* 1–100 passim.

61. For stories about Spenser's Burghley-go-round after the 1590 publication, see John Manningham, *Diary* (1602–03), in *Spenser Allusions in the Sixteenth and Seventeenth Centuries,* compiled by Ray Heffner, Dorothy E. Mason, and Frederick M. Padelford, edited by William Wells, *Studies in Philology* 68 (1971): 90; Thomas Fuller, *The History of the Worthies of England* (1662), in *Spenser Allusions, Studies in Philology* 69 (1972): 253–54. And see the delightful, learned, and fascinating accounts in John Hughes, *The Works of Mr. Edmund Spenser* (London, 1715; reprinted New York: AMS Press, 1973), lxiv–lxix, lxxxv–lxxxvii; and Henry John Todd, *The Works of Edmund*

Spenser (London, 1805; reprinted New York: AMS Press, 1973), iv–xi, who eloquently discounts the stories as hokum.

62. Judson, 154.

63. Judson, 155; quotation from "Colin Clouts."

64. For an exhaustive yet concise scholarly review of the Arthurian question in Elizabethan England, see Charles Bowie Millican, *Spenser and the Table Round: A Study of the Contemporaneous Background for Spenser's Use of the Arthurian Legend,* Harvard Studies in Comparative Literature VIII (Cambridge: Harvard University Press, 1932).

65. See Millican, 159, ns. 58, 59, 60.

66. Edwin Greenlaw, "A Sixteenth Century Battle of the Books," *Program* for the 44th meeting of the Modern Language Association (1972), 4; quoted in Millican, 25.

67. Millican, 90; see William Camden, *Britannia,* trans. Richard Gough (1806; reprinted Hildesheim: Georg-Olms Verlag, 1974), vol. 1, lii–liii, 7.

68. Millican, 97.

69. F. Smith Fussner, *The Historical Revolution: English Historical Writing and Thought* 1580–1640 (New York: Columbia University Press, 1962). On the "new history" see, out of many sources: H. Butterfield, *The Statecraft of Machiavelli* (New York: Macmillan, 1956), 59–86; Denys Hays, *Annalists and Historians: Western Historiography from the Eighth to the Eighteenth Centuries* (London: Methuen, 1977), 87–168; F. Smith Fussner, *Tudor History and the Historians* (New York: Basic Books, 1970); Arthur B. Ferguson, *Clio Unbound: Perception of the Social and Cultural Past in Renaissance England,* Duke Monographs in Medieval and Renaissance Studies 2 (Durham, NC: Duke University Press, 1979).

70. Compare Wyman H. Herendeen, "Wanton Discourses and the Engines of Time: William Camden—Historian among Poets-Historical," in *Renaissance Rereadings: Intertextual Context,* ed. Maryanne Cline Horowitz, Anne J. Cruz, Wendy A. Furman (Urbana, IL: University of Illinois Press, 1988), 147–48. Herendeen, in his original and succinct article, points to Sidney's historians in much the same way I do to elucidate Camden's historiography in much the same way I do Spenser's. Herendeen corroborates what I had already surmised. On Camden, however, compare Ferguson, 11.

71. Sidney, 83, 84, 90, 85.

72. See the fascinating correspondence between Sidney and Languet quoted by Millican, 74–75.

73. Ferguson, 351.

74. Ferguson, 36.

75. See Ferguson, 83, on Spenser's methodology in *A View;* and compare Herendeen, 148–49, on Camden's in *Britannia.*

76. Ferguson, 421, 37–38.

77. There has been no adequately comprehensive study of the significant breach in Spenser's chronicle chronology, particularly as it reflects the nature of temporal reality in Spenser's Britain and Faeryland and the complex chronicle/historical loyalties of his major Briton characters—Arthur, Britomart, and Artegall. I pursue these topics elsewhere. See Carrie Anna Harper, *The Sources of the British Chronicle History in Spenser's* Faerie Queene (1908: rpt. New York: Haskell House, 1964), 1, 144–50.

78. Sidney, 79.

JAMES SCHIAVONI

Predestination and Free Will: The Crux of Canto Ten

> "We may not so defend grace as to seem to take away free will, or, on the other hand, so assert free will as to be judged ungrateful to the grace of God."
>
> —Augustine, *De Peccatorum Meritis et Remissione, et de Baptismo Parvulorum*

BOOK I CANTO X of *The Faerie Queene* begins with what many critics take to be the most theologically Protestant, not to say Calvinistic, stanza of the entire poem, yet the canto goes on to present the most blatantly Roman Catholic imagery in Spenser's epic. Red Cross Knight's sojourn in the House of Holiness contains Roman Catholic elements which should have been anathema to any good son of the Church of England. Few, I think, are satisfied with C. S. Lewis's explanation that, because Roman Catholicism is so inherently allegorical, an allegorist's symbol will often resemble one already imagined by Roman Catholics.[1] Lewis's explanation fails to account for Spenser's specific choices of images: "seuen Bead-men" (36.3) representing the seven corporal works of mercy; St. George as his "owne nations frend/ And Patrone" (61.7–8); what appears to be the sacrament of penance (24 ff.); flagellation (27.1–2); and the intercession of saints (51.7–9). Alan Sinfield opines that these traditional figures indicate a discrepancy between Protestantism and Spenser's closest literary models, the Italian poets Ariosto and Tasso, rather than a respect for Roman Catholic religious practices per se;[3] but such a rationalization assumes that Spenser, who elsewhere admirably adapts and transforms the material of his predecessors to his own purposes, inexplicably is not in control of his images in this crucial canto. Monks saying the rosary, patron saints, a sacrament accepted only by the Roman Church—these images do more than merely resemble Roman Catholicism.

The crux of the canto resides in the incompatible theologies which the opening stanza and the Roman Catholic images suggest. The differences between Protestant and Roman Catholic theology mainly concern the state of man after the Fall and the nature of the atonement for original sin. Roman Catholicism insisted that man's free will remained, however weakened, and that he could cooperate with grace through good works and through reception of the sacraments. In general, Protestantism insisted on a total depravity and loss of free will as a consequence of the Fall and on salvation through faith alone, a faith God gratuitously infused in the elect, who could not prepare for or cooperate with it unless God first moved them to do so. A. S. P. Woodhouse recognizes the problem when he suggests that Spenser hesitates between two different theological systems of natural moral strength: "In the one tradition grace could build on the sure foundation of nature. In the other it seemed, rather, to demand a new start."[4] Surely Spenser knew his theology better than to confuse Protestant with Roman Catholic doctrine.

I suggest that the combination of an emphasis on predestination and grace with imagery suggesting human effort and the sacraments forms part of a larger pattern of divine grace and human effort in Book I, a pattern in which predestination and free will paradoxically work together in the process of justification and sanctification. I suggest also that this paradoxical coexistence of predestination and free will came to Spenser from St. Paul by way of St. Augustine. If my thesis is correct, Spenser read St. Augustine differently than did either Calvin or the Counter-Reformation theologians, for Calvin denied free will and sacramental efficacy, and Roman Catholicism, by the time of the Council of Trent, placed much less emphasis on predestination than formerly; but Augustine's works contain a strong emphasis on both. Spenser wrote his epic not long after the publication of Calvin's fifth edition of *Institutes of the Christian Religion,* the Thirty-Nine Articles of the Church of England, and the Canons and Decrees of the Council of Trent. *The Faerie Queene* responds to such texts not by denying predestination or free will but by juxtaposing them, thus suggesting that they are not mutually exclusive.

Theologians of the various denominations appealed to the authority of the greatest theologian of grace, St. Augustine, to validate their views on these issues. We can identify a Calvinist version of Augustine and a Roman Catholic version. Calvin, of course, concentrated on those works of Augustine which emphasized total depravity and absolute predestination. Roman Catholics preferred those works which suggested sacramental efficacy and the power of free will to cooperate after grace began the work of salvation. These divergent works suggest a certain paradox in Augustine's thought. On the one hand, he seems to believe that men are predestined to salvation or damnation by the circumstances of their lives, which determine whether or not they receive saving faith; on the other hand, he states repeatedly that the grace of final perseverance "cooperates" with men and that they decide whether or not to receive the gift.[5] Certainly, Augustine believes that without grace man's fallen will inevitably chooses sin (although it remains "free" in the sense that God does not compel it to do so). But the role of the will after grace remains open to interpretation.

In this doctrinal controversy, although Calvin was willing to take Augustine to task on certain secondary issues, he claimed Augustine's authority on the central issues of absolute predestination, utter depravity, and loss of free will: "Augustine is completely on our side" in these matters, he wrote.[6] The *Institutes* contain a myriad of appeals to Augustinian authority, particularly in those chapters that discuss the loss of free will (II.ii–v), justification (III.xi–xix), and election and predestination (III.xxi–xxiv). Calvin singles out Augustine among all the Church Fathers as the most lucid exponent of the enslavement of the will (II.ii.4, 9) and holds him forth as the pattern for the proper preaching of predestination (III.xxiii.14). Although Calvin leans heavily on the antipelagian works, he seems to have all of Augustine's writings at his fingertips: he quotes, for example, from Augustine's letters to prove God's righteousness in predestination (III.xxiii.11). As Calvin says: "If I were inclined to compile a whole volume from Augustine, I could easily show my readers that I need no words but his" to explain these high matters (III.xxii.8).[7] In calling on Augustine's authority, Calvin calls on the authority of the other Church Fathers as well, because "Augustine will not allow himself to be disunited from the rest" in matters of doctrine (III.xxii.8). Moreover, Calvin frequently cites St. Paul alongside of St. Augustine, suggesting that Augustine's theology follows the genuine Pauline doctrine (III.xxii.1; III.xxiii.1, 13).

Spenser's audience included many who favored a Calvinistic interpretation of Augustine. Calvin's opponents, however, reminded Calvin that Augustine's predestinarianism had never been officially adopted by the Church.[8] In contrast to Calvinists, Roman Catholics focused on those works of Augustine which emphasized the superiority of love to faith, the compatibility of free will with predestination, the necessity of the sacraments for salvation (especially the anti-donatist works), and the authority of the universal church to establish and to interpret scripture. Roman Catholics were particularly anxious to use Augustine's Pauline doctrine of the supremacy of love among the three theological virtues to strike at the cornerstone of the Protestant doctrine of justification through faith alone:

> Hence it was necessary, in the name of the true Augustine, to point out to the Reformers that "you will never find it said about faith that it is 'the bond of perfection'" as it was said about love. Love "does not permit anything to be preferred to it," not even faith. It was a mark of these "newfangled Christians" to speak of "faith alone," and in so doing to ignore the variety of meanings the word "faith" had in Scripture, where it did not refer only to "trust." Sometimes they interpreted [the] formula of "by faith alone" as though it implied the exclusion of the sacraments (or even of Christ himself) from the process of salvation, but usually it was the relation of faith to good works that was seen, and correctly, as the real issue.[9]

Certain Anglican theologians (such as Jewel and Cranmer) tended toward the Protestant reading of Augustine, others (such as Hooker) toward the Roman Catholic. And the Continental theological situation was even more complex: for instance, there was dispute among Roman Catholic theologians themselves over the relationship between free will and grace, with some, such as Molina (*Harmony of Free Will with the Gifts of Grace,* 1588), arguing in favor of free will, in agreement with the official doctrine of the Council of Trent, and others, such as Baius, adopting what was essentially a Calvinistic doctrine of utter depravity and irresistible grace *sans* free will. Augustine seems to have become a sort of battlefield and focus of doctrinal disputes not only between Roman Catholics and Protestants but also within the various traditions themselves.

The mixture of emphases in Book I suggests that Spenser adheres to an Augustinianism not coextensive with that of any specific church. Despite the Calvinist stanza, the remainders of Canto x in particular and of Book I in general contain images of sacramental efficacy and free will cooperating with grace which show that, contrary to scholars such as Lilian Winstanley, F. M. Padelford, Paul Siegal, James Boulger, Alan Sinfield, and most recently Daniel Doerksen and Anthea Hume,[10] Spenser was unwilling to commit himself wholly to a Calvinist reading of Augustine's theology. What is demonstrated by paradoxical imagery in Book I of *The Faerie Queene* is demonstrated by ambiguity in The Thirty-Nine Articles of 1563: Anglican theology sought to retain certain traditional elements which the most extreme Protestantism rejected. Those who argue for a Calvinist theology in Book I ignore the general implications of free will and the specific portrayals of "magical" (*ex opere operato*)[11] sacramental efficacy, both of these being incompatible with Calvinism.[12] Those few who argue for a Roman Catholic theology in Book I ignore the clear statements of Calvinist doctrines such as utter depravity and irresistible grace.[13] Those who argue for a *via media* theology in Book I are closer to the truth,[14] although Spenser takes a bolder stand for both utter depravity and sacramental efficacy than do the ambiguous Thirty-Nine Articles, which are more nearly a least common denominator than a complete theology for the English Church.

That Spenser was unaware of the apparent discrepancy between the Calvinist beginning and the Roman Catholic content of Canto x seems unlikely, for he was well-versed in the theological disputes of the Reformation. Calvin's 1559 revision of his *Institutes of the Christian Religion* had an enormous influence not only on the Continent but in Britain as well, so the opening stanza of Canto x comes as no surprise:

> What man is he, that boasts of fleshly might,
> And vaine assurance of mortality,
> Which all so soone, as it doth come to fight
> Against spirituall foes, yeelds by and by,
> Or from the field most cowardly doth fly?
> Ne let the man ascribe it to his skill,
> That thorough grace hath gained victory.
> *If any strength we haue, it is to ill,*
> *But all the good is Gods, both power and eke will.*
> (I.x.1, italics mine)

This articulation of utter depravity, the inability of man, ruined in the core of his nature, to will anything whatsoever with good motives until God moves him to do so, supports Padelford and other early scholars who label Spenser a Calvinist; Padelford went so far as to describe the first book of *The Faerie Oueene* as a poetic version of the third book of Calvin's *Institutes.*[15] In contrast to Calvinist doctrine, official Roman Catholic doctrine during the Counter-Reformation insisted that free will was not lost with original sin: "[F]ree will, weakened as it was in its powers and downward bent, was by no means extinguished in them" (Canons and Decrees of the Council of Trent VI.i)[16]

Disagreement over free will led to disagreement over the process of justification by which man is reconciled to God and accounted righteous once more. While both Roman Catholics and Calvinists agreed that God must initiate the process, Roman Catholics added that man must cooperate with God while Calvinists denied that man's will made any independent contribution to human salvation. The Decrees of Trent declare that although "the beginning of that justification must proceed from the predisposing grace of God," human beings "convert themselves to their own justification *by freely assenting to and cooperating with that grace*" (VI.v, italics mine). In nothing do we see so clearly the essential difference between Roman Catholicism and Calvinism as in this issue of the role of the will in justification, for Calvin writes: "[T]he Lord corrects our depraved will, or rather removes it, and of himself introduces a good one in its place. . . . [I]t is wrong to attribute to man a voluntary obedience in following the guidance of grace" (*Institutes* II.iii.7).

Additionally, Roman Catholics and Protestants meant different things when they spoke of "justification." For Roman Catholics, justification included moral progress, mainly through works of charity and reception of sacraments. In other words, sanctification was an intrinsic part of justification. Protestants, on the other hand, separated the two processes. For them, justification was extrinsic, accomplished by Christ and conferred, by God's inscrutable grace, on the elect through faith alone; it did not proceed in any way from moral progress in charity. The human agent remained a part of the process, but all inward "acts" of faith and outward "works" of charity were part of sanctification, which was the response, not the way, to justification, contrary to the Roman Catholic view.

Some critics prefer not to see strict Calvinism in the opening stanza of Canto x. R. Headlam Wells claims that the stanza is compatible with Erasmus's statement in *De Libero Arbitrio:*

> Nor . . . does our will achieve nothing, although it does not attain the things that it seeks without the help of grace. But

> since our efforts are so puny, the whole is ascribed to God . . . . Since human labor does nothing except when divine favor is also present, the whole is ascribed to the divine beneficence.[17]

But the stanza implies that not just our actions but also our wills are totally corrupt—a Calvinistic concept if ever one existed. To find any suggestion of free will, we must look not within this stanza but to other statements and images in Canto x and throughout Book I.

Although Canto x begins with a stanza asserting the utter depravity of the human will, the Roman Catholic images of good works and of the sacrament of confession (penance) in the remainder of the canto show Red Cross Knight actually becoming a saint in his earthly life by "freely assenting to and cooperating with" God's grace. Many of the allegorical inhabitants of the House of Holiness represent good works. Spenser's portrayal of the seven corporal works of mercy is telling: Red Cross enters a hospice "In which seuen Bead-men that had vowed all / Their life to service of high heauens king / Did spend their dayes in doing godly thing" (36.3–5). These Beadsmen, perhaps monks as Jerome Oetgen suggests,[18] engage in sheltering the homeless, feeding the hungry and thirsty, clothing the naked, comforting and redeeming the captive, ministering to the sick and dying, burying the dead, and aiding the widowed and orphaned. Charles Mounts notes[19] that, although Spenser follows Lactantius by adding the care of widows and orphans to Thomas Aquinas's list of the seven corporal works, the works are nonetheless Roman Catholic and are rarely even mentioned by Protestant reformers.

While Roman Catholics certainly had no monopoly on doing deeds, good or bad, Protestants looked upon good works as a result of, rather than a cause of, man's justification in God's sight. In the *Institutes* (III.xi.15), Calvin expresses chagrin that Augustine assigns grace to sanctification rather than to imputed righteousness.[20] Canto x seems to portray good deeds as instrumental in Red Cross's spiritual rejuvenation. Una first brings Red Cross to the House of Holiness because he "was feeble, and too faint" (2.2) and "vnfit for bloudie fight" (2.6)—hardly descriptive of a man spiritually mature and justified, since his physical state throughout Book I corresponds to his spiritual state. By putting forth effort during his spiritual retreat, Red Cross achieves not only justification but also sanctification: he becomes St. George.[21] More important still, as a *microchristus* he is able to conquer the Old Dragon and free human nature from spiritual imprisonment. Only Roman Catholics believed that men could become saints in this life; for

Protestants, final sanctification occurred only after death. Anthea Hume, in order to maintain her argument for Spenser's Calvinism, claims that Spenser does not mean that Red Cross literally has become a saint,[22] and D. Douglas Waters claims that the well of life represents Augustine's second rebirth of the soul in heaven and that the knight's victory over the dragon represents the Christian's final sanctification after death;[23] but the poem itself portrays the knight becoming a saint and conquering the dragon in *this* life.[24]

Spenser provides clear statements on the value of good works for salvation. Stanza 38 of Canto x, as Whitaker points out,[25] looks like a reference to works of supererogation, condemned by all Protestants as a doctrine leading to human pride: "The grace of God he layd up still in store,/ Which as a stocke he left vnto his seede;/He had enough, what neede him care for more?" In Roman Catholic doctrine, the good works of the saints, abundant beyond anything necessary for their own salvation, created a storehouse of grace from which the Church could distribute as it saw fit. Protestants saw this doctrine as one of the causes of such abuses as indulgences. At any rate, Spenser's wording certainly cuts against the grain of Calvinistic theology, which saw the good deeds even of the elect as tainted by corruption and utterly insufficient to earn any reward.[26]

Stanza 45 also suggests the merit of good works,[27] describing Red Cross's progress in imitating the beadsmen:

> During which time, in euery good behest
> And godly worke of Almes and charitee
> She him instructed with great industree;
> Shortly therein so perfect he became,
> That from the first vnto the last degree,
> His mortal life he learned had to frame
> In holy righteousness, without rebuke or blame.

The tone of this stanza is more Roman Catholic than Protestant and suggests that Spenser "revered the mediaeval ideal of saintliness far more than the Puritanical and Calvinistic ideal of justification through faith."[28] Likewise, Contemplation implies the value of good works when he tells Dame Mercy that she "doest the prayers of the righteous sead/Present before the maiestie diuine,/And his auenging wrath to clemencie incline" (51.7–9). Besides suggesting that a man's good deeds act as a counterbalance to his sins—a Roman Catholic notion indeed—this process also resembles the intercession of saints. The longer one reads Canto x, the more it seems to sprout those papist doctrines most odious to Reformation Protestants. References to the value of good works in attaining salvation continue even into Book II, where Guyon states: "But after death the tryall is to come, / When best shall be to them, that liued best" (II.i.59.3–4). Guyon's words possess a Roman Catholic emphasis on good deeds as the criteria for salvation.

Some critics have sought to account for these apparently Roman Catholic emphases on free will and the efficacy of works by referring them to Spenser's humanism. "To the Christian humanist, salvation is a cooperative enterprise between nature and grace."[29] Yet I do not think we can explain the theology of Book I by reference to the works of Christian humanists such as Erasmus, because they posit a non-sacramental view of salvation or at least place little emphasis on sacraments, whereas Spenser, like Augustine, portrays sacraments as central to the process of salvation.

In Augustinian and Roman Catholic doctrine the sacraments as well as good works are considered necessary for spiritual regeneration:

> If anyone says that the sacraments of the New Law are not necessary for salvation but are superfluous, and that without them or without the desire of them men obtain from God through faith alone the grace of justification . . . let him be anathema. (Decrees of Trent VII)

Red Cross appears to receive the sacrament of penance complete with its traditional components of confession, contrition, absolution, and satisfaction. To assuage Red Cross's conviction of guilt, Caelia brings "a Leach, the which had great insight / In that disease of grieued conscience, / And well could cure the same" (23.7–9). This doctor of the soul is Patience,

> Who comming to that soule-diseased knight,
> Could hardly him entreat, to tell his grief:
> Which knowne, and all that noyd his heauie spright
> Well searcht; eftsoones he gan apply reliefe
> Of salves and med'cines, which had passing priefe,
> And thereto added words of woundrous might:
> By which to ease he him recured briefe.
>
> (24.1–7)

This stanza describes a process remarkably similar to the Roman Catholic sacrament of penance, in which the penitent enumerates his particular sins to the priest, who listens, advises, absolves (or, in rare cases, witholds absolution until certain conditions are met), then imposes some act of penance on the sinner. That Red Cross must tell *all* his grief suggests the Roman Catholic doctrine that the penitent must confess all mortal sins during the sacrament of penance. Two cantos earlier, Spenser suggests that Orgoglio's club crushes Red Cross to the ground as punishment for "the guilt of mortall sins" (viii.9.2).[30] Protestants made no such distinctions among sins. E. Hickey proposes[31] that Patience is a priest and that the words of wondrous might he pronounces are the words of absolution: *Absolvo te in nomine Patris et Filii et Spiritus Sancti.* Red Cross's reception of the sacrament resembles Everyman's. Like the medieval Catholic figure, the Renaissance Protestant one must complete the sacrament by putting on the garment of contrition and making satisfaction for his sins through self-mortification. In fact, Red Cross's corporal chastisement makes Everyman's seem a holiday in comparison: whereas Everyman scourges himself, Red Cross dons sackcloth and ashes, fasts, has his wounds plucked with hot pincers, is whipped, bathes his wounds in salt water, and generally plunges himself into a self-chastisement more reminiscent of medieval Catholicism than of any practice among Reformation Protestants. Virgil Whitaker tries to deny that Spenser portrays confession as a sacrament, distinguishing the image of confession in Canto x from the images of baptism and the eucharist in Canto xi:

> [B]aptism and the Lord's Supper are clearly indicated as crucial steps in the final conflict with the Dragon, whereas Penance, although it is one of the Catholic sacraments, seems to be separated from them and treated in Canto x as a spiritual exercise.[32]

But surely Spenser separates penance from these other two sacraments because of the demands of his narrative: Red Cross could hardly take time out during his battle with the dragon to talk to a priest. Nor does Spenser portray confession as a mere spiritual exercise to ease the knight's conscience. Una, hearing the knight shriek in these torments, forbears from interfering because "well she wist, *his crime could else be never cleare*" (28.9, italics mine). Una's reasoning suggests not Protestant but Roman Catholic teachings on expiation of sin. Roman Catholic doctrine insisted that, if reception of penance is physically possible, then a sinner must receive the sacrament in order to be forgiven: "This sacrament of penance is for those who have fallen after baptism necessary for salvation" (Decrees of Trent XIV.ii). Calvin, on the other hand, is representative of Protestants in denying that confession to a priest is necessary:

> Now, when they prescribe as a necessary prerequisite to pardon that which God has chosen should be free, I maintain that it is an intolerable sacrilege; for nothing is more peculiarly the prerogative of God than the remission of sins, in which our salvation consists. (*Institutes* III.iv.24)

Furthermore, Red Cross's reception of penance actually works; the sacrament cleanses the knight of his sins. Spenser writes that the process of Penance, Remorse, Repentance, and Amendment "in short space . . . did to health restore/The man" (27.8–9). In Calvin's theology, intrinsic sacramental efficacy contradicts absolute predestination and reprobation, for one whose salvation is unalterably preordained has no absolute need of sacraments, which are seals or emblems of invisible grace.[33] Calvin writes: "[C]onfidence of salvation does not depend on the participation of the sacraments, as though that constituted our justification, which we know to be placed in Christ alone" (IV.xiv.14).

Not only the images of good works and sacraments but also a clear reference to free will suggest that Spenser's Augustinianism is not Calvinistic. When Una asks Fidelia to instruct Red Cross in theology, she teaches him "Of God, of grace, of iustice, of free will" (x.19.6). We do not know exactly what she says to the knight about free will, but the language Spenser uses implies its existence: a Calvinistic Fidelia would teach about the *loss* or *absence* of free will. Fidelia's instruction bears fruit: Red Cross's justification follows from his free choices to do works of mercy and to receive the sacrament of penance. By countering the Calvinist opening stanza of Canto x with Roman Catholic images of the seven corporal works and the sacrament of penance, Spenser refuses to accept completely either a Calvinist or a Roman Catholic reading of Augustine's doctrines on predestination, free will, and the sacraments. It remains to be shown how Canto x is part of the larger pattern of Red Cross's adventures in Book I.

The combination of Calvinist theology and Roman Catholic imagery forms part of a larger pattern of divine grace and human effort in

Book I, in which predestination and free will paradoxically work together in the process of justification and sanctification. Spenser's individualistic reading of Augustine shapes all of the spiritual adventures of Book I. Wherever Spenser shows Red Cross Knight putting forth effort, the poet adds a phrase or passage to remind the reader of God's sovereignty and initiative. Canto x reverses the pattern, beginning with a stanza emphasizing God's sovereignty, then proceeding to suggest, through the most convenient imagery available, the contribution that human effort and free will have to make. Spenser found medieval Catholic images useful because Roman Catholicism insisted so strongly, through its doctrines of free will, sacramental efficacy, and salvation by faith *and* works, on human effort cooperating with grace. In other cantos, Spenser implies free will without resorting to Roman Catholic imagery, but nowhere does he present either predestination or free will without presenting or implying the other.

Like Augustine, at one time a Manichaean, Red Cross Knight's first encounter with evil is his near-entrapment by Error. During this battle, Una urges her knight to add faith unto his force (i.19.3), implying that, although God has already provided Red Cross with faith (the shield), the knight must play a part by remembering that faith when under trial as well as by employing his force (actions, works). Red Cross overcomes the vomit of foul doctrines by faith, which he "provides *on his own responsibility* at the urging of Una" (italics mine).[34] Whitaker argues therefore that Spenser's allegory involves the "somewhat illogical" adaptation of the Roman Catholic belief in cooperation with grace to the Protestant teaching of justification by faith alone.[35] Spenser's allegory, however illogical, is biblical: Ephesians 2.8 insists that salvation through faith is God's gift and not a reward for good deeds; yet James 2.24 asserts that a person is justified by his works and not by faith alone.[36] The seeming contradiction between these two biblical passages points to the mysterious compatibility of divine grace and human effort. When Red Cross finally triumphs over Error, Una greets his victory with "Faire knight, borne under happy starre" (27.3), not to deny the merit of Red Cross's effort, but to remind Red Cross, of who, ultimately, is responsible for all spiritual victories. Thus predestination and human effort work together in Red Cross's victory. This first struggle in Red Cross's spiritual quest sustains neither the Protestant doctrine of justification by faith alone (Article XI and *Institutes* III.xii) nor the Roman Catholic doctrine of justification by faith and works (Decrees of Trent VI.7, 10) but, rather, suggests the patristic doctrine which gave rise both to the

Protestant and to the Roman Catholic view: Augustine's belief that human effort remains viable only within the context of grace.

The Orgoglio episode illustrates what Anthea Hume calls "the central theme of sixteenth-century Protestantism—the radical dependence of the individual on unmerited grace for his conversion and justification."[37] At first glance, the episode seems an exception to the pattern of predestination and free will working simultaneously, because Red Cross does not appear to contribute anything to his own rescue. Arthur, symbol of divine grace breaking into history, rescues Red Cross from Orgoglio's dungeon, into which Red Cross has been cast through his own fault (sin). Arthur simply hauls the captive knight back up into the light. Three details in this episode, however, speak in favor of human effort. First, the dwarf, the knight's own natural reason, brings truth (Una) and grace (Arthur) to his rescue—a very un-Calvinistic process indeed, as Nelan notes,[38] and one suggesting an extraordinary doctrine if we take it literally: that human reason can effectively make contact with truth and that truth can call on grace. Second, Red Cross responds to Arthur's voice (viii.38), alerting Arthur to his location in the dungeon. Third, even if divine grace must act first in the process of justification, that does not preclude a subsequent role for human effort. "Free will is not taken away because it is assisted, but is assisted in order that it not be taken away".[39] Immediately after the rescue, Arthur admonishes Red Cross: "Henceforth sir knight, take to you wonted strength, / And maister these mishaps with patient might" (45.1–2). Arthur's words imply the human responsibility to cooperate with grace. William Marshall points out that the Calvinistic Forty-Two Articles of 1552 say that grace works "in" us but the more ambiguous Thirty-Nine Articles of 1563 say that grace works "with" us (Article X), just as Arthur works with but not in those he rescues, offering but not forcing grace.[40]

Red Cross's temptation by Despair, which Paul Siegal claims could only have been written by a Calvinist brooding on predestination,[41] contains both a heavy emphasis on predestination and also a role for human effort. Una plays a crucial part in the Despair canto, remaining silent during nearly the whole of the temptation scene, but finally snatching the knife from Red Cross and berating him. Her timely intervention saves the knight from himself, in what is surely an instance of predestined grace; the real difference between Red Cross and the suicide of Sir Terwin is that Red Cross, by God's grace, happens to have Una by his side.[42] Una's assurance to Red Cross that he is among the elect agrees with Calvinist doctrine and contradicts the Decrees of Trent, which warn that "No one . . . ought in regard to the sacred mystery of divine predestination, so far presume as to state with absolute certainty that he is among the number of the predestined" (VI.xii). (This warning is all that the documents of Trent have to say about predestination.) Calvin writes on human knowledge of predestination: "The great and secret counsel has been revealed. The Lord knows who are his, but what was known to God has been revealed to men" (*Institutes* III.xxii.10).

> For as the Father has determined to unite to the body of his Son all who are the objects of his eternal choice . . . we have a testimony sufficiently clear and strong, that if we have communion with Christ, we are written in the book of life. (III.xxiv.5)

Thus Una is able to assure Red Cross: "In heauenly mercies hast thou not a part?/Why shouldst thou then despeire, that chosen art?" (I.ix.53.4–5).[43] But Una speaks to urge Red Cross to take crucial action, to "come away" (53.1), to "Arise, Sir knight arise, and leue this cursed place" (53.9). "So vp he rose," continues Spenser, "and thence amounted streight" (54.1), demonstrating the human effort by which Red Cross saves himself and is saved.

Following the temptation by Despair comes Canto x with its Calvinist opening and Roman Catholic imagery. Red Cross's spiritual rejuvenation in the House of Holiness prepares him for the climactic battle against the dragon. In this battle, the culmination of the knight's spiritual odyssey, St. George performs one of the corporal works of mercy, the release of prisoners.[44] Corporal works as a cause of justification presuppose free will, but throughout Canto xi Spenser interpolates suggestions of divine destiny into the general tenor of heroic human effort. St. George could not survive and triumph without the sacraments. Although sacramental efficacy theoretically precludes absolute predestination,[45] Spenser in this canto reconciles the two, as did St. Augustine, who denied any actual discrepancy. For Augustine, God's prescience and predestination extend not only to the salvation of the elect but also to the means that make possible a righteous life, so that in Augustine's writings, unlike those of some Protestant theologians, predestination does not undercut sacramental efficacy: the believer must depend upon both the grace of God and the ordinances of the Church.[46] Augustine defends both baptismal efficacy and predestination when he writes:

> Now those very persons, who think it unjust that infants which depart this life without the grace of Christ should be deprived not only of the kingdom of God, into which they themselves admit that none but such as are regenerated through baptism can enter, but also of eternal life and salvation,—when they ask how it can be just that one man should be freed from original sin and another not, although the condition of both is the same, might answer their own question, in accordance with their own opinion of how it can be so frequently just and right that one should have baptism administered to him whereby to enter the kingdom of God, and another not be so favored, although the case of both is alike.[47]

On the first day of battle against the dragon, the knight, after long and arduous combat, finds himself "Faint, wearie, sore, emboyled, greiued, brent / With heat, toyle, wounds, armes, smart, and inward fire" (xi. 28.1–2). Struck by the dragon, the knight falls backwards into a stream coming from a "springing well" (xi.30.3) rightly named "*The well of life*" (30.9, author's italics). Because the water of the well washes away the knight's sins and regenerates him as if he were a new man, some critics believe that this well symbolizes baptism, which in Roman Catholic theology forgives original and actual sin and makes the recipient a new creation.[48] Spenser coyly informs us that the well just happened to be in the right place at the right time: "It fortuned (as fair it then befell)" (20.1) implies that the knight's fall into the well involves more than mere fortune. But however predestined the knight's baptism is, there is no doubt that it is also efficacious: when battle resumes the next day, the knight rises "new-borne" (34.9) because "vnto life the dead it [the well] could restore, / And guilt of sinfull crimes cleane wash away" (30.1–2). Augustine insisted many times in his writings that, apart from baptism, "there is no other valid means of making Christians and remitting sins."[49] When St. George recoils from the dragon's fiery breath on the second day, the same paradoxical theology pertains: "It chaunst (eternall God that chaunce did guide)" (45.7) that the knight falls into a "trickling streame of Balme, most soueraine" (48.2). Spenser, no longer so reticent, informs us plainly that the knight was predestined to fall into the stream of balm and thus recover from the dragon's assault. But the balm, like the well, is efficacious ("soueraine"): "Life and long health that gratious ointment gaue, / And deadly woundes could heal, and reare againe / The senselesse corse appointed for the graue./Into that same he fell: which did from death him saue" (48.6–9). The balm is "gratious" because it actually conveys grace to the recipient. Whether this balm represents the Lord's Supper or merely the anointing with oil which follows immersion in water during baptism,[50] its effects are unmistakably sacramental. And those effects seem to transpire *ex opere operato,* as Roman Catholics claimed: since Red Cross is unconscious when he receives the balm, he cannot be receiving the sacrament through that conscious faith which Calvinists believed necessary to make the sacrament beneficial:

> But they [sacraments] avail and profit nothing unless received in faith. As with wine or oil or some other liquid, no matter how much you pour out, it will flow away and disappear unless the mouth of the vessel to receive it is open; moreover, the vesel will be splashed over on the outside, but will still remain void and empty. (*Institutes* IV.xiv.17)

For Red Cross, however, a splashing on the outside, even when he is unconscious, produces some astonishing results in the inward man. The knight almost seems to be playing the part of a newly baptized infant, unaware of the indelible change in his soul that his baptism has caused.

Canto xi ends with Una's praise of both God and her knight for the victory: "Then God she praysd, and thankt her faithfull knight,/That had atchieu'd so great a conquest by his might" (55. 8–9). The happy ambiguity of "his might,"[51] which could refer either to God or to the knight, expresses nicely the paradox of God's sovereignty coexisting with human free will and responsibility. The last word on the battle comes from the victor knight himself, not in Book I but in the first canto of Book II: "More than goodwill to me attribute nought:/For all I did, I did but as I ought" (II.i.33.4–5). Unlike the opening stanza of Book I Canto x, these words imply that we can and should attribute at least good will to the knight. This summary of the battle admits the part played by human effort but locates that effort within the context of divine providence, as Augustine did: "[A] man is assisted by grace, in order that his will may not be uselessly commanded".[52] Book I Canto xi takes the doctrine of predestination and the images of free will and human effort introduced in Canto x and reconciles them in the knight's final victory over the devil. By asserting both human responsibility and divine sovereignty, Spenser insists on the mystery of the salvific process. Red Cross Knight becomes holy *because* his good works cannot be separated from God's; St. George defeats the dragon because he becomes an allegory of Christ.

Book I of *The Faerie Queene,* then, revolves around Spenser's reading of Augustinian theology, a pattern of free will operating paradoxically within the context of divine election and grace. In this light, the odd inconsistencies in the implications of certain images and statements take on significance, for they participate in the theological paradox which Spenser uses as a poetic structure for Red Cross's quest for holiness. In the Letter to the Philippians, St. Paul urges: "[W]ith feare and trembling work your saluation. For it is God that worketh in you. . . ."[53] These words contain the seeds of the paradoxical theology which came down to sixteenth century Christianity by way of St. Augustine, a theology which acknowledges the difficulty of separating man's good works from God's good works because man is God's creation. Augustine comments on Paul's theology: "Paul does not take away freedom of the will, but says our will does not suffice unless God helps us, making us merciful so that we can do good works through the gift of the Holy Spirit."[54] Augustine's comment could stand as a guide to the theology of Book I of *The Faerie Queene.*

Vanderbilt University

NOTES

1. C. S. Lewis, *The Allegory of Love: A Study in Medieval Tradition* (Oxford: Oxford University Press, 1943), p. 322.
2. All references to *The Faerie Queene* are from A. C. Hamilton's edition (New York: Longman's, 1977). Professor Harold Weatherby of Vanderbilt University, who has been most helpful to me in my writing of this essay, suggested the resemblance of I.x.51. 7–9 to intercession of saints.
3. Alan Sinfield, "Bead-men," in *The Spenser Encyclopedia,* ed. A. C. Hamilton, Donald Cheney, W. F. Blissett, et al. (Toronto: University of Toronto Press, 1990), p. 81.
4. A. S. P. Woodhouse, "Nature and Grace in *The Faerie Queene,*" *ELH,* 16 (1949), p. 225.
5. Eugene TeSelle, *Augustine the Theologian,* (New York: Herder and Herder, 1970), pp. 324–28.
6. As quoted by Jaroslav Pelikan in *Reformation of Church and Dogma (1300–1700),* vol. 4 of *The Christian Tradition: A History of the Development of Doctrine* (Chicago: University of Chicago Press, 1983), pp. 224, 227. Pelikan quotes from *Corpus Reformatorum* (Berlin and Leipzig, 1834–).
7. All quotations of Calvin are from *Institutes of the Christian Religion* translated by John Allen (Philadelphia: Presbyterian Board of Christian Education, 1936).
8. Pelikan, p. 225.
9. Pelikan, pp. 252–53.

10. To mention only the more prominent proponents of Spenser's Puritanism or Calvinism. See Anthea Hume, *Edmund Spenser: Protestant Poet* (Cambridge: Cambridge University Press, 1984); Daniel W. Doerksen, "Recharting the *Via Media* of Spenser and Herbert," *Renaissance and Reformation,* 8.3 (1984), pp. 215–25; Alan Sinfield, *Literature in Protestant England 1560–1660* (Totowa: Barnes & Noble, 1983); James D. Boulger, *The Calvinist Temper in English Poetry* (The Hague: Mouton, 1980); Paul N. Siegal, "Spenser and the Calvinist View of Life," *SP,* 41 (1944), 201–22; F. M. Padelford, "Spenser and the Theology of Calvin," *MP,* 12 (1914), pp. 1–18, and "The Spiritual Allegory of the *Faerie Queene,* Book I," *JEGP,* 22 (1923), pp. 1–17; and Lilian Winstanley, "Spenser and Puritanism," *ML*·2, 3 (1900), pp. 6–16 and 103–10. Padelford does admit that Spenser's sacramentalism is not completely compatible with Calvin's views. Virgil K. Whitaker, *The Religious Basis of Spenser's Thought,* Stanford University Publications, Language and Literature, vol. 7, no. 3 (Stanford: Stanford University Press, 1950) argues that Spenser was a *via media* Anglican opposed to Puritanism although critical of ecclesiastical corruption. D. Douglas Waters, in *Edmund Spenser's Theology,* an unpublished doctoral dissertation (Vanderbilt University, 1960), claims that Spenser follows the French theologian De Mornay and other liberal Huguenot Augustinians. Robert Ellrodt, *Neoplatonism in the Poetry of Edmund Spenser* (Folcroft, Pa.: Folcroft Press, 1969), p. 198, concludes that Spenser was a Calvinist in mind but not in heart, a Protestant "in the ethical, not in the religious sphere." John N. King, *Spenser's Poetry and the Reformation Tradition* (Princeton: Princeton University Press, 1990), p. 9. argues that Spenser was the Elizabethan equivalent of a Low Churchman and then suggests that efforts to align him with Puritan, Catholic, or Anglican theology fail because the distinction between Puritans and Anglicans is anachronistic and because of a general Christian agreement on many fundamental issues. I would add that that general theological foundation, at least in the West, was largely Augustinian.

11. The phrase *ex opere operato,* common since the thirteenth century and used by the Council of Trent, expresses the Roman Catholic notion of sacramental causality: the sacramental rite actually bestows the grace it signifies. "Magical" is Calvin's bitter denunciation of this conception of the sacraments (*Institutes* IV.xiv.14).

12. Calvin may leave room for some sort of sacramental efficacy as means by which predestination is often implemented in human life. But Calvin denies that sacraments are necessary for salvation, and any Calvinistic sacramental efficacy would differ from the more "magical" efficacy of Catholic sacraments which seems to be at work in Red Cross's rejuvenation. Padelford, "Theology," pp. 6–7, a vocal proponent of Spenser's Calvinism, admits that Spenser grants the sacraments a primary office as vehicles of grace which Calvin did not.

13. E. Hickey, "Catholicity in Spenser," *American Catholic Ouarterly Review,* 32 (1907), pp. 490–502; Thomas P. Nelan, *Catholic Doctrines in Spenser's Poetry,* doctoral dissertation (New York University, 1943); Beatrice Ricks, "Catholic Sacramental and Symbolism in *The Faerie Queene,*" *JEGP,* 52 (1953), 322–31; Jerome Oetgen, "Spenser's Treatment of Monasticism in Book I of *The Faerie Oueene,*" *American Benedictine Review,* 22 (1971), pp. 109–20. To be fair, I should add that none of these writers claims that Spenser's theology was *entirely* Roman Catholic.

14. Whitaker, p. 173, summarizes this position best:

"Spenser adhered consistently to the Elizabethan Settlement both in its retention of episcopacy and traditional ceremonial and in its rejection of fundamental Calvinist teachings. His sympathies apparently lay, both in liturgical practice and in theology, with the conservative party in the Anglican Church; and his few deviations from Anglican doctrine were Catholic rather than Calvinistic in origin."
15. Padelford, "Theology," p. 9.
16. *Canons and Decrees of the Council of Trent* translated by H. J. Schroeder (St. Louis: B. Herder, 1941). All subsequent quotations of the Trentine documents are from this edition.
17. R. Headlam Wells, "Spenser's Christian Knight: Erasmian Theology in *The Faerie Queene,* Book I," *Anglia,* 97 (1979), p. 365.
18. Jerome Oetgen, "Spenser's Treatment of Monasticism in Book I of The Faerie Queene," *American Benedictine Review,* 22 (1971), p. 113.
19. Charles E. Mounts, "Spenser's Seven Beads-Men and the Corporal Works of Mercy," *PMLA,* 54 (1939), pp. 975–80.
20. The passage reads:

> Nor, indeed, is that opinion of Augustine, or at least his manner of expression, to be altogether admitted. For though he excellently despoils man of all the praise of righteousness, and ascribes the whole to the grace of God, yet he refers grace to sanctification, in which we are regenerated by the Spirit to newness of life.

21. Wells, p. 363, remarks:

> Although it would be wrong to say that Spenser does not concern himself with the question of salvation, this is neither his first nor his last concern. What he is primarily concerned to portray is not the *salvation* of the Christian Knight, but his *sanctification,* his realization of an ideal of *pietas,* or "holiness."

> Wells's remark assumes, in a Calvinistic way, that salvation through God's remission of our sins (imputed righteousness) can be separated from sanctification (our moral regeneration and progress in holiness). I am arguing that Augustine and Spenser make no such distinction between religion and morality.

22. Hume, pp. 70–71.
23. Waters, p. 217
24. Harold L. Weatherby, "What Spenser Meant by Holinesse: Baptism in Book One of *The Faerie Queene,*" *SP,* 84 (1987), p. 296.
25. Whitaker, p. 46.
26. See *Institutes* III.xiv.9, for example, which ends: "We have now ascertained, that there is not a single action performed by the saints, which, if judged according to its intrinsic merit, does not justly deserve to be rewarded with shame."

Thomas Aquinas, *Summa Theologica,* I–II, Q. 114, A. 3, says that a person can merit eternal life not absolutely but condignly, proportionate to human capacity. Perhaps Aquinas' view is not so far from Calvin's in the final analysis.

27. Mounts, p. 975; Nelan, pp. 53–55; Whitaker, p. 46; and Waters, p. 201 all make this point.
28. Ellrodt, p. 197.
29. Wells, p. 364.
30. Waters, p. 305.
31. Hickey, pp. 499–500.
32. Whitaker, p. 49.
33. See William H. Marshall, "Calvin, Spenser, and the Major Sacraments," *MLN,* 74 (1959), pp. 97–101.
34. Virgil K. Whitaker, "The Theological Structure of *The Faerie Queene,* Book I," *ELH,* 19 (1952), p. 156.
35. Whitaker, "Structure," p. 156. More specifically, Whitaker likens Hooker's notions of free will and right reason to St. Thomas Aquinas' four justifiers (*Summa Theologica* I–II, Q. 113, A. 6), "of which two, an infusion of grace and a remission of sins, are God's gifts, and two, a free choice of God by faith and a free choice against sin, must be man's contribution."
36. Roman Catholics often quoted James 2.24 to refute Protestant assertions of salvation through faith alone. Augustine distinguishes saving faith, active in love, from dead faith or the faith of demons, mere intellectual knowledge. Calvin argues in the *Institutes* (III.xvii.11–12) that James means that true faith always manifests itself in works.
37. Hume, p. 91.
38. Nelan, p. 325.
39. Augustine, *On Romans* translated by Paula Fredricksen Landes (Chico: Scholars Press, 1982), p. 440.
40. Marshall, pp. 99–100.
41. Siegal, p. 206.
42. Thomas P. Roche, Jr., "The Menace of Despair and Arthur's Vision, *Faerie Queene* I.9," *Spenser Studies,* 4 (1984), p. 86.
43. Marshall, p. 100, suggests that "chosen" in this passage means chosen in the "Anglican" sense that all in the Church are elect if they choose to save themselves by an exercise of free will.
44. Carol V. Kaske, "The Dragon's Spark and Sting and the Structure of Red Cross's Dragon-Fight: The *Faerie Queene* I, xi–xii," *SP,* 66 (1969), p. 635.
45. Marshall, pp. 97–101.
46 Pelikan, Jaroslav, *The Emergence of the Catholic Tradition (100–600),* vol. 1 of *The Christian Tradition: A History of the Development of Doctrine* (Chicago: University of Chicago Press 1971), p. 302.
47. Augustine, *De Peccatorum Meritis et Remissione, et de Baptismo Parvulorum* in *A Select Library of the Nicene and Post-Nicene Fathers of the Christian Church,* vol. V, edited by Philip Schaff (New York: Christian Literature Company, 1887), p. 26.
48. In *Allegorical Imagery: Some Medieval Books and Their Posterity* (Princeton: Princeton University Press, 1966), p. 110, Rosamond Tuve objects that, as Red Cross already

has studied in the House of Holiness and fought the devil for one whole day, he must have been baptized before. In "What Spenser Meant by Holiness: Baptism in Book One of *The Faerie Queene*," *SP*, 84 (1987), pp. 286–307, Harold Weatherby shows that Tuve bases her objection on Reformation baptismal practices, whereas, in the ancient Church, adult catechumens received baptism on Holy Saturday, and only after a lengthy period of Lenten preparation and instruction resembling Red Cross's sojourn in the House of Holiness. But Weatherby's explanation does not entirely solve the problem, because Red Cross has been wearing the armor of faith since the beginning of the poem, which implies his previous baptism. Because of the difficulties involved in interpreting the well as baptism, some critics have proposed alternative readings. D. Douglas Waters, for example, in "Spenser's 'Well of Life' and 'Tree of Life' Once More," *MP*, 67 (1969), pp. 68–69, sees the well as the Word of God, i.e., the Bible.

This issue raises the question of narrative consistency. Whitaker argues that "The Theological Structure of *The Faerie Queene*, Book I" follows not a realistic sequence of events in the knight's life but rather the order of topics in a typical Reformation confessional. Carol Kaske's article on "The Dragon's Spark and Sting" proposes that Red Cross on the first day of the dragon fight represents unregenerate natural man in need of grace.

Thomas Roche has suggested to me that the solution lies in distinguishing the moral (tropological) from the allegorical reference. On the moral level, where Red Cross stands for Everyman, the well must represent grace in general aiding the individual soul in extremity. On the allegorical level, the well represents the sacrament of baptism as an office of the Church. My point about the well and the balm as sacraments is that they are efficacious *ex opere operato,* yet also predestined; it matters little what level of reference is operating.

49. Augustine, *Peccatorum,* p. 78.

50. Nelan, p. 402–7.

51. A.C. Hamilton notes this ambiguity in his marginal comments in his edition, pp. 17, 154, as does Paul J. Alpers, *The Poetry of* The Faerie Queene (Princeton: Princeton University Press, 1967), p. 336.

52. Augustine, *De Gratia et Libero Arbitrio* in *A Select Library of the Nicene and Post-Nicene Fathers of the Christian Church,* vol. V, edited by Philip Schaff (New York: Christian Literature Company, 1887), p. 447.

53. Philippians 2.12–13 (Bishops' Bible).

54. Augustine, *On Romans,* p. 35.

CHRISTOPHER MARTIN

Turning Others' Leaves: Astrophil's Untimely Defeat

THE THIRTY-THIRD SONNET of *Astrophil and Stella* reaches back to what seems a time ponderously remote from the speaker's benighted present. It arrives as an abrupt and rather startling disclosure:

> I might, unhappie word, o me, I might,
> And then would not, or could not see my blisse:
> Till now, wrapt in a most infernall night,
> I find how heav'nly day wretch I did misse.
>   Hart rent thy selfe, thou doest thy selfe but right,
> No lovely *Paris* made thy *Hellen* his:
> No force, no fraud, robd thee of thy delight,
> Nor Fortune of thy fortune author is:
>   But to my selfe my selfe did give the blow,
> While too much wit (forsooth) so troubled me,
> That I respects for both our sakes must show:
> And yet could not by rising Morne foresee
>   How faire a day was neare, o punisht eyes,
>   That I had been more foolish or more wise.[1]

These verses harbor a tremendous cargo of pain; for while the experience of failure is, to a competitive temperament, always intolerable, the onus of self-defeat—of having let slip a precious opportunity to secure one's most desired goal—weighs upon its victim with a suffocating heaviness. Astrophil struggles here to articulate a regret almost too deep for words, as the first line's stumbling circularity attests. Although he never can bring himself to say explicitly what it is he "might" have done, the rest of the poem strives to unpack the implications of this "unhappie" word to his current plight. The effort marks an especially intense moment in Sidney's most celebrated literary achievement.

Arresting in its own right, the poem also bids for a privileged space within the broader framework of Astrophil's emotional self-revelation. Insofar as the sequence plays out what Nashe calls in his preface to the pirated 1591 edition a "tragicommody of loue," AS 33's retrospection affords precious insight into the nature of this lover's predicament. We can, I propose, best make sense of Astrophil's poetic reflexes by returning to the circumstance encountered here, a circumstance which both defines with greater precision the disputed function of time in the work, and further points up the remarkable subtlety of Sidney's original foreconceit. Where the self-doubt and psychological contortions Astrophil betrays are already evident in Petrarch, and even the anti-Petrarchism he notoriously affects had become long before this a common pose, the image of a lover who has in fact had the chance to gain his lady, but has unwittingly missed the occasion, charges the sequence with a distinctive poignancy. Although, as Germaine Warkentin has recently noted, two of Sidney's immediate predecessors had anticipated AS 33 in isolated remonstrances against bashfulness,[2] it remained for the younger poet to explore and develop the situation's dramatic potential—a task to which his temperament was, I will suggest finally, especially well suited. AS 33's admission highlights ironically the surface of a work whose individual gestures prove not so much consecutive rhetorical moments in a straightforward attempt at seduction—Richard Lanham's provocative thesis[3]—as components in a grand project of recovery, a quest that is itself shadowed by the burdensome recollection of an opportunity forgone.

Just over a decade ago, A. C. Hamilton challenged the commonplace that time never becomes a significant motif in *Astrophil and Stella* as it does traditionally in Petrarchan love poetry.[4] David Kalstone, for example, had asserted that "Sidney's sonnets noticeably lack a sense of time and the bearing of time upon love," and the "carelessness" about time

Dorothy Connell finds in the sequence supports her belief that it "is not only the interest in immortality which is lacking in Sidney's poetry, but also the consciousness of mortality."[5] By contrast, Hamilton discerns a more subtle manifestation: Astrophil's absorption in the "presentness" of the moment—his refusal to adopt an extratemporal perspective that might justify or redeem his current suffering—anchors each of his poetic reflections firmly within a temporal continuum. Looking to a poem like AS 47, wherein the speaker clocks his own shifting perspective literally line by line, from minute to minute, Hamilton considers time "not so much a theme . . . as an actual presence, the medium within which the poet writes."[6] Jane Hedley's recent comments echo this idea: Astrophil "speaks out of the mood of the moment; and so for the reader there is a very strong sense of the passage of time, as successive sonnets afford access to successive moments in his emotional and interpersonal life."[7] But, though I concur with Hamilton's theory—the modesty with which he presses his claims if anything underrates their urgency—my own sense of time's presence in the work generates, less abstractly, from the crucial instant this reader strangely overlooks: Astrophil's own recollection of how temporal concerns came to intrude upon his greener sensibility in the first place.

If Hamilton's silence about AS 33 seems puzzling, it nonetheless conforms to a broader interpretive trend. Despite its obvious forcefulness, the poem has endured an uneven reception among Sidneians. Almost a century of sporadic but disorienting controversy over its exact significance has yielded, in the past twenty-five years, to apparent critical indifference. The lapse coincides with a shift away from earlier suppositions about the author's artistic purpose. To an audience that understood *Astrophil and Stella* as poetic autobiography, AS 33 clearly announced Sidney's genuine remorse for failing to woo Penelope Devereux in time, before her unhappy marriage to Lord Rich had aborted his former prospects. So deeply did this presumption strike root that when in 1877 Alexander Grosart first contested the poem's import, historical rather than literary concerns governed his objections. Since there exists no independent evidence that Sidney in fact could once have entertained marriage with Penelope, Grosart reasoned, these lines cannot refer to belated courtship. His premise compels a perversely narrow construction of Sidney's metaphors ("'Fitly-punisht eyes' . . . is an absurd phrase if he were lamenting his loss in not marrying her") and the conclusion that AS 33 expresses nothing more than Astrophil's annoyance at having missed "some especial occasion when he might have met"

Stella.[8] Like the few who have since taken his reduction seriously, Grosart neglects to dissociate Sidney from Astrophil or to imagine that the author could, regardless of his own sexual pursuits, invent such a situation for his fictional persona to suffer.[9] Even Ephim Fogel, who in the last extended treatment of AS 33 discusses this "biographical fallacy," cannot effectively think free of its unsubstantiated identifications.[10]

Yet as credence in the biographical speculation encumbering the poem has eroded, so, strangely, has scholarly comment.[11] The prevailing reticence intimates that, although Grosart's "minority reading" is easily discounted, there remains little clarity about AS 33's relationship to its larger context. No one has adequately dealt with Fogel's one formidable protest, namely that "it is very curious indeed that an event supposedly so central to the story as his failure to marry Stella in good time should be so utterly devoid of structural and thematic consequences."[12] But what I think distinguishes Sidney's project is just the way he locates his speaker's psyche within the purposeful and emotionally devastating image of loss, orchestrating the various movements of his sequence around this key note. Its "consequences" will in fact reverberate in virtually every corner of Astrophil's expression. He mourns a procrastination that has cost him his very sense of integrity, something far more dear than any temporary vision of Stella: *Hart rent thy selfe.* Whatever elusive (or illusory) prospect of success may fuel his erotic enterprise, a grim retrospect dogs Astrophil every step of the way.

The awareness of squandered potential focusing AS 33's *energia*—the lover's knowledge of "how heav'nly day wretch I did misse"—inflicts a psychological wound that rankles more painfully than the cruel chastity he attributes to Stella. The accusatory gaze he now beholds in the mirror of his former imperception discovers Astrophil as his own worst enemy. Sidney's protagonist lacks an antagonist; he can find no external agency to blame, for he suffers defeat not at the hands of a "rich fool" who has since claimed the woman he covets, but by way of a humiliating passivity blinding him to "How faire a day was neare." The aggressive candor with which he appropriates responsibility disarms: "No lovely *Paris* made thy *Hellen* his: / No force, no fraud, robd thee of thy delight, / Nor Fortune of thy fortune author is." At once arrogant and confessional, these central lines concentrate Astrophil's furor as he struggles vainly to uphold a fiction of the self-control he has long since relinquished.

Astrophil's denial of Fortune's "authority" exposes something crucial about the pressures determining his outlook. Fortune had always been conceived as an essentially time-bound figure, her cycles rigidly inscribed in the unfolding pages of personal and cultural history. But under Italian humanism's revisionary gaze, prevailing attitudes toward this temporal dimension began to alter significantly. As Frederick Kiefer describes in his useful study, "people began to conceive of Fortune's nature in a strikingly new way; they came to regard her as a less menacing and more tractable figure than she seemed in the Middle Ages."[13] Now, Fortune was thought to open narrow windows of opportunity which, if recognized and exploited by her human vassals, might enable them to win a measure of control over—or at least a sense of participation in—destiny's workings. This shift is registered most dramatically by the period's iconographic fusion of *Fortuna* and *Occasio,* wherein Fortune appropriates the traditional forelock and other representative accouterments of her sister goddess. In Kiefer's words, "the conflation with Occasion rests upon the assumption that, while Fortune impinges upon him in a powerful and perhaps dangerous fashion, man still has the capacity to decide how he will respond to change."[14] Along with this more auspicious characteristic, however, Fortune also inherits the companionship of *Metanoea* or "Paenitentia," the figure who remained behind once Occasion had passed to plague those failing to grasp their moment of favor[15]: a heightened sense of responsibility also enhances the anxiety of personal failure. Entertaining just such a relationship with Fortune, Astrophil utters his punishing recriminations under the scourge of an ever-watchful penitence. Lamenting how "to my selfe my selfe did give the blow, / While too much wit (forsooth) so troubled me," he beholds his former "might" or potential dwindle to an "unhappie word" beneath the strokes of his truant pen. He will indeed "author" himself, but the tale will be one of isolation and impotence, since the heart into which he looks is "rent" between the consciousness of former possibility and present deprivation.

From the vantage of this poem's vital admission we may better appreciate the ironies conditioning various postures Astrophil assumes throughout the sequence. Self-laceration marks the very inception of his literary endeavor recounted in the famous first sonnet, which finds the speaker, as he tells us, "beating my selfe for spite." The description wonderfully characterizes his entire project's deep ambivalence: the same verses through which he hopes to secure Stella's grace will also immerse him in a joyless introspection. On the one hand, Astrophil has wasted time in tedious research, "Oft turning others' leaves, to see if thence would flow / Some fresh and fruitfull showers upon my sunne-burn'd braine," impatient to inaugurate the progress he forecasts with such meticulous care: "Pleasure might cause her reade, reading might make her know, / Knowledge might pitie winne, and pitie grace obtaine." But on the other hand, for all its liberating efficacy, the Muse's command that he look in his heart and write is equally an unwelcome one. Scrambling through the pages of other texts, any writer knows, can be as much an evasion tactic as a legitimate quest for inspiration. Astrophil's heart, both inscribed with a portrait of his lady and encumbered with a debilitating recollection of personal failure, is the last place he may wish to look. To achieve originality, the poet must return to the origin of his own pain, in an unmediated encounter with the memory of his early forfeiture.

In context, it should hardly surprise us that what Astrophil first spies as he directs his gaze inward is the untimely evolution of his feelings for Stella. This was decidedly not, he makes clear in sonnet 2, a love at first sight:

> I saw and liked, I liked but loved not,
> I loved, but straight did not what *Love* decreed:
> At length to *Love's* decrees, I forc'd, agreed,
> Yet with repining at so partiall lot.

Hamilton has remarked how Sidney's approach diverges from the conventional Petrarchan *innamoramento,* passion's slow ignition as opposed to the Italian poet's piercing, instantaneous rapture.[16] But if we are impressed by his atypical response here, the lover is oppressed by the thought that such an immediate reflex might have—and should have—preserved him from the anguish he now experiences. As it stands, he has lost his time and his "libertie"; consequently, his goal has professedly become one of self-deception, to "employ the remnant of my wit, / To make my selfe beleeve, that all is well, / While with a feeling skill I paint my hell." The "too much wit" that had at an earlier date crippled him is now itself impoverished, sufficient only to mock the futility of his maneuvers.

Astrophil buffers his shamed self-awareness by means of the irritable disclaimers he recurrently voices. One of the sequence's most widely discussed features, its sonnets on poetry, speaks directly to this concern. The ironies informing Astrophil's defensive impulses, especially those regarding the uniqueness of his literary stance, run deeper than his tendency to utilize the same tropes he openly disdains. Sonnet 3's sardonic dismissal of "*Pindar's* Apes," the rejection of shopworn references to "living deaths, deare wounds, faire streames and freesing fires" in sonnet 6, and ridicule for those who seek to resuscitate "poore *Petrarch's* long deceased woes" at sonnet 15 all intend to underline his independence from and casual indifference to prevailing fashions. His protests culminate in AS 74's querulous insistence:

> I never dranke of *Aganippe* well,
> Nor ever did in shade of *Tempe* sit:
> And Muses scorne with vulgar braines to dwell,
> Poore Layman I, for sacred rites unfit.
> Some do I heare of Poets' furie tell,
> But (God wot) wot not what they meane by it:
> And this I sweare by blackest brooke of hell,
> I am no pick-purse of another's wit.

But this concerted belligerence itself betrays a nagging intelligence of his own displaced status. It is, after all, to another man's "purse" (in the sexually suggestive sense of the term) that he all too knowingly aspires. Whether or not Astrophil turns another's leaves, he inescapably seeks to gain another's wife. The opportunity resigned through an obtuse lack of foresight condemns him to labor within a poetic mode whose conventions are all the more pressingly evident for his many attempts to deny indebtedness.

Similarly, Astrophil's attacks on the significant other who has claimed Stella with an enviable immediacy are also qualified by a rhetoric that implicates the speaker himself. The poet's abrasiveness on this front concentrates in sonnet 24, where he ranks "that rich foole, who by blind Fortune's lot / The richest gemme of love and life enjoyes," below those misers who by merely amassing capital damn "their owne selves to *Tantal's* smart, / Wealth breeding wast, more blist, more wretched grow." If these figures at least recognize the value of their sheltered hoard, he implies, his rival ignorantly fails to appreciate Stella's true worth. "Let him," Astrophil prays, "deprived of sweet but unfelt joyes, / (Exil'd for ay from those high treasures, which / He knowes not) grow in onely follie rich." The lover's wounded egotism refuses to allow Stella's husband any perspicuity: where Astrophil will not give over to Fortune even the folly rehearsed in AS 33, he conversely villifies Rich as a churl who has lucked into his place by "blind Fortune's lot." The sense of denial hard at work here—biased as we would expect such emotional reinforcement to be—aims to suppress any thought that although his adversary may now "abuse" the good fortune of Stella's hand, he has at least (unlike the poet) possessed sufficient insight not to let opportunity pass him by. Astrophil, one who "would not, or could not see" his bliss, interestingly fantasizes for Stella's legitimate partner a doom analogous to the one he himself presently suffers—exile from the intimate favors of a woman whose value he did not grasp. Near the end of the sequence, when in the eleventh song Stella dismisses the poet from beneath her window where he "playneth," "Lest that *Argus* eyes perceive you," he can lament, "O unjustest fortune's sway / Which can make me thus to leave you, / And from lowts to run away." But a perverse justice operates, as he no doubt conceives. He had deferred Fortune's offer early on, and so must now live in humiliating deference to a man he is psychologically obliged to caricature as a contemptible and unworthy rival.[17]

Along with the dark specter of Stella's husband, Astrophil must engage both the retinue of critics and friends who admonish his obsession, and the dictates of "virtue" constantly sounding within. In sonnet 23, he scoffs at the efforts of "curious wits" to anatomize his distraction:

> Some that know how my spring I did addresse,
> Deeme that my Muse some fruit of knowledge plies:
> Others, because the Prince my service tries,
> Thinke that I thinke state errours to redresse.
> But harder Judges judge ambition's rage,
> Scourge of it selfe, still climing slipprie place,
> Holds my young braine captiv'd in golden cage.

Although they mistake his erotic melancholy for intellectual or political discontentment, the "missing ayme" of their surmises is not so off-target as he might wish. Essentially, he does muse over the "knowledge" of past error, strives in vain to "redress" this dejected state, and (as he explicitly confesses a few poems later) is consumed by "one worse fault, *Ambition*" for Stella's grace. Adjourning them contemptuously as "fooles, or over-wise," Astrophil only anticipates the self-condemnation of AS 33's "o punisht eyes, / That I had been more foolish or more wise."[18] A measure of envy spices his annoyance. Had Astrophil earlier regarded Stella with the same attentiveness his courtly associates now infuriatingly display towards him, he might have beheld the early promise whose loss he presently regrets.

In less contentious moods, Astrophil forthrightly acknowledges the intemperance—literally an untimeliness—stunting his emotional and moral growth. Sonnet 21 intimates the ironic terms by which he gauges the development of his public image in time:

> Your words my friend (right healthfull causticks) blame
> My young mind marde, whom *Love* doth windlas so,
> That mine owne writings like bad servants show
> My wits, quicke in vaine thoughts, in vertue lame:
> That *Plato* I read for nought, but if he tame
> Such coltish gyres, that to my birth I owe
> Nobler desires, least else that friendly foe,
> Great expectation, weare a traine of shame.
> For since mad March great promise made of me,
> If now the May of my yeares much decline,
> What can be hoped my harvest time will be?

Both quick and lame, the speaker casts himself as a parodic emblem of that most honored Renaissance adage, *festina lente* or "hurry slowly." His self-portrayal in fact justifies the apprehension about precocity Erasmus cites in his famous discussion of the proverb. In "the words of Plato,"

> "He who hurries too much at the beginning comes later to the end." A little different, but referring to the same thing, is the remark of Quintilian: "That precocious kind of intelligence comes not easily to maturity." And, as the common people say, children wise before their time turn out stupid in old age. Actius seems to approve of this when he says (in Gellius) that young minds should have the sharpness of green apples: both ripen in the end. Ripening brings sweetness in its own good time—the rest go bad too early.[19]

Astrophil's easy repression of sexual desire in the "mad March" of his amorous prime had inspired in his seniors "great expectation." Yet unable to keep in step with the seasonal resources and demands his life has presented, the lover stumbles into a shameful regress toward a "faire" image that is already removed from his grasp.

Upon this loom of implicit self-irony Astrophil weaves the fabric of compliments by which he hopes to recover his now-distant erotic opportunity. Though he can no longer claim Stella publicly, he may nonetheless struggle to garner her more discreet attention and affection. The songs punctuating the sequence afford a particularly intriguing view of Astrophil's desperate strategies. Their rhetorical action sustains effectively his agitated preoccupation with time, as even a brief look at several of these key moments reveals.[20]

Song ii features the most dramatic example of the lover's new determination to seize chance's fleeting offer, along with the inefficacy of this resolution. Happening upon the sleeping Stella, Astrophil steals a kiss, the first bold action we see him take. The poet determines as he beholds his vulnerable lady, "Now will I invade the fort; / Cowards *Love* with losse rewardeth." The "Now" beginning the third line of each stanza signals his nervous attentiveness to a volatile and transient present he must either utilize or permanently foresake. But *now,* threats of violence menace the courtly game, infecting the occasion he contemplates and rendering it less a second chance than a mocking replay of his original situation. He is still, of course, unable to renounce efficiently his characteristic dilatoriness:

> But o foole, thinke of the danger,
> Of her just and high disdaine:
> Now will I alas refraine,
> *Love* feares nothing else but anger.

Displacing his desire to violate Stella onto the compromise gesture of the kiss, he will nonetheless answer her waking indignation with crass regret, "Foole, more foole, for no more taking." Astrophil's very attempt to exploit time only certifies his awareness that legitimate fruition can never be his. Even under such absurdly reductive circumstances as we encounter in song ii, he continues Time's fool, trapped between impetuous desire and fearful doubt.

As evidence of the speaker's insensitivity to time in his sequence, Connell points to how *carpe diem* "is not among the many forms of persuasion which Astrophil urges upon [Stella] with passionate ingenuity."[21] But such a trope cannot figure prominently within Astrophil's rhetorical arsenal precisely because it flashes too near his own weakness. At only two points does he resort to this seduction ploy—in songs iv and viii—and in both instances he meets with Stella's direct rebuff; the replies in fact stand among the few times we get to hear her speak. In the first, Astrophil utters a market truth he has learned at great expense: "Niggard Time threats, if we misse/This large offer of our blisse,/Long stay ere he grant the same." And in song viii he will appeal desperately to her to make use of the present moment:

> Never season was more fit,
> Never roome more apt for it;
> Smiling ayre allowes my reason,
> These birds sing: "Now use the season."

In light of the poet's general predicament, these thoroughly stock notions take on a special resonance. By the time Astrophil has come to understand the urgency of occasion, it is too late. This venerated poetic move is, to Sidney's vanquished persona, no longer accessible.

As a result, Astrophil is left tantalized by a recovery that inevitably eludes him. His inability to manage time assails whatever integrity he once knew, and wastes his youthful stamina. "O my thought my thoughts surcease,/Thy delights my woes increase,/My life melts with too much thinking," he sighs in song x. And Stella's consoling remark in the next (and last) song, that "time will these thoughts remove:/Time doth work what no man knoweth," partakes of an irony surely not lost on her distressed lover. "Time doth as the subject prove" is his melancholy reply. Time cannot salve a wound of which it is the source; the passing minutes can only deepen and extend his obsession. He ends as one damned to "Tantal's smart," reflecting in the sequence's ultimate poem "Ah what doth *Phoebus'* gold that wretch availe,/Whom iron doores do keep from use of day?" For Astrophil, time has devolved into an endless round of frustration and self-loathing, consumed exclusively with futile efforts to regain by means of his attenuated wit that which his "too much wit" lost him in the first place.

Astrophil's lyric efforts, freighted with the reflexive irony that turns up again and again to haunt his expression, seem to exacerbate rather than assuage the suffering he undergoes. In the poem which follows the pivotal sonnet 33, Astrophil discusses his undertaking with himself—or more accurately with the "foolish wit" that let him down and now lingers as his sole companion-nemesis:

> Come let me write, "And to what end?" To ease
> A burdened hart. "How can words ease, which are
> The glasses of thy dayly vexing care?"
> Oft cruel fights well pictured forth do please.

"Art not asham'd to publish thy disease?"
Nay, that may breed my fame, it is so rare:
"But will not wise men thinke thy words fond ware?"
Then be they close, and so none shall displease.
"What idler thing, then speake and not be hard?"
What harder thing then smart, and not to speake?
Peace, foolish wit, with wit my wit is mard.
Thus write I while I doubt to write, and wreake
My harmes on Ink's poore losse, perhaps some find
Stella's great powrs, that so confuse my mind.

On the stage of this "tragicommody" we see played out the drama of an individual's desperate attempt to cope less with fortune's adversities than with freedom's anxieties. No Fortune authors his experience: yet the responsibility he claims herein consolidates or affirms a selfhood he almost wishes he could escape. The missed occasion that overshadows Astrophil precipitates an endless occasion for poetry itself, through which his deficiency will become the audience's gain, but in which he must also cast a depressing image of irreparable defeat.

Since a hard-edged appreciation of time's melancholy workings is something Astrophil shares with his creator, a parting glance at this particular connection stands to reinforce my reading. The correspondence between Philip Sidney's life and *Astrophil and Stella* depends not, in the end, upon the facile equations of author with persona sought by earlier biographical criticism, but looks instead to relationships more basic and fluid. This poet's experience—like any artist's—did not dictate his work, although personal concerns of course shaped and directed the topics he chose to explore on paper. Historical matters uncontestably funded Sidney's imaginative interest in the subject, and therefore potentially contribute to his conception of Astrophil.

Even as she professes Astrophil's obliviousness to time's encroachments, Connell concedes that "outside the world of his poetry, Sidney was fully conscious of time."[22] His 1580 letter to Edward Denny, in which he encourages the older friend to "resolve thus that when so ever you may iustly say to your selfe you loose your tyme, you doe indeed loose so much of your life: since of lyfe . . . the consideration and markinge of it stands only in tyme," confirms the point.[23] Sidney had drunk in such proverbial wisdom from his earliest days at Shrewsbury, when he would have first encountered the tag "rem tibi quam nosces aptam dimittere noli: / fronte capillata, post est Occasio calua" (let an advantage escape at your own risk: Occasion's forelock is ample, but the back of her head is bald) in his *Catonis disticha.* It was the political experience of his maturity, however, that endowed the warning with a stern contemporary relevance.

Delay's hazards excited the concern of all those who witnessed closely and participated in the management of Elizabeth's regime. The queen, notorious for what one historian calls "an unrivalled ability to hesitate, vacillate, and postpone decisions," and another her "profound unwillingness to take action until events forced it," consistently procrastinated her way through crises domestic and foreign.[24] But what in retrospect proved to be part of a shrewd (and effective) executive program appeared to the hypertensive middle decades of the reign as nerve-wracking irresponsiblity. Alive to the dangers of missed occasion presaged by such dilatory politics, Elizabeth's counselors were kept in an almost constant state of anxious frustration. Especially aggravating for the militant Leicester faction, of which Sidney was a member, was her hesitancy to move decisively on the question of England's role in a proposed Protestant League. The exasperation Walsingham voices to the queen in a letter on this issue is exemplary: "For the love of God, madam, let not the cure of your diseased state hang any longer on deliberation."[25] Casual disgust would come to inform Sidney's own private rhetoric, evident in the impatient remark to his brother Robert on "how idlie wee looke on our Naighbours fyres."[26] I have argued elsewhere that the young courtier's literary debut, *The Lady of May,* aimed specifically to parody this royal predilection.[27]The continued unemployment he suffered over the four years separating his masque from *Astrophil and Stella,* and the attendant fears that opportunity was wasting along with talent, did little to abate his professional or literary fascination with time. In the fullness of his artistic maturity Sidney was ready once more to ponder the subject of dilatoriness and its consequences, no longer in terms of a restricted topicality but as a richer meditation on the regret precipitated by failure to recognize and master occasion.[28]

Petrarchism's incendiary passions are typically self-destructive, and the convention's pathos relies on its subject's anguished sensitivity to this fact. But when the poet in *Astrophil and Stella* levels at his mistress the warning "Whose owne fault casts him downe, hardly high seat recovers" (song v), he speaks from the special vantage of one already beaten, so to speak, by the clock. Astrophil's ongoing breakdown traces its genesis to a past error that hopelessly compromises his amorous scheme. However much he wishes to repress time's role in his present embarrassment, he cannot write his way around this force which, in fact, circumscribes him.[29]

Boston University

Notes

1. All quotations from *Astrophil and Stella* refer to *The Poems of Sir Philip Sidney,* ed. William A. Ringler, Jr. (Oxford: Clarendon Press, 1962).
2. Germaine Warkentin, "The Meeting of the Muses: Sidney and the Mid-Tudor Poets," in *Sir Philip Sidney and the Interpretation of Renaissance Culture: The Poet in His Time and in Ours,* ed. Gary F. Waller and Michael D. Moore (Totowa, N.J.: Barnes and Noble, 1984), pp. 17–33. Warkentin refers to Barnabe Googe's "Unhappye tonge, why dydste thou not consent" from his *Eglogs Epytaphes and Sonettes* (1563) and George Turbervile's "The Lover blames his Tongue" from *Epitaphes, Epigrams, Songs and Sonets* (1567).
3. Richard A. Lanham, "*Astrophil and Stella:* Pure and Impure Persuasion," *English Literary Renaissance* 2 (1972): pp. 100–115.
4. A. C. Hamilton, "The 'mine of time': Time and Love in Sidney's *Astrophel and Stella,*" *Mosaic* 13 (1979): pp. 81–91.
5. David Kalstone, *Sidney's Poetry: Contexts and Interpretations* (New York: Norton, 1965), p. 122; Dorothy Connell, *Sir Philip Sidney: The Maker's Mind* (Oxford: Clarendon Press, 1977), p. 49.
6. Hamilton, "The 'mine of time'," p. 86.
7. Jane Hedley, *Power in Verse: Metaphor and Metonymy in the Renaissance Lyric* (University Park, Pa.: Pennsylvania State University Press, 1988), p. 105.
8. Alexander B. Grosart, ed., *The Complete Poems of Sir Philip Sidney,* 3 vols. (1877; Freeport, N.Y.: Books for Libraries, 1970), vol. 1, p. lvii.
9. For a concentrated recent attack on the biographical approach, see Thomas P. Roche, Jr., "*Astrophil and Stella:* A Radical Reading," *Spenser Studies* 3 (1982): pp. 139–191, and "Autobiographical Elements in Sidney's *Astrophil and Stella,*" *Spenser Studies* 5 (1984): pp. 209–29.
10. Ephim G. Fogel, "The Mythical Sorrows of Astrophil," in *Studies in Language and Literature in Honour of Margaret Schlauch,* ed. M. Brahmer et al. (Warsaw: Polish Scientific Publishers, 1966), pp. 133–52. Fogel provides in his references a summary of the controversy's progress.
11. Since Fogel, critics have addressed the poem only in passing. See, for example Neil L. Rudenstine, *Sidney's Poetic Development* (Cambridge, Mass.: Harvard University Press, 1967), pp. 230–31; J. G. Nichols, *The Poetry of Sir Philip Sidney: An Interpretation in the Context of His Life and Times* (N. p.: Barnes and Noble, 1974), pp. 60–61; and A. C. Hamilton, *Sir Philip Sidney: A Study of His Life and Works* (Cambridge: Cambridge University Press, 1977), pp. 94-95. Alternative efforts to locate "centralities" within the sequence have given their energy chiefly to identifying various sonnets as structural turning points; for a sample list of the results see Roche, "*Astrophil and Stella:* A Radical Reading," p. 191 n.42.
12. Fogel, p. 143.
13. Frederick Kiefer, *Fortune and Elizabethan Tragedy* (San Marino, Cal.: Huntington Library, 1983), p. 193.

14. Kiefer, p. 199. The notion will, as Gary Waller observes, leave its imprint even upon Protestant discourse: "A recurring phrase in the sermons and tracts of the age is the Pauline exhortation to 'redeem the time,' to seize each moment's opportunity. A widespread nervousness about the discrete moments of man's life permeates the writing of the age" (*English Poetry of the Sixteenth Century* [London: Longman, 1986], pp. 100–101).
15. The classical source for the company of Occasion and Penitence is Ausonius' thirty-third epigram. When the poet asks Occasio why this figure who has just identified herself as the goddess "quae factique et non facti exigo poenas" (who inflicts punishments for both deeds performed and things left undone) accompanies her, she replies "quandoque uolaui,/ haec manet; hanc retinent, quos ego praeterii" (she remains after I depart, held closely by those I have left behind).
16. Hamilton, "The 'mine of time'," p. 83.
17. In an earlier discussion of Astrophil's fate, Hamilton offers pointedly: "Worse than ever Pygmalion was, he is left with Stella's image while another enjoys the reality" (*Sir Philip Sidney,* p. 231).
18. Cf. Richard B. Young's observation that Astrophil "has been as blind as the curious wits he mocked for thinking him ambitious" ("English Petrarke: A Study of Sidney's *Astrophel and Stella,*" in *Three Studies in the Renaissance: Sidney, Jonson, Milton* [New Haven, Conn.: Yale University Press, 1958], p. 51).
19. Trans. Margaret Mann Phillips, *Erasmus on His Times: A Shortened Version of the "Adages" of Erasmus* (Cambridge: Cambridge University Press, 1967), p. 16. On the topos of the *puer senex* or "young man old," to which Erasmus is eluding, see Ernst R. Curtius, *European Literature in the Latin Middle Ages,* tr. Willard R. Trask (Princeton, N.J.: Princeton University Press, 1953), pp. 98–101, and Edgar Wind, *Pagan Mysteries in the Renaissance,* rev. ed. (New York: Norton, 1958), pp. 99–100.
20. For an extended discussion of *Astrophil and Stella's* songs from both thematic and structural perspectives, see Roche's "*Astrophil and Stella:* A Radical Reading," esp. pp. 165ff.
21. Connell, p. 49.
22. Connell, p. 50.
23. James M. Osborn, *Young Philip Sidney, 1572*–1577 (New Haven, Conn.: Yale University Press, 1972), pp. 537-38.
24. Osborn, p. 449; Wallace MacCaffrey, *The Shaping of the Elizabethan Regime* (Princeton, N.J.: Princeton University Press, 1968), p. 20.
25. Osborn, p. 244.
26. *The Complete Prose Works of Sir Philip Sidney,* ed. Albert Feuillerat, 4 vols. (1912; Cambridge: Cambridge University Press, 1968), vol. 3, p. 133.
27. Christopher Martin, "Impeding the Progress: Sidney's *The Lady of May,*" *Iowa State Journal of Research* 60 (1986): pp. 395–405.
28. A noteworthy experience which perhaps first drew together erotic opportunity and the risks of delay in Sidney's imagination took place in 1570/71, when the astrologer Thomas Allen cast the youth's horoscope. The surviving document, which James Osborn discusses and partially translates, includes an interesting passage "De Coniugio." Here, Allen addresses Sidney's current marital prospects, warning "unless you seize the time, Philip, in which you are sixteen years old, there will be scarcely (no, not even scarcely) any time available until your twenty-sixth year. Unless my

method of forecasting deceives me, you had the strongest possible inclination and propensity to marriage now that sixteen years are passed and gone" (Osborn, p. 522). It is not likely that Sidney would have taken this remark more seriously than he did anything else Allen had to say; Osborn quotes Thomas Moffett's assurance that Sidney scorned astrology, and we have no reason to suspect this verdict. But the notion may well have lodged in Sidney's highly impressionable imagination, to surface later when he came to conceive his sequence—the portrait of a lover who, unlike Sidney himself, finds his neglect of the auspicious moment an expensive mistake. Though astrology does not figure prominently in this account of "Stella" and her lover, as Osborn notes (p. 521), the minor incident in Sidney's own history may at some distance stand behind the sequence's formulation.

29. A preliminary version of this essay was delivered before the Renaissance Society of America meeting at Harvard in March 1989. I wish to thank Arthur Kinney, Heather Dubrow, and Donald Cheney for early counsel and encouragement, and Thomas Roche for his judicious remarks on the penultimate draft.

GREG WALKER

"Ordered Confusion"?: The Crisic of Authority in Skelton's *Speke, Parott.*[1]

SCHOLARS HAVE FREQUENTLY prefaced their comments on John Skelton's *Speke, Parott* (written in 1521) with the observation that the poem seems almost chaotic in its mixture of cryptic allusions, quotations, snatches of foreign languages, and sententiae.[2] But the assumption is usually that this apparent disorder was simply a shield behind which the poet protected his secret political intentions.[3] As the text itself declares'

> . . . *metaphora, alegoria withall,*
> Shall be his protectyon, his pavys and his wall.
> (199–203)[4]

The disorder is thus said to be only cosmetic and adopted for political reasons. The text is in fact extremely carefully constructed. Behind the apparent nonsense stand two authoritative figures who provide it with its unifying principles, the "gatherer" and narrator, Parott, and the poet and "maker," Skelton. The poem appears chaotic as it is conceived as the random gleanings from centuries of European cultural discourse, gathered by the near-immortal observer, Parott.

Suche shredis of sentence, stowed in the shop
Of auncyent Aristippus and such other mo,

I gader together and close in my crop
Of my wanton conseyt . . .

(92–95)

Yet this apparently arbitrary selection of phrases and stories has been shaped by the poet as a vehicle for political satire. The confusion is, as Parott suggests, carefully structured. It is "confuse distrybutyve," (198) "ordered confusion."[5] Much of the apparent nonsense can, as has been suggested elsewhere, be read as a complex attack upon Thomas, Cardinal Wolsey, the chief minister of Henry VIII, an attack designed to be appreciated by the Poet's coterie intended audience at the royal court and in the universities.[6]

In the eight years prior to 1521, Wolsey had risen from the relatively lowly office of Royal Almoner to a position in which, as Henry's confidant, Lord Chancellor, and papal legate *a latere,* he dominated the royal administration, the law courts, and the church. Such an accumulation of power in the hands of one man was virtually unprecedented and brought with it new political imperatives.[7] Yet, even as Wolsey was reaching the peak of his ascendancy, signs of the fragility of his position became apparent. In 1521 he undertook a prolonged diplomatic mission on Henry's behalf, ostensibly aimed at reconciling the warring powers of France and the Habsburg Empire. The conferences at Calais and Bruges which this mission entailed kept him abroad between August and November of that year.[8] This lengthy absence from London and Westminster created new tensions between king and minister, as the latter lost that capacity to cater readily for Henry's every political desire upon which his position of favour rested. These tensions proved to be merely temporary. But for a brief period during the summer of 1521 it appeared that Henry might be about to dismiss Wolsey, and this possibility seems to have prompted Skelton to write *Speke, Parott.* For the poem follows closely the deteriorating relationship between king and minister, mirroring first Henry's questioning of Wolsey's judgment, then his demands that the Cardinal return home, in cryptic allusions to untrustworthy servants and over-powerful underlings, and references to unnamed individuals tarrying unprofitably overseas.[9]

The poet's aim was seemingly to present Henry and the court with a reflection of royal criticisms of Wolsey, and in so doing draw favorable attention to himself, thereby increasing the chances of his own return to royal favor. But for this strategy to work it was essential that his readers understand the political significance of his apparently nonsensical poem. Hence the numerous intrusions in the text by what appears to be the authoritative voice of the poet, which insist that readers look beyond the surface confusion to find the satiric message beneath.

> The myrrour that I tote in, *quasi diaphonum,*
> *Vel quasi speculum, in enigmate,*
> *Elencticum,* or ells *enthimematicum,* [is]
> For logicions to loke on, somwhat sophistice.
> (190–93)

> . . . of that supposicyon that callyd is arte,
> *Confuse distrybutyve,* as Parott hath devysed,
> Let every man after his merit take his parte.
> (197–99)

> . . . who lokythe wysele in your warkys may fynd
> Muche frutefull mater.
> (296–97)

> For trowthe in parabyll ye wantonlye pronounce
> Langagys divers; yet undyr that dothe reste,
> Maters more precious than the ryche jacounce.
> (364–66)

Skelton's increasingly fraught insistence on the point is instructive. Clearly there is much "hidden" material in *Speke, Parott* which can be understood only once the poem's political context is appreciated. But such political readings as that suggested above are nonetheless problematic. They inevitably dismiss large tracts of the text (along with its most fruitful rhetorical strategy) as simply camouflage, as a deliberately unpalatable shell placed around Parott's true intentions in order to protect them from the unwelcome attentions of the poet's political enemies. Undoubtedly Skelton's satirical project was fraught with danger. Even under relatively favorable circumstances it was no light matter to criticize a minister of the crown. Thus the poet's allegorical approach was no doubt partly a product of caution. But the poem's lack of clarity and its sense of randomness and disorder are more fundamental than this explanation would suggest. It is the purpose of this paper to re-examine the treatment of order and disorder in the text, and to re-assess the notion of Parott's strategy of *"confuse distrybutyve"* or ordered confusion. I will suggest that a knowledge of the poet's political intentions does not provide a key to the cipher of the text which resolves the sense of disorder and confusion, because the disorder is itself instrumental to the poet's ends. Throughout the poem there is enacted a struggle between authority and an imperfectly suppressed other, "ryot," which provides its central motif. And this struggle itself plays a fundamental role in the poem's political strategy, as it foregrounds a commensurate political struggle, a crisis of authority in the mechanisms of government, allegedly instigated by the rise to power of Wolsey. Indeed, so resistant is this sense of crisis in the text to the poet's strategy of containment that it ultimately frustrates the attempt to use Parott as an effective political mouthpiece. For "ryot," as Parott ultimately concedes, cannot be subordinated to rational ends, and will always seek to subvert the order upon which they rest.

For the reasons outlined above, Thomas Wolsey stands at the center of Parott's diatribe as the representative of all that is wrong in the narrator's conception of the Henrician body politic. He is figured in the numerous instigators of disorder in the text. His identity provides the link between Judas Iscariot (133), the betrayer of his master, the merciless Moloch who repays a king's kindness with cruelty (60), the tyrannical wielder of the *byrsa* (80), the predatory "Lyacon of Libyk" (289, 400) and the arrogant "chief cardynall" (431). It is his return from the diplomatic conference at Calais which is demanded in the various requests for the return of travellers such as "Jerobesethe" (279), "Seignour Sadoke" (304) and "solen Syre Sydrake" (326), and it is his supposed ambition for the ultimate authority which prompts Parott to see a "wolvys hede, wanne, bloo as lede," gaping over the crown (434). Yet it is not only Wolsey's personality which the poem attacks. As what follows will make clear, Parott seeks to portray the Cardinal as the cause of a far wider political and cultural crisis.

Parott's vision of a disordered world becomes apparent only gradually, however. The poem begins more calmly with four stanzas of descriptive material, introducing Parott as

> . . . a byrde of Paradyse.
> By Nature devysed of a wonderowus kynde. (1–2)

He has been sent "to greate ladyes of estate" (6) and is a fit "mynyon to wayte apon a quene" (19). Thus far there is no indication of the text's radical implications. The narrative structure remains coherent and the subject matter apolitical. Yet it is significant, given what follows, that Parott has arrived at the Henrician court (he salutes both Henry and Katherine of Aragon in the following stanzas [34 and 36]) at the moment when Wolsey dominates the administration of church and state. Having travelled the world "Syns Dewcalyons floode" (462), it is during the Cardinal's ascendancy that Parott is "by fortune" dispatched from "Ynde" to London to employ his gift for prophecy in the service of the King. That his arrival is governed more by providence than by fortune gradually becomes apparent as the political burden of his declarations becomes clearer.

Hereafter Parott breaks into his multi-lingual monologue, interspersing prophetic warnings with seemingly irrelevant comments, alluding to a prevailing unnatural state of disorder and excess,[10] suggesting ominous analogies for the rise of a base-born minister, and hinting that the King himself is either too cowed or too gentle to oppose his servant's will,[11] only breaking off to offer further, apparently unconnected, references to his own history.

> My lady mastres, Dame Phylology,
> Gave me a gyfte in my neste when I lay,
> To lerne all langage and hyt to speke aptlye,
> Now *pandes mory,* wax frantycke som men sey:
> Phronessys for frenessys may not hold her way.
> (42–46)

Such details as this stanza provides are, however, crucial, both to the text's political purpose and to its rhetorical strategy; particularly so Parott's allegiance to Philology. For his service to two mistresses, Dame Philology and the ladies of the court (Language and Politics), provides the framework within which his complaints are articulated. He sees both spheres, the linguistic and the political, under threat, as the rules governing each prove incapable of resisting the rise of new principles of arbitrariness and caprice symbolized by Wolsey, who dominates the government and patronizes the new humanist linguists who are driving Skelton's favored traditional Latinists from the universities.

Parott has, he declares, the gift of all languages. Yet that gift is only of benefit if he can put those languages to use, "and hyt to speke aptlye" (his use of the singular pronoun indicates the organic nature of his conception of the language system). And now he is unable to find the "aptness" in languages. The universal ground-rules governing and permitting their use have been overthrown by madness, by the "frantycke" implications of contemporary practice. Just as in the political sphere, the shared assumptions concerning the need for strong personal rule by the Monarch, tempered by aristocratic counsel, have been shattered by the rise of the all-powerful commoner, Wolsey, so in language studies the new methods of the humanists undermine the old, trusted ways of learning. Consequently the chaotic implications always inherent in a multi-lingual culture have now been set free. What was once a means of universal communication now becomes a meaningless jumble of words and phrases. Parott had been able to speak in all tongues and was understood everywhere. Now he is incapable of speaking consistently in one and cannot communicate clearly at all.

While Latin held sway and methods of instruction were similar, the spread of civilization was possible, Parott claims. But even within that assertion of the superiority of old ways there is an indication of an instability at the heart of the order he praises. The fragility of the hegemony of Philology is ironically foregrounded by the very terms which Parott employs. The supposedly inimical opposites of Understanding and Frenzy are carried by the near-homophones, "Phronessys" (the Greek *Phronesis*) and "frenessys" (*phrenesis*, "frenzies").[12] When read aloud the text would appear to be trying to distinguish between identical terms. The lines between rationality and madness, authority and chaos, it would seem, are finely drawn.

There is a similar sense of the instability of previously assumed constants running throughout the text. Both language and politics draw their stability from shared assumptions validated by recognized authorities. The existence of a strong central authority in the person of the Monarch legitimates and gives power and purpose to the symbols and channels of political authority (in *Speke, Parott* the crown, the Great Seal, the council, and the royal courts of law). In the same way the recognition of learned authorities gives stability to human discourse. In *Speke, Parott* Skelton presents a world bereft of both central unifying concepts. A debased and decenterd monarchy and a banished and rejected rationality are, it is claimed, the twin products of the crisis of authority engendered by Wolsey, and are symbolized by the unworn crown coveted by the Cardinal (434–35) and the banished text-books ("Albertus *De modo significandi;*/And Donatus") "dryven out of scole" (169–70).

Parott's tirade against the rise of Greek scholarship, an educational trend patronized by Wolsey, among others, takes further this theme of disruption.[13] The Greek scholars, Parott claims, ignore traditional methodology, which insisted upon a sound grounding in general principles before the student moved on to develop elegance of expression, and instead rush immediately into the polishing of a pure style. Consequently their language betrays them. It is elegant but without utility. They cannot employ it to convey even the simplest of meanings.

> . . . *aurea lyngua Greca* ought to be magnyfyed,
> Yf it were cond perfytely, and after the rate,
> As *lyngua Latina,* in scole matter occupyed;
> But our Grekis theyr Greke so well have applyed
> That they cannot say in Greke, rydynge by the way,
> "How hosteller, fetche my hors a botell of hay!"
> (142–47)

The Greek of the humanists becomes, for Parott, an emblematic language, the language of anti-reason, of wilfulness. It is a code which has no logic, indeed which cannot be used to construct a logical argument.

> Neyther frame a silogisme in *phrisesomorum*
> *Formaliter et Grece, cum termino;*
> Our Grekys ye walow in the washbol *Argolycorum;*
> For though ye can tell in Greke what is *phormio*
> Yet ye seke out your Greke in *Capricornio.*
> (148–52)

Hence it is in Greek that Understanding and frenzy are almost identical. Without the basic understanding necessary to command it, humanistic Greek is a language without authority. Its anarchic implications are precisely those which the poet was later to see in the rise of Lutheran heresy.[14] Both the humanists and the Lutherans reject authority and accepted practice and offer the immature student the opportunity to dabble in matters far beyond his grasp. The accessibility of William Tyndale's heretical English translation of the New Testament made every young scholar think that he was capable of interpreting the Scriptures, and so led him to reject the authority of the church and the writings of the Fathers. Similarly the humanists example makes every scholar think that he can write Greek as eloquently as the great masters, and so "every mad medler must now be a maker" (161). The result is a babble of non-language.

Plautus in his comedies a chyld shall now reherse,
And medyll with Quintylyan in his *Declamacyons*
That *Pety Caton* can scantly construe a verse.
With, "*Aveto*" in *Greco,* and such solempne salutacyons,
Can skantly the tensis of his conjugacyons;
Settyng theyr myndys so moche of eloquens

That of theyr scole maters lost is the hole sentens.
(176–82)

The names of the authorities and the titles of their books are remembered, but their teachings and wisdom are forgotten. Equally, as what follows will suggest, the symbols of authority are retained but, because of the rise of Wolsey, they are denied their meaning. Again a crisis in one sphere is reflected in the other. Dame Philology and the Tudor court suffer a similar fate.

The King remains on his throne, but, Parott claims, he no longer exercises his centralizing authority.

Heu, vitulus bubali fit dominus Priami
(348)

[Alas! The bull-calf of the ox has become the master of Priam]

Non annis licet et Priamus sed honore voceris:
Dum foveas vitulum, rex, regeris, Britonum;
Rex, regeris, non ipse regis.
(348–51)

[Granted that it is not because of your age but because of your rank that you [Henry] are called Priam, as long as you cherish the bull-calf [Wolsey], King of Britain, you are ruled, you do not yourself rule]

The real political authority has been removed elsewhere by Wolsey, literally outside the King's grasp, to Calais. Hence political symbols no longer correspond to political verities. The Great Seal, ostensibly Henry's official governmental signature, the stamp which bears his likeness, has been taken from him. Its bestowal supposedly demonstrated the Crown's trust in its chief minister. Where the Seal lay, so lay the King's favor. But now, Parott declares, Henry has no control over it, and is unable to gain its return.[15] Thus, significantly, he is denied his role both as an author (of governmental warrants) and as an authority. Both of Parott's mistresses have failed Henry.

The intimate connection between the linguistic and political spheres is reiterated in the lines which follow.

> *Moderata juvant* but *toto* dothe exede;
> Dyscrecion ys modyr of nobyll vertues all.
> (50–51)

Moderation and discretion, the keystones of political conduct and polite discourse alike, ought to determine action, Parott suggests,

> But reason and wytte wantythe theyr provynciall,
> when wylfulness ys vicar generall.
> (53–54)

The lack of a central authority, a provincial, disrupts the political order. Discord and disjunction replace the discretion which Parott venerates, both in the political arena and on the written page. By referring to that missing authority as a provincial (a bishop or archbishop) and by the subsequent reference to the Vicar General, the text again stresses Wolsey's role in the turmoil. The passage is normally read as a straightforward declaration that Wolsey's governance as "vicar generall" banishes good sense and good authority from the church. But a closer reading reveals the text, here as elsewhere, to be equivocal in intent and self-critical, thereby voicing a deeper cultural malaise.

Reason and wit lack their provincial, their justifying authority, just as the realm lacks its chief minister, Wolsey, who is in Calais. Thus on one level the passage identifies the *lack* of Wolsey as part of the problem and voices the need for his return. At least it is the lack of the Great Seal which he carries with him that "cawsythe pore suters [to] have many a hongry mele" (311). But, as the context makes clear, Wolsey is not the provincial who will restore the sovereignty of reason and wit. It is his presence as much as his absence, indeed his very existence as "vicar generall", which precludes the restoration of stability. For "reason and wytte wantythe theyr provynciall, / *When* wylfulness ys vicar generall".

That Wolsey is synonymous with wilfulness in Parott's mind is appropriate on a number of levels. To be governed by wilfulness, by the will, is to be motivated by sheer caprice, to ignore form, convention, logic and consensus in favor of the gratification of passing whims and desires. It replaces ordered conduct with the unpredictable, the conventional hierarchical consensus of government with the overbearing cult of the individual. In Parott's conception Wolsey represents in himself and in his methods of government just such a process of disruption and displacement. As head of the King's Council and Henry's chief adviser, he is accused of replacing the collective responsibility of the council with his own single advisory voice. Moreover, as Lord Chancellor he presided over the courts of Chancery and Star Chamber, the prerogative courts of the crown, in which the Common Law, the law of precedent and case law, was replaced by Equity, the legal principle based upon the individual judgement and discretion of the Lord Chancellor who, acting as the King's surrogate conscience, mitigated the iron law of precedent to offer swift justice. In theory at least, then, in these prerogative courts the will of the individual replaced the rule of precedent, the unpredictable and the contingent replaced the predictable and immutable.

Thus the text, on the sub-stratum of stubborn, insistent, suggestion, again seeks to question its own absolutes. Parott declares with confidence that "Dyscrecion ys modyr of nobyll vertues all" (51). But when discretion is that of the Lord Chancellor in the Equity courts, the discretion of the individual will to overturn convention and the traditional wisdom of the Common Law, then discretion itself becomes another manifestation of wilfulness, its own antithesis. The potentially subversive implications of the use of the nearly identical terms "phronessys" and "frenessys" to identify supposed opposites are here taken a stage further, as the text presents, not simply a blurring of one term into another, but an unstable co-existence of antipathetic forces in the single word "dyscrecion." The instability of Parott's language is again suggested, as it proves incapable of containing the forces which it seeks to order.

By producing seemingly apposite sententiae from his storehouse crop, Parott tries to give meaning to his experience. But the distinctions which he attempts to create crumble and merely increase the sense of dislocation, of language out of control and experience beyond the control of language, which he strives to dispel. When Understanding and frenzy are indistinguishable and "discretion" can denote either, the reason which Parott vaunts cannot aid him.

Parott's continual citation of Scripture is further evidence of his failure to cope with the events which he witnesses. He suggests Biblical parallels for the relationship between Henry and Wolsey: Aaron and the Golden Calf, Gideon and Og of Bashan, Moses and Moloch. To see the current crisis as part of a tradition of conflict would be to reduce its radical implications. But the text ultimately rejects such continuities. Wolsey's dominance of Henry, it asserts, is unprecedented, as is the disorder which it releases. "Syns Dewcalyons flodde the world was never so yll." (497) It is the growing realization of this fact that Parott tries to suppress, with increasing difficulty, throughout the text. In attempting to contextualize contemporary problems Parott tries to stamp his authority upon events and so contain and subordinate them to his creator's political ends. But in so doing he produces a monologue which is increasingly fragmented and chaotic.

Despite his fear of anarchy, his voice ultimately only adds to the confusion.

> Ware ryat, Parrot, ware ryot, ware that!
> "Mete, mete, for Parott, mete I say, how!"
> (101–2)

Parott warns himself against riot, and then seems to break off from this train of thought to call for food. Yet the juxtaposition of the lines invites the reading of continuity. For riot, anarchic disorder, is indeed "mete" (both "fitting" and "food") for Parott.[16] His monologue is sustained by disorder. Without it there would be no text. As corruption brings forth prophets, so riot brings forth Parott and prompts his complaint. Moreover, the power of his utterance is the direct result of his vivid re-creation of the riot which he claims to witness. He becomes as much a creature of disorder as the Cardinal whom he condemns.

Parott swings between the extremes of engagement with and retreat from the world. At one point he preaches moderation as the best means of ordering the chaos, at another he dismisses the apparent free-for-all as none of his concern ("*moveatur terra,* let the world wag, / Let syr Wrigwrag wrastell with Syr Delarag; / Every man after his maner of wayes" [88–90]). But these swings are evidence of a deeper inconsistency. In a world from which political principles and rationality have been banished it is no longer possible for even the prophet to expect reform or to argue for it. Finally Parott can only yield to the riot and to Wolsey's victory and become part of them, even celebrate them, in the hope that the sheer excess of the celebration prompts revulsion and a desire for change.

> Frantiknes dothe rule and all thyng commaunde;
> Wylfulness and Braynles now rule all the raye.
> Agayne Frentike Frenesy ther dar no man sey nay,
> For Frantikenes and Wylfulnes and Braynles ensembyll,
> The nebbis of a lyon they make to trete and trembyll.
>
> To jumbyll, to stombyll, to tumbyll down lyke folys;
> To lowre, to droupe, to knele, to stowpe and to play cowche-quale;
> To fysshe afore the nette and to drawe polys.
> He [Wolsey] makethe them to bere babylle, and to bere a lowe sayle;
> He caryeth a kyng in hys sleve, yf all the worlde fayle;

> He facith owte at a flusshe with, "Shewe, take all!"
> Of Pope Julius cardys, he ys chefe Cardynall.
> (420–31)

It is, then, unwise to read the final envoy, in which Parott is asked to "sette asyde all sophisms and speke now true and playne" (448), as marking a return to stability in the text. Certainly that envoy has a regular structure, being a catalogue of complaints presented in a venerable medieval form. And Parott does seem to speak in a single, coherent, voice, unpunctuated by his previous near-manic switches of persona. Yet the envoy is neither a retreat from the riot confronted in the previous stanzas nor a signal that authority has been restored. Rather it is a further celebration of the demise of authority and the triumph of chaos, irrationality, and caprice.

> So lytyll dyscressyon, and so myche reasonyng;
> So myche hardy-dardy, and so lytell manlynes
> (456–57)

> So many thevys hangyd, and thevys neverthelesse;
> So myche presonment, for matyrs not worth a hawe;
> So myche papers weryng for ryghte a smalle exesse;
> So myche pelory pajauntes undyr colowur of good lawe;
> So mych towrnyng on the cooke-stole for every guy-gaw;
> So myche mokkyshe makyng of statutes of array—
> Syns Dewcalyons flodde was nevyr, I dar sey.
> (477–83)

The disorder evident in the text is, then, far more than simply a device by which Skelton conceals his satiric intentions. It is both the major strategy by which those intentions are realized and the inevitable product of the problems which Parott describes. The chaos which Parott sees around him is the most potent indictment of Wolsey's governance which the poem provides. The fact that Parott has finally to yield to it is a further measure of its potency. The suggestion that Wolsey's administration produces only anarchy gains amplification from a text which is itself an unmediated exemplar of authority subverted by chaos. But the text does more than this. It goes much further in exploring the notion of "riot," particularly of riot in the institutions and machinery of a supposedly rationally ordered culture, and comes perilously close to implying that riot is always latent in the very heart of things. Such a conclusion was almost certainly not what Skelton intended to be drawn from the poem, but even his supposedly ultimate authority proves incapable of keeping the ideas which he raises within manageable bounds.

The text which is itself decenterd (it denies the existence of a unifying authorial presence, claiming to be the random recollections of a bird, and structurally has no center, but rather tails off in a series of envoys) takes as its theme the decenterd nature of the Henrician regime. In *Why Come Ye Nat To Courte?,* a subsequent satirical diatribe against Wolsey, Skelton posits a Henry / Wolsey relationship which is a dual monarchy, a two-headed monster which had no place in contemporary anthropomorphic images of the commonweal. The question "Why come ye not to court?" is thus answered by the poet with both an explanation of the courtier-narrator's self-imposed exile and a genuine query, a plea for some authoritative voice to resolve the contradictory impulses created by Wolsey's ascendancy.

> Why come ye nat to court?
>
> To whyche court?
> To the kynges courte?
> Or to Hampton Court? [Wolsey's residence]
> (*WCYNTC, 401*–4)

Here the crisis of authority is provoked by the presence of too many governors. In *Speke, Parott* it is provoked by the absence of a governor. Wolsey is geographically absent in Calais and so the system of personal administration collapses in on itself in the vacuum created by his departure. But beyond this obvious physical absence there is alleged a more fundamental and disturbing lack. Wolsey's sojourn across the English Channel, it is implied, merely highlights the longer-term absence of Henry himself from the political system. Wolsey's self-imposed exile in Calais, Parott's exile from Paradise, Albertus and Donatus's exile from the schoolroom, all these absences merely point towards the greater exile, that of the King from his responsibility to govern. That the administration collapses without Wolsey stands as an unstated indictment of the King's failure to provide a stable central authority, and to be the true "provincial" which Reason and Wit require. Thus Parott's political message might almost be reduced to the statement that Henry should dismiss Wolsey and take over the reins of government himself.

In early Stuart court masques the disordered world of the anti-masque was transformed into order by the arrival of the Sovereign in the masque proper. At its simplest, the anti-masque dramatized a world without royal authority in order to provide a contrast to the masque itself in which that authority was introduced and examined. In *Speke, Parott* Skelton seems to present a vision of just such an anti-masque world, a world in chaos, awaiting the arrival (in this case the return) of its central justifying authority, the inference to be drawn being that only by purposefully re-entering the political arena can Henry resolve the conflicts which Parott warns are destroying the realm in his absence. The poem was thus crafted as a tacit encomium to Tudor sovereignty rather than a satire upon it.

Although the intention behind the text may have been this simple, however, its effects clearly go further. Even for a former tutor to the King, as Skelton was, the line dividing loyal good counsel, the honest offering of unwelcome news and advise, from near-treasonable complaint is easily crossed. And in creating a poem which stresses the instability of authority, whether political or intellectual, Skelton comes close to describing a culture enmeshed in an insoluble crisis of authority. Parott's account of an all-pervading sense of disorder, of riot run rampant, is too effective to allow for the disarmingly simple solution which the call for Henry's reassertion of his sovereignty offers. In this as in so much else in the poem, riot proves too powerful an impulse to be mastered and contained by authority, whatever its origin.

It would be excessive to suggest that the disorder evident in *Speke, Parott* is a reflection of the tensions accompanying the dawning of a new age. Some critics have claimed to find in the idiosyncratic fecundity of Skelton's verse the intellectual tensions created by the transition from a declining medieval world to a just glimmering Renaissance. More practically, however, it might be suggested that the text articulates the anxiety provoked in the conservative intellectual by the mutation or decline of traditional institutions, modes of thinking and deference structures in the face of two specific new imperatives, the advance of humanist Greek scholarship and the rise of Wolsey. The former threatened the scholastic consensus which had previously dominated the schools and universities, the latter apparently brought into question the concilliarist conception of government. Each brought the prospect of unwelcome change in areas of activity central to the poet's life; the first in the academic community where he had established a reputation for linguistic excellence of a kind now beginning to look old-fashioned,[17]the second in the council of the king whom he had himself taught to respect classical governmental values. In the attempt to ridicule these new forces the text seeks to establish a contrast between a privileged old order, characterized by stability, coherence and, ultimately, civility, and an anarchic, vulgar, overambitious, threatening, other. Yet, in seeking to demonize the latter, it succeeds only in exposing the instability of the former, and thus the falseness of the distinction. The language of the supposedly stable consensus proves no more stable than the anti-language of the aberrant Greeks. Thus it is unable to contain the riot which it manufactures. Consequently, having fashioned *Speke, Parott* as an instrument of his will and authority, Skelton was forced to watch it turn in his hand, as the numerous instructions to his readers in the envoys reveal. The text which he had crafted so carefully as a vehicle for his ambitions appeared to its readers as merely the piece of nonsense which it spuriously claimed to be. In a poem full of subversions and betrayals this is possibly the most ironic. Wolsey had, Parott claimed, betrayed Henry, and the humanists betrayed language, yet language in turn betrays Parott, and finally the text itself, the sum of these betrayals, betrays its author.

Quod magnus est dominus Judas Scarioth.
(133)

University of Leicester

NOTES

1. This paper was originally given at the "John Skelton: Poetics and Politics" session at the 24th International Congress on Medieval Studies at Kalamazoo, Michigan, in May 1989. I am grateful to the session organizer, Roland Greene, for the opportunity to raise these ideas there, and to the other contributors, Elizabeth Fowler, Tony Spearing, and Derek Pearsall for their stimulating ideas and suggestions. I am also indebted to John McGavin of the University of Southampton for his help and assistance, and the President and Fellows of the British Academy, whose grant of a Post-Doctoral Research Fellowship enabled the completion of the paper.

2. H. L. R. Edwards, *John Skelton, the Life and Times of a Tudor Poet* (London, 1949), pp. 182–85; A. R. Heiserman, *Skelton and Satire* (Chicago: University of Chicago Press, 1961), pp. 166–67.

3. Notable exceptions to this rule are A. C. Spearing, *Medieval to Renaissance in English Poetry* (Cambridge: Cambridge University Press, 1985), pp. 265–77, and

F. W. Brownlow, "The Boke Compiled by Maister Skelton, Poete Laureate, called *Speake Parrot*", *English Literary Renaissance,* 1 (1971), 3–26.

4. All references to Skelton's poems refer to the texts in *John Skelton, the Complete English Poems,* V. J. Scattergood, ed., (London, Penguin, 1982).

5. The translation is Scattergood's.

6. Greg Walker, *John Skelton and the Politics of the 1520s* (Cambridge: Cambridge University Press, 1988), pp. 61–100; Heiserman, *Skelton and Satire,* pp. 134–65.

7. For the effects of Wolsey's ascendancy upon the King's council and the conciliar courts, see J. A. Guy, *The Cardinal's Court* (Hassocks, Harvester Press, 1977).

8. The real objective of Wolsey's mission was to secure a secret, aggressive, alliance with the Emperor, Charles I, while delaying the outbreak of war with France until England was thoroughly prepared. For a detailed examination of this mission, see P. J. Gwyn, "Wolsey's Foreign Policy: the Conferences of Calais and Bruges Reconsidered," *Historical Journal,* 23 (1980), 82–100.

9. Walker, *John Skelton,* pp. 82–100.

10. *Speke, Parott,* 57–58 & 61.

11. Ibid., 60, 76–77 & 78.

12. The translation is Scattergood's. As the marginal annotation to the manuscript text of these stanzas (British Library MS Harley 2252, fols. 133v–140) reveals, Skelton (if he was the annotator) was fully aware of the difficulty. The annotation reads "*Aphorismo quia paronomasia certe incomprehensibilis.*" This point was noted by V. J. Scattergood in his paper, "The Early Annotations to John Skelton's Poems," also read at the 24th Kalamazoo Congress.

13. This passage constitutes Skelton's only surviving contribution to the so-called Grammarians' War of 1518–21, a debate between traditionalist schoolmasters and their humanist critics over the respective merits of Latin and Greek and the best methods of teaching those subjects. See Walker, *John Skelton,* pp. 63–66.

14. See Skelton's "Replycacyon" written against the heretical scholars Thomas Bilney and Thomas Arthur in 1528–29, to be found in Scattergood, pp. 373–76.

15. *Speke, Parott,* 278–84 & 301–14.

16. It is both "meat" and "meet" for Parott. Thus the line might be read in a number of ways, as "Meat, meat for Parott," "Meat meet"; "Meat meet" or "Meet, meet." In each case the implications indicated above would be present.

17. Note Caxton's eulogy of the poet's skills as a translator in the prologue to the printer's edition of the *Eneydos* (c. 1490) printed most accessibly in *Caxton's Own Prose,* N. F. Blake, ed., (London: Andre Deutsch, 1973), pp. 78–81.

ROLAND GREENE

Calling Colin Clout

THOUGH SCHOLARS of his work are not likely to admit it, John Skelton's "Collyn Clout"(composed ca. 1522, published ca. 1530) has generally lacked a clear-cut identity apart from the other productions that constitute his literary quarrel with Cardinal Thomas Wolsey, from "Magnyfycence" to "Why Come Ye Nat to Courte?"; and when its particular qualities have come under scrutiny, it has often been treated as the literary antitype of Spenser's poems involving the ambiguous figure named Colin Clout.[1] This is to neglect a poem that has its own agenda, strategies, and properties. Skelton's "Collyn Clout" is a poem through which runs a chapter in the emergent modern history of relations between authors of fictions and the voices they adopt; in which an acrid social criticism is adroitly materialized as the collaboration of author, persona, and reader; and after which the role of the poet in England has been subtly redefined out of what Skelton perceives as social and institutional marginality. Writing from his sanctuary at Westminster—a situation that finds him both safely "in" and frustratingly "out" of different contexts that matter to him—Skelton fashions a speaker who will occupy, even personify, that liminality, until the proto-satire's readership summons him out of it, toward a newly authorized poetic vocation.[2]

The example of "Collyn Clout" will not fully take for two or more generations: one can watch, say, Thomas Wyatt and later, John Donne claim some of the gains for satire imagined in "Collyn Clout," while in the *Sonnets* William Shakespeare builds on Skelton's diagrammatic interactions of voice and reader to establish a still more urgent relation between first and second persons. All of these poets, of course, capitalize on the role-building for the English poet carried out across Skelton's poem. At this moment "Collyn Clout" deserves a certain attention it has scarcely had—neither prospective nor retrospective, neither strictly generic nor firmly historical, but on its own strange and original terms.

Skelton's Collyn Cloute, the self-identified speaker in the poem, personifies the removal of poetry from religious and political sites of authority. This is another way of saying that he personifies lack of influence, marginality, or even irrelevance—but what a surprising stand for a poet laureate to take, and what an unpromising vantage for satire. Greg Walker has recently shown both historical and literary precedents for nearly every element in Skelton's "Collyn Clout."[3] As I see it, however, "Collyn Clout"—as opposed to even Skelton's other anti-Wolsey screeds—is a poem of the sort that becomes fatally less original, and more difficult to read, when one assimilates it rigidly to either the historical circumstances of the period or received categories like satire. Skelton elaborates a marginality more extreme than anything he could have experienced in his unsettled but generally well-connected life, a virtual and vivid relation between "in" and "out." His product is not simply satire according to one available model or another, but social criticism argued from a designedly neutral space in which the vocation of the (specifically) English poet can be defined and strengthened by its being marginal—in other words, satire directed not only at a vulnerable object, but at the segregation of a vulnerable subject, at giving that standpoint an overdetermined but underwritten role to inhabit.

In Skelton's early sixteenth century, I would argue, little is available in the way of a discernible poetic vocation for Englishmen, and it is all but impossible to unravel poetic or aesthetic interests from those of the state, the church, or powerful individuals such as Wolsey. A. C. Spearing and probably many other scholars would insist that the emulation of Chaucer by itself represents such a vocation: in his suggestive book *Medieval to Renaissance in English Poetry,* Spearing gives over half of his investigation of Skelton's poetics to a rote survey of Chaucerian and non-Chaucerian elements in lyrics such as "Collyn Clout" and "Phyllyp Sparowe."[4] Like other systems of assimilation that Skelton's work has provoked, which may be forward-looking as well as retrospective, Spearing's Chaucer-oriented approach explains a few touches, but leaves most of the substance and means of the poems, especially their overwhelming strangeness, largely out of reach.[5] Surely one of the factors that holds our understanding of a Skelton at bay is that we come to him with a much solider canon of his models than he could have had, as well as a repertory of anachronistic devices that includes even the terms on which we lean most heavily, such as "poet," "satyre," and "ryme."[6] When one reads with strict historical and aesthetic scruples, nearly everything in these poems must be open to doubt and conjecture. Nothing, not even a "tradition" that appears forceful from a twentieth-century vantage, can be treated as beyond question.

As I see it, the sporadic imitation of Chaucer observed by Spearing actually argues against the availability of a poetic vocation in England: lacking a clearly defined social and artistic role, would-be poets of the fifteenth and early sixteenth centuries invoke the precedent of those few persons, especially Chaucer and Lydgate, who managed to invent poetic careers in *ad hoc* fashion. This practice often provides that these early modern poets have to become their own models when the example of an earlier author runs out of force or relevance and leaves them on their own. Something like this happens with the string of experimental poems that leads to Skelton's "Collyn Clout," which according to Spearing's program becomes an instance of an "un-Chaucerian form at its most un-Chaucerian."[7] Moreover, there are enough surviving polemics for and against Skelton's claim to be a poet to suggest that the occupation is still a speculative one during his career.[8] His own gumption on this question was remarked two generations ago by H. L. R. Edwards, in a summary that is still useful when its anachronism and hyperbole are factored away:

> For the first time in English literature we come upon a poet who rejects the medieval convention of modesty and claims outright that he is a genius. "Written by me, Skelton, laurelled bard of the Britons" ["Per me laurigerum / Britanum Skeltonida vatem," lines 834–35] is his proud signature to *Philip Sparrow.* The cipher in *Ware the Hawk!* resolves itself into a boast that he is unique: the phoenix of England. The only change in *Colin Clout* is that of emphasis. His manner in this poem is rustic, he admits; all the same, "they will sing me and praise me everywhere, so long as the English race retains its fame" ["Undique

> cantabor tamen et celebrabor ubique, / Inclita dum maneat gens Anglica," epilogue lines 5–7]. *Why Come Ye Not* is curt in its decisiveness: "This the bard wrote / Whom thousands quote" ["Hec vates ille / De quo loquntur mille," lines 29–30, and repeated as an epigraph at the end of the poem]. And surely nowhere else in the world has a poet devoted a work as long as the *Garland [of Laurell]*, sixteen hundred lines of it, to pure self-praise, winding up with the assertion that he is his country's Catullus, her Adonis, her Homer![9]

The woodcuts that often appear in Skelton's editions during his lifetime and after, invariably (and for modern readers, tautologically) naming him as a poet, perhaps against the grain of current opinion, may participate in this long-running argument.[10] The interests or properties that make one a poet by a certain set of standards tend to invalidate him by alternate, equally plausible criteria. In that sense, something definitive of the entire enterprise of poetry is at stake in every discussion of a poem or career, and whatever theory or speculation occurs is passed through these particularities.

These conditions, which will not obtain longer than a generation after Skelton's lifetime, go to explain some of the poet's satiric strategy in "Collyn Clout": where the culture lays out no role and no method, a purposeful and "inventive" poet must devise them.[11] He finds a place from which to make his strike, and then issues the poem from there. In fact, the plotting of such a position, and with it the reform of the poet's marginal situation in English society, determine the contours of "Collyn Clout." The poem begins almost boastfully with the speaker's professions of irrelevance,

> What can it avayle
> To dryve forth a snayle,
> Or to make a sayle
> Of a herynges tayle?
> To ryme or to rayle,
> To wryte or to indyte,
> Other for delyte
> Or elles for despyte?
> Or bokes to compyle
> Of dyvers maner style,

Vyce to revyle
And synne to exyle?
(1–12)

and concludes, in the Latin epigraph, with the aforementioned prophecy of *premia* or "rewards." Between these announcements come Collyn Cloute's testimonial to the abuses of knowledge and interpretation that are always breaking out at the center of English affairs, and his disclosures to the prelates and magistrates of what the "communalte" say about them. The viewpoint is ostentatiously that of a factitious persona who haunts the borderlines of institutional society—this is inseparable from his job as poet—and plays the margins against the center.[12]

The name "Collyn Cloute" is introduced early, around line 50:

And yf ye stande in doute
Who brought this ryme aboute,
My name is Collyn Cloute.
I purpose to shake oute
All my connynge bagge,
Lyke a clerkely hagge.
For though my ryme be ragged,
Tattered and jagged,
Rudely rayne-beaten,
Rusty and mothe-eaten,
Yf ye take well therwith
It hath in it some pyth.
(47–58)

In the view of Robert S. Kinsman and other critics, the name seems to be a metonymy for marginality from at least two directions: "Collyn," from the Latin *colonus* for farmer, perhaps a proverbial name for stock rustics, and "Cloute," meaning a rag, a patch or shred of cloth, a heavy blow, and a target in archery.[13] Read as a complex of elements lifted from the fifteenth- and early sixteenth-century sociolect, the name suggests not only bluntness and rude force, not only rusticity or removal from the center of things, but the possibility of a rough blow's turning into a deft strike, and of the margin's becoming the center or target. Collyn Cloute is the self-avowed constructivist figure who cultivates and harvests the scraps of unsolicited public opinion to fashion a polemic that has, finally, the "clout" that none of its pieces can claim. Like other historical and fictional names of this period that were read symbolically—Christopher Columbus, whose adopted Spanish name Colón ("colonist," "member") seizes one of the same morphemes, is perhaps the most prominent example—the name "Collyn Cloute" enacts the premise of the larger project.[14] Both name and poem exaggerate the poet's disenfranchisement from society so as to give his social criticisms more weight; and the poem itself finally sketches a reconstituted world in which a Collyn Cloute would be unnecessary, where the tension and contradiction would be routed from his name.

If the name is largely built on such tensions in the sociolect, it also enacts the border-making and -crossing that the poem claims as its purpose. Pulling away from the contemporaneous and specific morphemes I have already mentioned is a semantic current that is both older and newer, both vaguer and more insistent: the adverbs *in* and *out,* which place the speaker straddling a figurative boundary ("Collyn Cloute" / call in, call out) wherever his name occurs. He is a liminal character who stands where "in" and "oute" give onto each other—a vantage familiar to social critics of many eras, and especially to ambitious, critical poets of Skelton's time.[15] Recall the unexplicated moment (877–79) in which the speaker appears with a changed name, "Christen Clout," in the thick of an old ballad that takes place at such a boundary, namely a well that encloses the figurative space of sin and redemption.[16] An example of the fluid shifts of reference and situation that drive the poem—that make it, according to many critics, a "structureless hodgepodge"—the passage is purposeless anecdote unless one recognizes this speaker's border-haunting.[17] Moreover, as lines 47 through 58 allow, the assonances and rhymes that keep company with the name make a racket of ins and outs. Here figuration follows the rules set down by sound—as it always does in skeltonics, which might be defined as a poetry turned inside out, in which theme and imagery are often determined by the material patterns of sound.[18] As the passage announces, Collyn Cloute will open the poem's insides to public view to disclose the "pyth" it holds there. He will do the same to society, until its contradictions and connivances are exposed like seams.

Naming and identity are persistent issues in "Collyn Clout." In one sense, the question of who can and cannot be named implies Skelton's satiric strategy within the extant political conditions. Collyn Cloute gets the poem underway by naming himself with a dramatic flourish, but he is both the speaker and the least substantial figure: a unique and specific name, but only a name. The praiseworthy people who are invoked to balance his indictments of others remain anonymous by expediency ("some there be, . . . / Set nought by golde ne grotes, / Theyr names yf I durst tell," 147, 160–61) or obscurity. Here and there they may get assigned names such as "Jacke at Noke" or "Gyll," but cannot shake their anonymity. It is a condition of the common people's and the good clerks' station in society, not of "Collyn Clout." No poem can make them important enough or favor them with literal and individual names; their significance is in the collectivity. Other figures implicated in the poem, however, go unnamed in a different fashion. These are called by the epithet "no man," which is first broached by the poem's Biblical epigraph: "Quis consurget mihi adversus malignantes, aut quis stabit mecum adversus operantes iniquitatem? Nemo, Domine!"[19]

> Men say, for sylver and golde,
> Myters are bought and solde;
> Theyr shall no clergye appose
> A myter nor a crose,
> But a full purse.
>
> (289–93)

> Ye are so puffed with pryde,
> That no man may abyde
> Your hygh and lordely lokes.
>
> (593–95)

> For I rebuke no man
> That vertuous is. Why than
> Wreke ye your anger on me?
> For those that vertuous be
> Have no cause to say
> That I speke out of the way.
>
> Of no good bysshop speke I,
> Nor good preest I escrye,
> Good frere, nor good chanon,
> Good nonne, nor good canon,
> Good monke, nor good clerke,
> Nor of no good werke.
>
> (1089–1100)

To use suche despytynge
Is all my hole wrytynge;
To hynder no man
As nere as I can,
For no man have I named.
(1107–11)

The epithet "no man" is applied not only to the objects of criticism, as the second instance above shows, but in other contexts where a space or gap in the category of person works strategically toward Collyn Cloute's purpose. The second passage here uses the epithet in the fashion that the first one uses "Men say," as a stop against the identification of the class or group of which Cloute is the spokesman. For the most part, however, "no man" (and its variants, such as "no bysshop" and "no clergye") mark the places in which the speaker's and the poet's refusals of specification force the objects of satire—in fact, every reader—to collude in the making of the poem. Wherever a clerical reader acknowledges an indictment, wherever a lay reader identifies the proper objects of Skelton's invective, "no man" becomes someone, and both Collyn Cloute and his poem move closer to a position of credibility and authority. "Rebuk[ing] no man / That vertuous is," the speaker calls in to us that he is not well enough informed or connected to offer precise identifications of his objects ("Ye knowe better than I," 1064); we in turn call out to him at his margin the correct names and situations, and the distances between poet, object, and audience grow shorter.

The extremity of this resistance to naming appears in the long speech, between lines 1150 and 1226, that brings Collyn Cloute to the end of his poem. The passage is preceded by Cloute's appeal:

Then yf any there be
Of hygh or lowe degre
Of the spirytualte
Or of the temporalte,
That doth thynke or wene
That his conscyence be nat clene,
And feleth hymselfe sycke,
Or touched on the quycke,
Suche grace God them sende
Themselfe to amende;

For I wyll nat pretende
Any man to offende.
(1117–28)

In case some member of Skelton's audience still occupies this position as the "no man" of Collyn Cloute's satire—as though that standpoint has not already been cleared out by all the foregoing denials—he is warned here, with special urgency, to vacate the role on spiritual grounds. What follows immediately registers a sharp increase in volume and bitterness:

Wherfore, as thynketh me,
Great ydeottes they be,
And lytell grace they have
This treatyse to deprave;
Nor wyll here no prechynge,
Nor no vertuous techynge,
Nor wyll have no resytynge
Of any vertuous wrytynge.
(1129–36)

Here is the motive, I believe, for the poem's extensive play with "in" and "out," with the epithet "no man," and with the designedly empty speaker named Collyn Cloute. Anticipating a hostile reception that would assert the lack of worth of his "treatyse," Skelton opens an indictment that his audience will have to complete, builds a role each reader will want to enact with his own knowledge of depravities and abuses. Situating himself on the margins of society and laying out his complaint in ostensibly disinterested, impersonal fashion, Collyn Cloute will be drawn to the center of things by us, his constituency—or better, the center will move to find him at his outpost. The bond of "wrytynge" and "resytynge," which Skelton's enemies would try to divide, warrants that the factitious person called Collyn Cloute will be a conduit for shared responsibility. As we speak the poem it must gain the specificity its text omits, and what was decisively "out" is refigured as strenuously, urgently "in." And Collyn Cloute gains a material identity—that of his audience, of whom he has been both member and colonist.

Having closed out possible offenses to and from his audience, Collyn Cloute then launches his own attack on the "no men":

With them the worde of God
Is counted for no rod;

They counte it for a raylynge
That nothynge is avaylynge.
(1145–48)

The following speech, which I need not reproduce here, is the direct utterance of someone, seemingly a wayward prelate, who has been entirely cut off from an identity that can be named by the poem. No reader will claim it, and anyone else who endorses it becomes "no man" in this context. At the same time, the speech itself is heavy with allusions and mock-names such as "Syr Gye of Gaunt" and "syr doctour Deuyas." Here at its climax, "Collyn Clout" turns itself over to what it has opposed to this point—and dramatically, the speech proves to be estranged from the reconstituted world that the poem has tacitly fashioned. The non-speaker's commands ("Take him, wardeyn of the Flete," 1165) necessarily go unrealized, as emphasized by his appeals to several different wardens and prisons and his face-saving last order: "The Kynges Benche or Marshalsy, / Have hym thyder by and by!" In this imaginative rehearsal, Collyn Cloute and his constituency can hear themselves confronting the (potential) words of a powerful adversary, and still going free. In other words, the utterance and everything it stands for have been circumscribed, colored as "evyll," and finally ruled out by Skelton's delicate play of person and persona, name and no name, speaker and reader.[20]

The last stroke in this movement comes with Collyn Cloute's summary of the unclaimed speech:

And so it semeth they play,
Whiche hate to be corrected
Whan they be infected,
Nor wyll suffre this boke
By hoke ne by croke
Prynted for to be,
For that no man shulde se
Nor rede in any scrolles,
Of theyr dronken nolles,
Nor of theyr noddy polles,
Nor of theyr sely soules,
Nor of some wytles pates
Of dyvers great estates,
As well as other men.
(1234–47)

The reader or auditor, who has elaborated Collyn Cloute's idea of a cleansed church and society and made it his own, is here threatened momentarily and elliptically with the same oblivion that envelops the poem's wanton prelates. "This boke" is the field on which the struggle for identity and standing is played out: while it makes some churchmen into no men, they in turn would cancel out its readership in order to hide their own "nolles" and "polles" (in both instances, heads). Do you, the reader, want to construe their conduct "as well as other men"? Will you speak for the renewed order that Collyn Cloute has put before you? Then, the poem implicitly urges at this point, the poem and its speaker have carried out their purposes. Social criticism has been channeled, organized, and given a synthetically personal—but genuinely collective—voice. The distance between poetry and society has been bridged with an invective that seemed to be "out of the way" but is actually in the middle of events—with measurable consequences for the little defined vocation of poet, which rides along with "Collyn Clout." And the different elements that the poem alternately rouses and condemns, "the tone against the tother" (67), are cleanly arrayed for an encounter. All that done, Collyn Cloute will retire to the margins again,

> Shall glyde and smothely slyppe
> Out of the wawes wodde
> Of the stormy flodde,
> Shote anker, and lye at rode,
> And sayle nat farre abrode,
> Tyll the coost be clere,
> (1252-57)

from which he may be recalled when he can rectify and amend again.[21] He is only as substantial and immediate as those "thynges that are amys."

Because in Skelton's example the figure of Collyn Cloute marks out the radius between poetry and authority at a given moment, Spenser seizes on him at the beginning of his own career as a convenience for projecting a new social and poetic order. The later poet dramatizes his Colin's removal to the borders of his pastoral society: a master poet whose songs are the medium through which all the shepherds know what they think, Spenser's Colin abruptly loses his authority and flees to the outskirts, whereupon his countrymen try to summon him back by homage, imitation, and discussion. As I have argued in another essay, their object is the sort of dialogic lyric formerly produced by Colin, a poem of multiple perspectives: Spenser imagines this text in view of its social function, as a discourse that mediates ideological divisions and fashions a community.[22] In the end, Colin's efficacy is restored by the collective motions of his fellow shepherds, who build a factitious but nonetheless dialogic lyric (we might say) the hard way, setting bits of various texts against one another in unitary songs. His poetry returns in the here-and-now of the "November" and "December" eclogues, just in time to disappear again with him and with the *Calender* itself. Accordingly, I think those interpretations that construe the *Calender* as Colin's journey, or that see his artistic success or failure as central, miss the most important experimental stroke of these poems: that Colin is not the protagonist of *The Shepheardes Calender,* but the instrument on which Spenser's continuing quarrel with narrowly mimetic or monologic lyric discourse is made to register. Or to put it another way: Spenser's first Colin Clout cannot inhabit the center of the *Calender,* as distinct from the "coost" or "margyn," without passing these standpoints through himself and losing himself in them (as in the exquisitely layered role-playing of "Aprill," where as Paul Alpers notices, Hobbinol plays Colin playing an exaggeratedly rustic character).[23] Spenser takes apart Colin's protagonism, I have argued, and redistributes his song among other speakers as though to win an argument about the nature of lyric discourse and its capacity for intramural and extramural dialogues.

As *The Shepheardes Calender* takes Skelton's comparatively simple scheme of the poet's marginality and complicates it by proposing to situate him within society to explore what that condition entails, Spenser's *Colin Clouts Come Home Againe* treats the matter yet again by reweighing that scheme: now that the poet is securely "in" society, what if the world outside proves to be larger than imagined—large enough, in fact, that the society to which Colin belongs is not actually at the center of anything? In the name's reappearance in Book 6 of *The Faerie Queene,* moreover, Spenser offers yet another display of Colin Clout as fugitive instrument, whose siting enables Calidore (and the poem's reader) to measure his present condition of remoteness, but who somehow eludes even the narrator's capacity to fix him into the poem: witness Colin's ambiguous placing—is he there or not?—at the center of the ring of a hundred maidens. Skelton's self-interested invention of his liminal speaker continues to work for the rest of the century wherever poets want to invoke their (or their speaking agents') distance from society, rule, or efficacy. His Collyn Cloute is perhaps the first poetic persona in English whom we can watch being built, unbuilt, and adapted to starkly different social climates and literary conventions.

Harvard University

NOTES

1. The record of criticism on Skelton's "Collyn Clout" is necessarily involved with that of Spenser's poems. Among the best of the recent retrospective examinations is David Lee Miller, *The Poem's Two Bodies: The Poetics of the 1590* Faerie Queene (Princeton: Princeton University Press, 1988), pp. 37–49.

2. H. F. Westlake, "Skelton in Westminster," *Times Literary Supplement,* 27 October 1921:699, prints the item from a certain Alice Newebery's lease that can be seen, not merely as a historical detail, but as one of the generative principles of (what I will describe as) this poem's investment in "in": "In quoquidem tenemento Johannes Skelton laureatus modo inhabitat." One can easily imagine the sentence's being turned inside out: the literal and figurative space Skelton inhabits in Wolsey's England is out of sight, out of reach, out of influence.

3. Greg Walker, *John Skelton and the Politics of the 1520s* (Cambridge: Cambridge University Press, 1988), pp. 126–53, argues that "Collyn Clout" is both highly conventional in its appropriation of satirical models and entirely specific in its application to Wolsey.

4. A. C. Spearing, *Medieval to Renaissance in English Poetry* (Cambridge: Cambridge University Press, 1985), pp. 224–47.

5. As the Renaissance-oriented counterpart to Spearing's medieval-determined approach to Skelton, compare Paul McLane, "Skelton's *Colyn Cloute* and Spenser's *Shepheardes Calender," Studies in Philology* 70 (1973): 155: "Another point of similarity between [Skelton and Spenser] is their tremendous confidence in themselves as poets, their assurance of having achieved poetic immortality." Obviously the contrary forces of two anachronisms threaten to pull Skelton apart; he cannot be both Chaucerian and Spenserian in any meaningful way.

6. Alvin Kernan, *The Cankered Muse: Satire of the English Renaissance* (New Haven: Yale University Press, 1959), and A. R. Heiserman, *Skelton and Satire* (Chicago: University of Chicago Press, 1961), mount sustained and highly successful efforts to read the significance of satire, the term and the mode, in its early modern contexts. Derek Attridge, *Well-Weighed Syllables* (Cambridge: Cambridge University Press, 1974), pp. 94–96, demonstrates the contemporary senses of the terms "rime" and "rhythm." Probably because it would undermine much that we believe we know about the sixteenth century, no one, as far as I know, has done a similar reweighing of "poet" or any equally fundamental term. For one provisional approach to the question—sometimes insightful, often appallingly ahistorical—see Robin Skelton, "The Master Poet: John Skelton as Conscious Craftsman," *Mosaic* 6, no. 3 (1973): 67–92, where it is argued that for English Skelton virtually invents the role of the "Master Poet," which is preliminary to the elaboration of the cultural position of the modern poet.

7. Spearing, *Medieval to Renaissance in English Poetry,* p. 230.

8. Anthony S. G. Edwards, ed., *Skelton: The Critical Heritage* (London: Routledge & Kegan Paul, 1981), pp. 43–53, collects these contemporary judgments.

9. H. L. R. Edwards, *Skelton: The Life and Times of an Early Tudor Poet* (London: Jonathan Cape, 1949), pp. 22–23. The rest of the epitaph in "Phyllyp Sparrowe" is as important as what Edwards quotes: Through me as poet, "Hec cecinisse licet/Ficta sub imagine texta" ["These compositions could be sung under a feigned likeness,"

lines 836–37]. Likewise the epilogue of "Collyn Clout": "Lauris honoris, / Quondam regnorum regina et gloria regum, / Heu, modo marcescit, tabescit, languida torpet! / Ah, pudet! Ah miseret! Vetor hic ego pandere plura / Pro gemitu et lacrimis; prestet peto premia pena" ["At one time the laurel crown of honour, / the queen of realms, and the glory of kings; / alas, how feeble it grows, how it wastes away, how sluggishly it becomes inert. / Ah, how shameful! Ah, how deplorable! I can expound no more of these things here / because of sighing and tears; I pray that the rewards may justify the pain," lines 7–11]. All quotations of "Collyn Clout" and other poems refer to the *Complete English Poems,* ed. John Scattergood (New Haven: Yale University Press, 1983). Translations of Skelton's Latin, as here, are Scattergood's.

10. Mary C. Erler, "Early Woodcuts of Skelton: The Uses of Convention," *Bulletin of Research in the Humanities* 87 (1986–87): 17–28, treats the assembling of these images from diverse sources. Note especially figures 1 and 3, the latter of which comes to be modified (in a 1545 edition of "Collyn Clout," STC 22601, for instance) as Erler describes on 23. For more background on Skelton's portraits, see Julie A. Smith, "The Poet Laureate as University Master: John Skelton's Woodcut Portrait," *Renaissance Rereadings,* ed. Maryanne Cline Horowitz et al. (Urbana: University of Illinois Press, 1988), pp. 159–83.

11. I quote the epithet applied by Henry Bradshaw, from "The Life of St. Werburge of Chester" (written about 1513, published in 1521, in *Skelton: The Critical Heritage,* ed. A. S. G. Edwards, p. 47.

12. Compare the analogy for removal from sites of influence used by the physician William Bullein (d. 1576), excerpted in *Skelton: The Critical Heritage,* ed. A. S. G. Edwards, p. 56, about Skelton himself: "Skelton satte in the corner of a Piller, with a Frostie bitten face, frownyng, and is scant yet cleane cooled of the hotte burnyng Cholour, kindeled against the cankered Cardinall Wolsey; wrytyng many sharpe Disticons, with bloudie penne against him, and sent them by the infernall riuers *Styx, Flegiton,* and *Acheron* by the Feriman of hell called *Charon,* to the saied Cardinall."

13. Robert S. Kinsman, "Skelton's 'Colyn Cloute': The Mask of 'Vox Populi,'" *Essays Critical and Historical Dedicated to Lily B. Campbell* (Berkeley: University of California Press, 1950), pp. 20–21; *Complete English Poems,* ed. Scattergood, p. 466. On the traditional pastoral associations of "Colin," see Helen Cooper, *Pastoral: Mediaeval Into Renaissance* (Ipswich, England and Totowa, New Jersey: D. S. Brewer and Rowman and Littlefield, 1977), p. 153.

14. Writing in the 1520s, Bartolomé de Las Casas, *Historia de las Indias,* ed. André Saint-Lu, 3 vols., Biblioteca Ayacucho 108–10 (Caracas: Biblioteca Ayacucho, 1986), 1:26–27, mentions the spiritual significance of the first name Christoferens ("bringer or carrier of Christ"), which Columbus adopts for symbolic purposes in April 1493, and the surname Colón, "which means colonist [*poblador de nuevo*], a name which suited him in that by his industry and works he was the cause that these discovered peoples, the infinite souls among them, through the preaching of the gospel and the administration of the ecclesiastical sacraments, have gone and still go every day to populate that triumphant city of heaven" (my translation). Compare the biographical *Historie* by Columbus's son Ferdinand, *The Life of the Admiral Christopher Columbus,* trans. Benjamin Keen (New Brunswick: Rutgers University Press, 1959), p. 4: "So the surname of Colón which he revived was a fitting one, because in Greek it means 'member,' and by his proper name Christopher, men might know that he was a

member of Christ, by Whom he was sent for the salvation of those people. And if we give his name its Latin form, which is Christophorus Colonus, we may say that just as St. Christopher is reported to have gotten that name because he carried Christ over deep waters with great danger to himself, and just as he conveyed over people whom no other could have carried, so the Admiral Christophorus Colonus, asking Christ's aid and protection in that perilous pass, crossed over with his company that the Indian nations might become dwellers in the triumphant Church of Heaven." On Columbus's cryptic monogram, see Paolo Emilio Taviani, *Christopher Columbus: The Grand Design,* trans. by the author (London: Orbis, 1985), p. 248. H. L. R. Edwards, *Life and Times,* p. 22, mentions Skelton's lack of poetic interest in the New World.

15. In a historical appendix to the poem, the antiquarian Francis Thynne (?1546–1608) tells in his *Animadversions,* ed. G. H. Kingsley, rev. F. J. Furnivall, EETS 1865 no. 9 (London, 1865), pp. 9–10, tells how his father William was warned by Henry VIII that, because of his edition of an anti-clerical imitation of Chaucer, the Bysshopes "will call the in questione for yt"; and how William was in fact "called in" by Wolsey, "his olde enymye," to answer for his complicity in "Collyn Clout," which was written at his home. The political and social distance covered by those "called in" is the same as that measured by Collyn.

16. As noted by Kinsman, "The Mask of 'Vox Populi,'" p. 21, the name "Cristian Clowte" appears in the refrain of Skelton's early poem "Manerly Margery Mylk and Ale." This version of the speaker's first name trades one of Columbus's onomastic elements for the other (*Christ* for *Colon*) while modifying the former not with *-ferens* but with *-en,* the suffix that speaks to both interiority and outward fashioning: this is a Christen(ed) Cloute and a Christ-in-Cloute who guards the particular border between the well and the outside. Considering that both Skelton and Columbus seem to be drawing independently on an understanding of these names as involved with each other in a larger semantic complex, Scattergood's note helps little: "*Christen Cloute* and *frere Fabian* (881) appear to be arbitrary names suggested by alliteration" (p. 476). The ballad "The Friar in the Well" is printed in *The English and Scottish Popular Ballads,* ed. Francis James Child, 5 vols. (Boston, 1882–98), Vol. 5, Part 1, pp. 100–103.

17. Heiserman, *Skelton and Satire,* p. 198, summarizes the views of earlier critics on the formlessness of "Collyn Clout." He argues that the diffused character of the poem's object—a "complex syndrome of general and particular evils" associated with "the clergy, the nobility, the heretical laity, and the disorder of the times" as well as Wolsey himself—accounts for the appearance of disorder (pp. 197–98).

18. This is a retrospective definition, of course: what skeltonics turn inside out is the priority of the fictional or intellectual elements in poetry (over its material or experiential elements) that will not be codified or regularly enforced in English for at least two more generations. If later theorists such as Gabriel Harvey and Philip Sidney propose to deauthorize the latter elements, George Puttenham's *Arte of English Poesie* (1589, though probably written about a decade earlier), especially Book Two, witnesses the continuing fluidity of the situation. For useful treatments of the skeltonic, see Robert S. Kinsman, "Skelton's 'Uppon a Deedmans Hed': New Light on the Origin of the Skeltonic," *Studies in Philology* 50 (1953): 101–9, and Stanley Eugene Fish, *John Skelton's Poetry,* Yale Studies in English 157 (New Haven: Yale University Press, 1965), pp. 250–57.

19. "Who will rise up for me against the evil doers? or who will stand up for me

against the workers of iniquity? No man, Lord!" (*Complete English Poems,* ed. Scattergood, p. 465). Kenneth John Atchity, "Skelton's *Collyn Clout:* Visions of Perfectibility," *Philological Quarterly* 52 (1973): 715–27, treats this quotation from Psalm 94 as another generative principle of "Collyn Clout."

20. Fish, *John Skelton's Poetry,* pp. 200–202, offers the best discussion to date of this "anti-speech." Like Robert S. Kinsman, "The Voices of Dissonance: Pattern in Skelton's *Colyn Cloute," Huntington Library Quarterly* 26 (1963), 311, he sees its speaker as the "one man" of lines such as 473 and 989 to 993.

21. H. L. R. Edwards, *Life and Times,* p. 217, argues that these last lines of the poem reflect Skelton's confidence at living within the sanctuary of the Westminster Abbey precinct, out of Wolsey's ecclesiastical and temporal reach.

22. Roland Greene, *"The Shepheardes Calender,* Dialogue, and Periphrasis," *Spenser Studies* VIII, ed. Patrick Cullen and Thomas P. Roche, Jr. (New York: AMS Press, 1990): 1–33.

23. Paul Alpers, "Pastoral and the Domain of Lyric in Spenser's *Shepheardes Calender," Representations* 12 (1985): 93.

ELIZABETH FOWLER

Misogyny and Economic Person in Skelton, Langland, and Chaucer

JOHN SKELTON'S raucous "Tunnyng of Elynour Rummynge" (ca. 1517–1521[1]) is like an architect's folly in which the gingerbread of misogyny overwhelms a barely-recognizable structure of economic ideas. Though it has always been viewed as a piece of exuberant but realistic description, I would like to show that the poem brings together several learned discursive traditions (all far from "realistic" in mode) through a complex of careful allusion. "The Tunnyng" works with the materials of the poetic canon to open up the materials of canon law: the subset of legal texts which grew up around early economic questions and doctrines is the object of the satire's sharpest points. By a sophisticated use of what we would now call literary character, Skelton savages the character constructed by early economic texts: that of economic person. In the service of this project, Skelton draws on Langland and Chaucer in ways that have not been recognized.[2] In "The Tunnyng" we see Skelton breaking down the machinery of personification, the dominant medieval form of characterization, as if it were an anachronism to be cleared away before the English lyric took a Petrarchan, personal, psalm-like shape and began its reign over later Tudor letters.

It is a curious fact that Skelton's critics have been distracted by the extravagance of his misogyny and have neglected the poem's economic argument. If we cannot see (as most critics of the poem have not seen) misogyny as ideological discourse, we ignore its specific historical content and cannot discover how it works. For example, it can combine with other arguments to articulate what would not be as persuasive or natural were it not attached to the more familiar rhetoric of misogyny. In "The Tunnyng," misogyny works to legitimize a critique of the money economy. Critical writing on Skelton's work abundantly demonstrates that though the signification of gender alters with social facts over time, readers are deceived by the apparently intractable presence of misogyny in the history of English culture. To render its workings more legible, it must be remembered that the cultural function of misogyny is necessarily disrupted as the meaning of gender changes.

Though Skelton's reputation has varied precipitously in the centuries since his death, critics have been unanimous on the particular merits of "The Tunnyng of Elynour Rummynge." In persistent celebration of the poem's visual qualities, such terms as "realism" have been overworked by nearly five centuries of readers. Historically-minded scholars[3] have routinely ignored the poem because it lacks reference to the courtly and ecclesiastical themes emphasized by Skelton's biographers. Instead, the poem concerns an alewife and her female clientele. An early eighteenth-century editor calls the poem "a just and natural Description of those merry Wassail Dayes."[4] In 1844, *The Quarterly Review* compares the poem to a painting:

> It is a low picture of the lowest life—Dutch in its grotesque minuteness: yet, even in the description of the fat hostess herself, and one or two other passages, we know not that we can justly make any stronger animadversion than that they are very Swiftish. But it will further show how little (of course excepting cant words) the genuine vulgar tongue and, we may add perhaps, vulgar life is altered since the time of Henry VIII. Take the general concourse of her female customers to Elynour Rummin, uncontrolled by any temperance societies.[5]

Here, as elsewhere, the assertion of Skelton's pictorialism stands as evidence of the poem's social realism. In 1936, G. S. Fraser argues that "Skelton's figures are . . . portraits, not caricatures. Eleanor Rumming, regrettably, exists . . . Every detail . . . adds to her reality."[6]

C. S. Lewis complains that the poem is *too* close to life: it is "disorder in life rendered by disorder in art."[7]

Stanley Fish continues this tradition, deriving the poem's social "realism" from the poem's "visual" technique. He elaborately identifies the poem with painting:

> *The Tunning of Eleanor Rumming* is a picture, a verbal painting—and designedly nothing more. . . . To read the poem is to see a canvas prepared before (or through) your very eyes. . . . Indeed the sophist Hermogenes might be describing *Eleanor Rumming* when he writes "An ecphrasis is an account in detail, visible as they say, bringing before one's eyes what is to be shown. . . . The virtues of the ecphrasis are clearness and visibility; for the style must . . . operate to bring about seeing."[8]

Yet the poem is merely vivid, and demonstrates little ecphrastic rhetorical technique. In fact, painting that can be described as "a mood piece," or in which "no space on [the] canvas remains unfilled" with visual detail (254) does not appear in England until much after the 1520s: the contemporary visual arts tradition is heavily symbolic and moral. These metaphors, while they allow Fish to bring out the experimentalism of the poem, lead him away from the poem's primary formal instruments and its overriding tone of disgust and enthusiastic opprobrium. Feminists and other readers who are struck by the poem's virulence, rather than impressed by its aesthetic detachment, may be relieved when Fish concedes that the poem contains "one value judgment." It is, however, an aberrant couplet designed to prove the rule of the poem's moral and philosophical neutrality:

> As the "pryckemedenty" rises from her seat, the poet steps forward to make the one value judgment in the poem,
>
> She was not halfe so wyse,
> As she was pevysshe nyse, [588–89]
>
> and dispatches the offender with a couplet:
>
> We supposed, I wys,
> That she rose to pys. [594–95]
>
> By including himself in the scene ("We"), he serves notice to his characters and his readers that no moral or philosophical considerations will be allowed to disturb the surface (there is after all nothing else) of his tableau. (252)

The metaphor of the painting works to convey the idea (through the word "surface") of a form with no content, no meaning and "no moral or philosophical considerations." In conjunction with this assertion, Fish does not hesitate to conclude, in line with his predecessors, that the result is a kind of documentary social history: "Skelton has done nothing more nor less than portray in words the chaos and confusion of a sixteenth-century 'still,'" (254). Approving the "visual 'realism' so many critics have noted," Fish claims: "One doesn't think about the poem, one only takes it in," (255). In this essay I hope to establish a stronger connection between descriptions of the poem as artifact and as social history. As this connection is fleshed out, the poem appears as a "disturbed surface," full of the "moral or philosophical considerations" Fish has banished from it.

"The Tunnyng of Elynour Rummynge" is vivid, yet not primarily visual; its descriptive mode relies on incongruous juxtaposition. The prologue-like portrait of Elynour, for example, is impossible to imagine visually unless, like the Italian painter Arcimboldo (to whom the epithet "realist" is seldom attached), we can picture a body made up of roast pig's ear, rope, a sack, egg whites, a jetty, buckles, a trowel-like tool, and a crane:

> Her face all bowsy,
> Comely crynklyd,
> Woundersly wrynklyd,
> Lyke a rost pygges eare,
> Brystled with here. . . .
> Her skynne lose and slacke,
> Greuyned lyke a sacke . . .
> Jawed lyke a jetty; . . .
> The bones of her huckels
> Lyke as they were with buckels
> Togyder made fast.
> Her youth is farre past;
> Foted lyke a plane,
> Legged lyke a crane . . . (17–21, 31–32, 38, 45–50)

This poetry is brilliantly evocative, but its mode is not "visual realism." If I were to seek an analogy from the visual arts, it would serve the poem better to call to mind the paintings of Skelton's contemporary Hieronymus Bosch or the grotesques of late medieval manuscript illustration. Yet "The Tunnyng" makes no reference to painting; Skelton's instruments are a series of carefully referenced *poetic* techniques. This passage is an anti-blazon, and stands in the scurrilous and ingenious ranks of such poems as Marot's "Du laid Tetin" (1535). But while Marot narrowly concentrates on the breast, producing a grotesque, Skelton careens across Elynour's body, top to bottom and up again, framing each part in a different diction. The connections between her parts are so loose that she is in the process of falling quite apart: her hips have to be fastened together by buckles. Her nose is continually leaking egg whites. Her body appears to exude, even to manufacture, an odd assortment of commodities.

The introduction of Elynour, then, is hardly the document of visual realism it has been taken for. Nor is the poem a picture in a more complex and social sense: it does not document social history (the "vulgar life") in any direct, visual way. The wealth of incidental detail about ale-making and commercial exchange is, upon closer inspection, of little value to a historical anthropologist or a social historian. Instead, our glimpse of "real" life is as ragged and constructivist as our picture of Elynour's body. All the social history that can be gleaned from this poem is that at the beginning of the sixteenth century there were such things as egg whites and buckles; that accusations about quality and morality were made against alewives and their customers; and (more tenuously) that "in kind" commercial exchanges were made as well as monetary ones. As for a picture of brewing:

> Than Elynour taketh
> The mashe bolle, and shaketh
> The hennes donge awaye,
> And skommeth it into a tray
> Where as the yeest is,
> With her maungy fystis.
> And somtyme she blennes
> The donge of her hennes
> And the ale togyder,
> And sayth, "Gossyp, come hyder,
> This ale shal be thycker,
> And floure the more quycker;
> For I may tell you,

> I lerned it of a Jewe,
> Whan I began to brewe,
> And I have found it trew."
> (195–210)

What we learn about the process of brewing is that hen's dung is dropped into the mashfat, separated from it in the mashbowl, skimmed into a tray with the yeast, and judiciously blended into the ale. While the status of this reportage as an accusation may be "representative" in a narrow sense (frequent charges as to the quality of their product were brought against brewers in this period), when we take it as information about brewing—the tunning—we are clearly in the territory not of realistic documentation of "vulgar life," but of parody. In fact, the results of this parodic "brewing" suggest that the parody may be not only of brewing, but of something larger than the ale business, and perhaps even more pervasive, though that is hard to imagine in sixteenth-century England. These lines begin to suggest what is more explicitly dramatized in the course of "The Tunnyng": that the poem's concerns are economic. The process of Elynour's "brewing" produces thicker ale and quicker flour (plus a younger and sexier countenance, 213–22): a set of usurious effects Elynour tells us she learned from a Jew. After brief descriptions of Elynour and the brewing process, as above, the bulk of the poem—some four hundred lines—is devoted to the portrayal of sales. For now, let it suffice to say that the poem abjures visual realism, and in fact uses more of the resources of allegory than Skelton's critics have suspected. Critical emphasis on realism—as well as a delight in Skelton's pungency—has led to a neglect of the poem's allusive structures, its sources and its intertextual claims.

The most important allusion Skelton makes is through the curious organization of "The Tunnyng of Elynour Rummynge" into sections called "passus:" the use of this designation in an English poem comes from the well-known example of Langland's late fourteenth-century *Piers Plowman.*[9] The allegorical story of the personification Mede the maiden dominates the first section of Langland's poem. Mede—the Middle English word for wages, compensation, and bribe—stands for a kind of surplus value, a conceptual tool that allows Langland to analyze the exchange of services for money.[10] The problem of containing Mede's promiscuity allegorically illustrates the rewards and difficulties the crown faces in its attempts to regulate the money economy. In *Piers Plowman,* the plot of commerce combines with conventional language describing female sexuality, and furnishes Skelton with the form of "Elynour Rummynge": a commercial plot waged under cover of the topic of the incontinence of women. Skelton inherits this combined discourse from Langland, and from Chaucer's *Canterbury Tales.* "The Tunnyng" calls on the General Prologue's description of the Wife of Bath (which he cites in lines 71–72), the Wife's Prologue, and the Shipman's Tale.

The analogy between female sexuality and commerce structures both "The Tunnyng" and *Piers Plowman* more bitterly than it does the Shipman's Tale. While Chaucer's Shipman's Tale is far from affectionate about its topic, it is satirical by means of a plot extended logically into absurdity: a sharp sexual joke on the bourgeois milieu of the merchant class. The main object of Langland's satire is an aristocratic woman brought to the king's courts where, despite the command of the king, Conscience refuses to marry her. "The Tunnyng" takes aim at women of an opposite social stratum altogether, but like Langland, though more strongly, Skelton proposes that women cannot be redeemed. In this sense Langland's reluctant conclusion becomes Skelton's starting place. Mede per se is not immoral, according to the character Theology; she is the legitimate daughter of Amendes. In sharp contrast, the immorality of the women of "The Tunnyng" is all too transparent, too unequivocally displayed. More often than not, that immorality is the female body itself:

> There came an old rybybe;
> She halted of a kybe,
> And had broken her shyn
> At the threshold comyng in,
> And fell so wyde open
> That one might se her token.
> The devyll thereon be wroken! (492–98)

The antifeminist historical tradition gives a theological context for Skelton's attitude, beginning with the fall of mankind through Eve's sin. Such a view of history provoked Chaucer to the arguments of the Wife of Bath's Prologue, and the scholar Christine of Pizan to elaborate rebuttals of the arguments of the *Roman de la Rose.* The primary cultural function of clerical antifeminism in the late middle ages is perhaps curiously not so much the oppression of women (though it is effective at that) but the consolidation of an estate of men who live without legitimate sexual ties to women. Like the poem, antifeminism is a discourse about women designed for men. In "The Tunnyng" all the figures are female, and the speaker and the implied audience emphatically male. The colophon purports to invite women to listen to the poem, but it "addresses" them in the third person and in Latin (a languge reserved nearly entirely for men); moreover, it proposes not to reform them, but to record their deeds:

> *Omnes feminas, que vel nimis bibule sunt, vel que sordida labe squaloris, aut qua spurca feditatis macula, aut verbosa loquacitate notantur, poeta invitat ad audiendum hunc libellum, & c*
>
> *Ebria, squalida, sordida femina, prodiga verbis,*
> *Huc currat, properet, veniat! Sua gesta libellus*
> *Iste volutabit: Pean sua plectra sonando*
> *Materiam risus cantabit carmine rauco.*
>
> *Finis*
>
> Quod Skelton Laureat
>
> [All women who are either very fond of drinking, or who bear the dirty stain of filth, or who have the sordid blemish of squalor, or who are marked out by garrulous loquacity, the poet invites to listen to this little satire. Drunken, filthy, sordid, gossiping woman, let her run here, let her hasten, let her come; this little satire will willingly record her deeds: Apollo, sounding his lyre, will sing the theme of laughter in a hoarse song. (tr. Scattergood 452)]

In these last lines Skelton authorizes the poem with the Latin of a cleric and a humanist, placing his work firmly in the tradition of antifeminism engaged by the Wife of Bath.[11]

"The Tunnyng" is part of a last gasp of clerical antifeminism insofar as the genre's importance in England coincides with the dominance of that vast multinational corporation, the medieval church. After the Reformation, there were fewer motives for the English church's production of such systematic propaganda against women and their charms: priests who practiced cohabitation, as Skelton did, were urged to marry rather than to repudiate their sexual partners.[12] In its capacity as a powerful social tool, antifeminist rhetoric became less relevant to the English church's need to police its clergy. As this occurred, "The Tunnyng of Elynour Rummynge" became less intelligible as satire. While not unopposed by clerical defenses of women and commerce, censures of women and economically produced value are a prominent feature of the tradition Skelton invokes. When the renunciation of women lost its privileged status as a clerical imperative during the reformation of the English church, the analogy upon which the "Tunnyng" rests became obscured.

When this linked discourse makes its way into the poem, it makes a particular contention about how the feminine is related to economic value. This ideological particularity, or spin, is embedded in the formal design of the poem, a structure which is best understood, I think, by contrasting "The Tunnyng" with the sources it acclaims. At the risk of misrepresenting the two lesser-known poems ("The Tunnyng" and *Piers Plowman*) by fastening on descriptive moments—set-pieces, really—in what are deeply narrative structures, let me compare the three passages that introduce Chaucer's Alice, Skelton's Elynour, and Langland's Mede. Here is part of the General Prologue's portrait of the Wife of Bath:

> In al the parisshe wif ne was ther noon
> That to the offrynge bifore hire sholde goon;
> And if ther dide, certeyn so wrooth was she
> That she was out of alle charitee.
> Hir coverchiefs ful fyne were of ground;
> I dorste swere they weyeden ten pound
> That on a Sonday weren upon hir heed.
> Hir hosen weren of fyn scarlet reed . . .
>
> (449–56)[13]

Skelton's prologue-like description of Elynour asks to be measured against Chaucer's lines. Elynour's headdress is equally imperious:

> And yet I dare saye
> She thynketh her selfe gaye
> Upon the holy daye,
> Whan she doth her aray,
> And gyrdeth in her gytes
> Stytched and pranked with pletes;
> Her kyrtell Brystowe red,
> With clothes upon her hed
> That wey a sowe of led,

Wrythen in wonder wyse
After the Sarasyns gyse . . .
(64–74)

It is a comparison at the level of character; the Wife of Bath and Elynour share a boisterous self-assertion and a pretension that is, at the root, economic. The Wife alone has a subtle psychological life, developed in her prologue, that can provoke sympathy in the reader; Elynour's fabliau-like energy and thinness produce an enjoyable revulsion, and allow Skelton to draw her as a grotesque. On the other extreme, Langland's dreamer, a surrogate for the reader, feels fascination and fear at the introduction of Mede:

I loked on my left half as the Lady [Holy Church] me taughte,
And was war of a womman wonderliche yclothed—
Purfiled with pelure, the pureste on erthe,
Ycorouned with a coroune, the Kyng hath noon bettre.
Fetisliche hire fyngres were fretted with gold wyr,
And thereon rede rubies as rede as any gleede [glowing coal],
And diamaundes of derrest pris and double manere saphires,
Orientals and ewages envenymes to destroye.
Hire robe was ful riche, of reed scarlet engreyned,
With ribanes of reed gold and of riche stones.
Hire array me ravysshed, swich richesse saugh I nevere.
(B.II.7–17)[14]

The introduction of Mede is an unmistakable example of personification allegory, one that Holy Church proceeds to interpret for the dreamer. While the portrait of Elynour is less iconic and her role is less theologically derived, nevertheless she is given no more internal, "subjective" experience than a personification allegory. She is not, as a Chaucerian pilgrim is, more or less individuated by realistic details. She does not represent individual personality.

In the Wife of Bath, Chaucer evokes the peculiar social powers of a bourgeois widow in late medieval England,[15] a person who was able to act economically on behalf of her own wealth and often allowed to conduct a business. The Wife's industriousness and financial independence are accompanied by a spirited sexual assertiveness; Elynour is married, nonetheless she too can act directly in the economy through her position as an alewife and boasts of her sexuality. In both characterizations, occupation, or position in the economic world, is stressed as a key to sexual behavior. The vicissitudes of the Wife of Bath's relations with her husbands depend upon the history of her economic power; Elynour's happy sexual relations are attributed to her ale-making in a bald piece of advertisement:

> "Drinke now whyle it is new;
> And ye may it broke,
> It shall make you loke
> Yonger than ye be
> Yeres two or thre,
> For ye may prove it by me."
> "Behold," she sayd, "and se
> How bright I am of ble!
> Ich am not cast away,
> That can my husband say
> Whan we kys and play
> In lust and in lykyng."
> (211–22)

Here as elsewhere the poem subordinates the characterization of Elynour to the topic of the sale of the brew. The sale, the plot of the poem, provides a frame or a context within which character takes its meaning: I have already quoted the anti-blazon which expresses Elynour's body in what one might call "commodity form." Skelton veers away from the Chaucerian dramatic monologue (best exemplified in the Wife of Bath), mixing the Wife's rowdiness with the more brittle and plot-manipulated characterization of a narrative like the Shipman's Tale. There Chaucer combines the double theme of sexuality and money in a quite different way, one which is epitomized in the pun on "taillynge" that closes the tale.[16] In both "The Tunnyng" and the Shipman's Tale, as well as in Langland's personification allegory, plot controls characterization.

Despite its feint at portraiture in the allusion to Chaucer's Wife of Bath, "The Tunnyng of Elynour Rummynge" is organized entirely by a simple and highly repetitious plot. The women appear serially, and each makes an exchange of some commodity for ale. This series of transactions is the spine of the poem. Just as in the exchange each commodity undergoes a metamorphosis into ale, in the same way the women are reduced to beastly, squalid things—bodies unadulterated by spirit or mind. As they fill with ale, they empty of humanity. Incontinence is the theme throughout. There is no "tunning" of ale into tuns or barrels in this poem; the ale is poured into human receptaclcs and its paradoxical function is to evacuate them. Like Chaucer's Alice, the Alice of "The Tunnyng" boasts of pilgrimages, but she strikes a less noble posture:

> Than thydder came dronken Ales
> And she was full of tales,
> Of tydynges in Wales,
> And of Saynte James in Gales,
> And of the Portyngales;
> . . .
> She spake thus in her snout,
> Snevelyng in her nose,
> As though she had the pose.
> "Lo, here is an olde typpet,
> And ye wyll gyve me a syppet
> Of your stale ale,
> God sende you good sale!"
> And, as she was drynkynge,
> She fyll in a wynkynge
> With a barlyhood;
> She pyst where she stood.
> Than began she to wepe,
> And forthwith fell on slepe.
> (351–55, 363–75)

If the characters enter the poem as Chaucerian (on the model of the Wife of Bath), contact with commercial exchange transforms them into iconic, allegorical vice figures, closer to Langland's Deadly Sins than they are even to the automated creatures of the Shipman's Tale. They become the emptied, conscience-less figures familiar in allegory: devoid of interior life and the capacity for intentional cognition, they are formally related to Langland's more elegant Mede.

The transformation of character into the plot of commercial exchange is epitomized in the fate of the words Elynour's husband uses for her in bed. In the course of the advertisement for her special recipe, cited above, she declares her husband's appreciation of her:

> "Behold," she sayd, "and se
> How bright I am of ble!
> Ich am not cast away,

That can my husband say,
Whan we kys and play
In lust and in lykyng.
He calleth me his whytyng,
His mullyng and his mytyng,
His nobbes and his conny,
His swetyng and his honny,
With, 'Bas my prety bonny,
Thou art worth good and monny'
This make I my falyre fonny,
Tyll that he dreme and dronny;
For, after all our sport,
Than wyll he rout and snort;
Than swetely togither we ly,
As two pygges in a sty."
(222–34)

The rhyme group that makes up her husband's declaration consists of a series of epithets for Elynour—conny, honny, and monny—that are repeated after only nine intervening lines, in which the author disclaims the scene. Suddenly her customers come running with payments they wish to exchange for ale:

In stede of coyne and monny
Some brynge her a conny,
And some a pot with honny . . .
(244–46)

The epic list of commodities, just beginning in these lines, is generated out of the body, out of the characterization, of Elynour.

The poem, then, is a mix of Chaucerian and Langlandian forms. Like the Wife of Bath and the other Canterbury pilgrims, named according to their professions, Elynour is an alewife, a social type. She is a rebuttal to the Wife of Bath's prosecution of antifeminism, taking a role in the same controversy, the discourse of misogyny. Her character embodies the same double valence (the commercial and the feminine), a metaphorical relation further elaborated by Skelton into a plot. In Puttenham's terms, then, the poem has an allegorical structure: "this manner of inuersion extending to whole and large speaches, it maketh the figure *allegorie* to be called a long and perpetuall Metaphore."[17] The metaphorical relation ale draws between the incontinence of women and the incontinence of money is extended into narrative, becoming the form of the poem.[18] In fact, were Elynour named "The Banker of Whitbread" or "The Brewster of Angels" the poem would be classed with Skelton's "Bowge of Courte" as a fair example of personification allegory. However, following neither Chaucer nor Langland, Elynour acquires a "real" name, one that could have belonged to an alewife, and in fact did.

In 1946 John Harvey found a reference to an "Alianora Romyng" (the spelling seems like a further pun) in the Court Rolls of the Manor of Pachenesham in County Surrey:

> The Ale-Taster's presentment at the Court held on August 18, 1525 (Surrey County Muniments, S.C.6/15), runs, in translation:—
>
> "Robert a Dene Ale-Taster there comes and being sworn presents that Richard Godman and John Nele Thomas Snellyng and John Romyng are common brewers of ale and also keep common hostelry and in the same sell divers victuals at excessive price, therefore are they in mercy Also he presents that Alianora Romyng (fine 2d.) is a common Tippellar[19] of ale and sells at excessive price by small measures, therefore she is in mercy."[20]

Despite the fact that the language of the records describes the short-changing of customers, the formula "with outen mesur" classes the crime as incontinence, as if false-bottomed cups were somehow gluttonous. It is precisely the stupefying effect of greed that permeates Skelton's poem. Avarice seems grandiosely contagious in the poem, finding its source in each woman, in all women, and somehow at the same time arising out of the brewing and the marketing of the ale itself.

While Alianora Romyng apparently lived, her name is almost too good to be true. Whether or not Skelton knew of her (and there is nothing to suggest he did not), the effect of her existence is partly to take the edge off the poem's allegorical aspect, distinguishing it further from the brittle, rarified type of allegory that poets such as Stephen Hawes were writing. At the same time, using the name of an infamous alewife would allow Skelton to draw more directly on a traditional animosity to brewsters that is as much evidenced in verse as it is documented by the criminal rolls. As to the latter, the trespass recorded here is against the legal notion of just price; the poem makes the same accusation in terms of the dilution and adulteration of the ale (with

parison with such poems as his "Agaynst the Scottes," "Against Dundas" or "Chorus de Dys contra Gallos." One of the tales that drunken Alice brings to the other gossips of "The Tunnyng" (351–62) refers to the Evil May Day riot of 1517, in which Italian, French, and Flemish merchants and diplomats were assaulted in the City of London by a mob of possibly two thousand apprentices who blamed foreigners for the economic recession.[27]

The topic of ale and the figure of the alewife both, then, present us with a poem about economics. How does "The Tunnyng" work this out? The poem opens with the portrait of Elynour as a pastiche of objects, but moves quickly into an account, almost an accounting-ledger, of her sales by customer and proceeds. In the course of seven passus a queue of women brings a wild assortment of commodities to Elynour as payment in kind for ale: the poem is a long list of many repetitions of the same commercial exchange. In the logic of the poem, ale is at first merely one in a series of commodities of which equal exchanges are made, but with repetition it is elevated to being the one commodity which stands as the fate and measure of all the rest. It is the symbol of conversion into value of any thing, and the one solvent of all value as well. "In stede of coyne and monny," according to the Tertius Passus:

> Some brynge her a conny,
> And some a pot with honny,
> Some a salt, and some a spone,
> Some their hose, some their shone;
> Some ranne a good trot
> With a skellet or a pot;
> Some fyll theyr pot full
> Of good Lemster woll.
>
> (244–52)

In these lines, not only is Elynour's character reduced to commodity form (as we have seen, the first commodities in the list are affectionate names for Elynour her husband uses in bed), but money itself is reduced to being just another commodity; it has given over its privileged status to ale. Not only such household items as spoons and skillets, but things that belong specifically to the characters' husbands are offered up, and as the ale progressively dissolves the drinkers' ties to the traditional social fabric, one brings her wedding ring.

In a mock-heroic process of elevation, Skelton's ale achieves the status of the economic "universal or general equivalent," the one commodity which is selected to be the marker of value in all others. According to the economic historians, the rise of a general equivalent accompanies the commercialization of an economy and the process of its saturation with money. As if undoing the process that Marx describes in the "Fetishism of Commodities" section of *Capital,* Skelton projects the behavior of commodities back on the human agents of commodity exchange. According to Marx, in a market economy commodities appear to act as (what I would call) personifications of the social relations of the human agents involved: "To [the producers], their own social action takes the form of the action of objects, which rule the producers instead of being ruled by them."[28] But in "The Tunnyng" women begin to act as if they are personifications of behavior associated with commodities. They become as adulterated, incontinent, bestial, and filthy as Elynour's ale is described as being. The depreciation of the value of the "typpet," the "brasse pan," or the bacon, when each is turned into ale, is made known to us through the actions of its former owner, who embodies that depreciation in our eyes.

Maude Ruggy thyther skypped:
She was ugly hypped,
And ugly thycke-lypped
Like an onyon syded,
Lyke tan ledder hyded.
She had her so guyded
Betwene the cup and the wall,
That she was therewithall
Into a palsey fall;
With that her hed shaked
And her handes quaked.
(467–77)

In came another dant,
With a gose and a gant.
She had a wyde wesant;
She was nothynge plesant;
Necked lyke an olyfant;
It was a bullyfant,
A gredy cormerant.
(515–21)

Than sterte forth a fysgygge
And she brought a bore pygge.
The fleshe thereof was ranke,
And her brethe strongely stanke,
Yet, or she went, she dranke,
And gat her great thanke
Of Elynour for her ware,
That she thyder bare
To pay for her share.
(538–46)

The women have an automatic quality, an inhuman lack of moral intent. Significantly, like their goods, they appear fully estranged from their social context. The commodities appear apart from the process of labor that produced them and the normal uses to which they are put. The women arrive shorn of kinship, of occupational status, and of membership in associations and social hierarchies. In Chaucer's Shipman's Tale the husband is promised a usurious sexual profit from his (unwitting) loan of his wife to the monk, and the queer behavior of money is enacted by the wife: it can be used and not used up but increased. Similarly, in the Skelton poem the women act out ale-like behavior. Their social existence is dissolved along with their humanity, and above all, they are emptied of their productive capacity, becoming merely dissolute, depreciated, consumed. If ale is the general equivalent, it reduces all things to its meaningless self, its empty signification. Infinitely desirable, it is infinitely perishable as well.

The corruption of the market and the corruption of women act as evidence for each other: swindling, inflation, and compulsiveness are summed up in what the poem says is the fleshly incontinence of money.

We supposed, iwys,
That she rose to pys;
But the very grounde
Was for to compound
With Elynour in the spence,
To paye for her expence.
(594–99)

More famously, of course, Langland's poem also deplores the money economy's power to corrupt. While it too describes a crisis in the determination of value, *Piers Plowman* locates the crisis in the provision of services rather than the consumption of products, and offers graft and bribery as the primary model of corruption. In Skelton's poem the locus of crisis is the unstable value of the commodity and of money: the depreciation and adulteration of their value; the opportunity for injustice in exchange; and female agency with respect to the corruption of value.

Both Skelton and Langland rely on their double subject in a fundamental way: in each the sexual is constituted in economic terms, and the economic is construed in sexual terms. While the economic plot has been neglected by critics describing Elynour Rummynge, Mede's critics have caught the economic satire, but tended to neglect the marriage plot and the sophisticated use of gender Langland makes. Mede, an allegorical personification, is the type of an aggregate of human behavior, what the social, economic body does rather than the individual body. The feminine gender is particularly useful to Langland, because he needs a figure that will analyze agency, that will help differentiate between the intending subject and the performer of the intended act. Within the doctrine of "unity of person" in marriage, early modern law was capable of making a distinction between principal and agent by gender, as not only in criminal law but in law regulating business transactions and contracts, women could in certain cases be considered not intentional centers of subjectivity or authority, but rather potenially authorized agents for their husbands.[29]

By placing Mede within an allegory of a set of legal questions, Langland uses her sexuality to illustrate the need for her marriage, and thus the need for royal control of the money economy. In his judicial role, the king proposes to marry Mede to the (male) privy councillor Conscience, who would rectify her status as an agent without a principal by fixing her intentions authoritatively. As an example of agency unanchored by subjective experience and intention, Mede represents the idea of the feminine as an opportunity for corruption. The logic of Langland's argument depends on the fact that the relation of female sexuality to marriage was elaborately worked out by theology and law, whereas the problem of money's pervasive effect on late fourteenth-century social structure was a newer and more difficult problem to wrap language around. Mede represents a version of economic surplus value which becomes increasingly powerful and visible as a social force in a commercialized money economy. When it is personified, this surplus is analytically separated from price or wage level and so can be acted upon decisively—in this instance, by Conscience and Reson.

While a theory of gender provides Langland with a conceptual tool, it does not provide an instrument of policy that will help to determine just price and excess profit in practice: there are no women he can banish from the polity in order to insure that financial transactions do not generate surplus value and inequity.

Allegorical personification in Mede's case reinforces a view of women as the opportunity for corruption, but when we turn back to the characterization of Elynour we find that a notion of the feminine as the very locus of corruption coincides with the flattening of personification into social caricature. A less allegorical figure is one we hold more responsible for her actions. Elynour Rummynge does not stand for the agency of the economy; she is herself an agent in the economy depicted. Like the other women of the poem, she is an origin and agent of corruption. The characters share this agency with ale, which seems to be powerfully vicious in itself. More than merely the opportunity for the vicious acts of the women, it seems to provoke corruption actively. Paradoxically, these ideas coincide with a conception of value as located in commodities. There is a net loss of value when the customers bring their solid pots and pans to Elynour and exchange them for slippery, vanishing ale. Accordingly, it is not surprising that, in the scene of Skelton's poem, labor is invisible. The customers are extracted from their roles in productive labor, and Elynour's work is portrayed as being as passive and corrupting as the fall of the hen dung into the vat.

Conversely, Langland's emphasis on value as "personal," subject to conscience, and understood by means of personification, coincides with a labor-oriented representation of value. The Mede episode seems to provoke pangs of personal guilt in the dreamer, who worries about his own wages in the succeeding Passus V of the C-text; Piers Plowman's search for truth begins with the episode known as the plowing of the half-acre, a utopian laboring community brought to ruin by shirkers. If the poem offers a final decision about what a socially-determined just wage ("mede") would be, it is measured in Passus V by the unit of the dreamer's bodily stomach, his "womb": not a product, not services, not appetite, not social position, but need. In the remainder of the poem Langland abandons his valiant attempt to link labor and value, and turns to a more mystical, orthodox, and less economic view of the world. Yet the well-circulated manuscripts of *Piers Plowman* may have made an important contribution to consciousness of the socially-constructed theoretical basis of labor and wages: Langland's lifetime witnessed changes that brought that basis into question. In the late

Middle Ages the value of labor became increasingly less "naturalized" because of the accumulated losses of the plague, which were greater among laborers than in the landholding classes. The repeated enactments of the Statutes of Labourers as well as the 1381 revolt bear witness to an alteration of the value of labor in English society. The increase in the mobility of workers, the spiritual movements for voluntary poverty[30] the invention of clocks[31] — all such things make the determination of wages less inevitable and natural, less reasonably based on a worker's birth and station.

The value of labor is a question that vexes the whole of *Piers Plowman.* But the similarity between the concepts of wage and price was little recognized in early economic thought. Work is commodified and takes on a value in money when compensation is commuted to money; thus wages are a species of price in the service economy with which Langland surrounds Mede. No theory claiming that labor is the primary locus of the production of value appears as early as the fourteenth, or even the sixteenth century; in fact, not before the eighteenth century is such a claim clearly articulated. The early theorists go only so far as to imply that labor can be part of the cost of producing a commodity, and to allow in certain cases that such cost contributes in a somewhat mysterious way to price or at least to the right to profit. In "The Tunnyng," as we have seen, the priority *Piers Plowman* accords to labor is transferred to bodily decay and corruption: moreover, here the very type of the body, as in so much antifeminism, is female. This notion is part of a larger theological tradition surrounding the figure of Eve, a tradition that associates women in particular with the flesh — the beastly, corrupt, and sexual aspect of human nature. In Genesis, the two different kinds of labor (agricultural and child-bearing) that define the human condition are punishments that find their origin in Eve's sin. Rather than resuming Langland's trial of labor as an approach to the analysis of value, Skelton sets consumption at the heart of his inquiry.

"The Tunnyng" proceeds by negatives. Economic value is corrupt, fleshly, and feminine, and is set apart from the ideal values implicit negatively in the satire. The character of character in "The Tunnyng" is vicious, and yet it clearly inhabits a usually virtuous role: that of the agent of commercial exchange. Thus character in the poem is a representation of economic person, drawn from and against the discourse of early economic thought. For Skelton, economic person is not the independent, choosing male agent, whose autonomy, continence, and volition are protected as if with a shield by the invisible hand of the market. In effect, the poem's characters dramatize Aristotle's concept of passive or effeminate incontinence (*Magna Moralia* I.33), equating the involuntary, the nonlaboring, the feminine, and consumption. As a form of character the representation of economic person is not a metaphor or an allegory, and it is more than the individualized type of a trade. The poem constructs a notion of an aggregate class: all the characters in the poem are women, and all occupy the same standpoint in the network of the economy as agents in economic transactions. Their situation standardizes the characters, defining them in a common denomination. According to the poem, the confrontation with commercial value has transformative power over the representation of person. The process of evaluation in economic terms, the very process that is enacted in commercial exchange, transforms character into a compulsive plot; alienates personal agency to a corrupt social, economic form; and creates an inhuman, sterile object out of a fertile subject.

When later thinkers fashion a discipline out of the study of the market, the epistemological veil between a buyer or seller and what is happening "in the market" becomes the assurance that the greater workings of the market are socially just, insofar as the freedom of choice of individual buyers and sellers is preserved. Skelton dramatizes the corruption of choice and free agency by the commodity of money itself. The concept of false consciousness elaborated by Marxist thought—just one step from Aristotle's involuntary and incontinent actors—is nearly present here, portrayed in the drunkenness of the women. They are inebriates of the agency of money, possessed by an agency which has contaminated their own. It is value that is the agent in this confrontation beween the idea of person and the theory of economic value; value corrupts the moral capacities of the person, and makes what the economic canon would offer as its paradigmatic subject—the farmer or the shoemaker negotiating for each other's wares—into the depreciated object of the workings of money itself. Whereas in the Shipman's Tale the wife becomes a kind of productive commodity, in "The Tunnyng" Elynour and her customers become consumed, decayed commodities, used up by the economy and thrown away by the poet like putrefying corpses.

In these corpses women are invited to see themselves: it is precisely misogyny, the *"carmen raucum,"* that is the poem's vehicle. This has made the poem both more and less accessible—taken in itself, misogyny has not ceased to be provocative. The trouble with such a poem for feminists is that its misogyny is so bald and virulent that at first pass we are not left with anything intelligent to say about it. It is merely shocking, or exaggerated and witty enough to amuse us. What is the meaning—both historically and for us—of antifeminism in "The Tunnyng"? The old answer, "realism," no longer rings true. Over time, misogyny has managed to obscure Skelton's economic satire because the feminine has come to function differently than it does in clerical antifeminism. Despite the importance of women in retail trades and as consumers, when the "market" later appeared as the topos of economic disciplinary thought, the agent was not female, the story of the corrupt feminine origins of labor was discursively marginalized, and Skelton's tirade against the monetary measurement of value in the mechanism of exchange was taken at "surface" value: not as a threat to moral agency and to the body politic, but as a picture of vicious woman. During the modern period the market itself increasingly represented public life, and the feminine became its domesticated, private opposite. In unpacking some of the social history embedded in "The Tunnyng of Elynour Rummynge," I hope to have raised questions about the claim of realism: to show that "pictures" of the world which have looked utterly natural for centuries reveal complicated ideological assertions about gender, agency, person, and value—assertions that do not passively reflect their culture but attempt to alter the fundamental tenets of its organization.

John Skelton has not fit neatly into poetry survey courses because his poems do not hold the prosodic and generic shapes that would make them obvious comparisons for the poems of the Scots poets[32] and the late Chaucerians on the one hand, or those of the innovators of Tottel's *Miscellany* on the other. C.S. Lewis wrote of him that "He has no real predecessors and no important disciples; he stands out of the streamy historical process, an unmistakable individual, a man we have met."[33] This sells Skelton's writing short. In a sense, Skelton-the-narrator has seduced his critics into marginalizing his poetry under the sway of the peculiarity of his "personality." Fish's appraisal of "The Tunnyng" is too typical of the topos that has dominated Skelton criticism: a picture in which Skelton, a rather loud-mouthed, smart, perhaps politically brave man views the world as a kind of clever existential photographer, exploring the formalities of language. This persona is familiar to us as the corporally absent, mentally present, male voyeur of "The Tunnyng." His partial view led Fish to flatten the texture of the poem—topic, tone, social details—because that texture is contradictory and incompatible with the idea of the poet as an *auteur,* masterminding the poem.[34] I hope my attempts to bring out the poem's contradictions reveal it as a more profoundly inventive and culturally engaged text than can be understood from the epistemological standpoint of Skelton's misogynist narrator, a character in which Fish is too willing to be confined. Greg Walker's recent book has contributed to the demise of that paradigmatic character, by showing that Skelton's pretensions to being at the center of court life were merely that; this has robbed the poems of some of their promise as sources of intricate political allusion.[35] What is left is a body of work more curious than ever, full of peculiar versification, surreal voicing, and a more grandiose bitterness. Perhaps we are faced with a less riddling, more specific and complete poetry than earlier generations read.

"The Tunnyng" does not effect the subtle probing of sexual politics that Chaucer accomplishes in the Wife of Bath's Prologue and Tale, nor does it stand up to the sophisticated legal critique of Langland's plot. Using fragments of Langlandian and Chaucerian representations of person within the specially-concentrated acid of satire, Skelton manages nonetheless to create a mode of characterization that can argue powerfully about the effect of commercial life on social agency. Yet here I have formulated my point too neutrally, for social agency has a violent, gendered charge throughout his work. To brilliant effect, Skelton takes advantage of his model of the imperfect female subject, and of the less-human characters of birds, in poems such as "Ware the Hauke," "Phyllyp Sparowe," and "Speke Parott." Skelton is experimental about the representation of person in such poems partly because the material allows him to be: these poems are about women, children, and animals—partial subjects, lacking full intentional capacity. His poetic personae are not the nightingale or the lark but the Phoenix-out-of-ashes (in the riddle of "Ware the Hauke" 239–45); the ventriloquist Parrot who speaks in gobbets and macaronics; and the lad dressed in rags, Collyn Clout. In these poems, the liberation of voice from its earlier, conventional poetic embodiments accomplishes all the schizophrenia that is promised by the narrative fever of "The Tunnyng of Elynour Rummynge."

Skelton's work precedes the formation of a new dominant poetic form of person in the devotional and Petrarchan sonnets of the 1580s and 90s. It was not Wyatt or Sidney (or, alas, an economist) who discovered something useful in Skelton, but the more narrative imagination of Spenser, who found Skelton's negative logic suited his own indirection and obsession with experimentation and the forms of person. Skelton's achievement lies in his profound curiosity about the question of person, and his new, technical approach to the representation of person in letters. He is a poet of *bricolage:* it is as if we watch him dismantling full-blown personification allegory in order to see what he can do with pieces of it. In moments like the confrontation of economic person with the question of value, dramatized in "The Tunnyng of Elynour Rummynge," Skelton leaves the old cast of medieval characters lying dead around the stage. If the poem is an architectural folly, we can call it a chantry, erected at the site of the funeral of residual forms. It is left to Wyatt and Surrey to take up the task left incomplete by Chaucer: the rearranging of personification into persona; it is left to Spenser to reanimate personification as a partial object in a heterogeneous body politic, one that Skelton's representations of person made possible.

The Society of Fellows, Harvard University

Notes

I would like to express my indebtedness to Charles Donahue, Jr., Roland Greene, Barbara Kiefer Lewalski, Cyrus R.K. Patell, Derek Pearsall, Katherine Rowe, John Scattergood, William Sherman, A. C. Spearing, and J. B. Trapp.

1. John Skelton, *The Complete English Poems,* ed. John Scattergood (New Haven: Yale University Press, 1983), 449. The lineation in this essay follows Scattergood.
2. This essay examines the register of poetic reference in "The Tunnyng;" in a forthcoming piece I draw out Skelton's allusions to the legal and economic tradition and the poem's specific critique of economic person. The present argument is part of a larger work in progress concerning the representation of person in English legal and poetic texts of the early modern period.
3. Richard Halpern draws an analogy between Skelton's poetics and the Marxist theory of the economic mode called primitive accumulation, though he does not comment on "The Tunnyng," in *The Poetics of Primitive Accumulation: English Renaissance Culture and the Genealogy of Capital* (Ithaca: Cornell University Press, 1991). Arthur Kinney provides a list of generic sources and analogues for "The Tunnyng" in *John Skelton: Priest as Poet: Seasons of Discovery* (Chapel Hill: University of North Carolina Press, 1987), 168–87.
4. In Anthony S.G. Edwards, ed. *Skelton: The Critical Heritage* (London: Routledge & Kegan Paul, 1981), 74.
5. Edwards, 111.
6. Edwards, 190.
7. *English Literature in the Sixteenth Century* (Oxford: Oxford University Press/Clarendon, 1954), 139.
8. *John Skelton's Poetry* (New Haven: Yale University Press, 1965, rpt. Hamden, CT: Shoe String Press/Archon, 1976), 251–55: subsequent references appear parenthetically in the text.
9. Two earlier poems imitate the passus of *Piers Plowman: Richard the Redeles* and *The Wars of Alexander.*
10. Perhaps a pun on the word "meed" suggested the primary conceit of "The Tunnyng" to Skelton.
11. Regarding antifeminist writing in the vernacular and in Latin see, e.g., Benson's

Riverside Chaucer (Boston: Houghton Mifflin, 1987), 864; R. Howard Bloch, *Medieval Misogyny and the Invention of Western Romantic Love* (Chicago: University of Chicago Press, 1991); John Peter, *Complaint and Satire in Early English Literature* (Norwood, Pa.: Norwood Editions, 1979); Robert A. Pratt, "Jankyn's Book of Wikked Wyves: Medieval Antimatrimonial Propaganda in the Universities," *Annuale Medievale* 3 (1962): 5–27; Francis L. Utley, *The Crooked Rib* (Columbus: Ohio State University Press, 1944); Katharina M. Wilson and Elizabeth M. Makowski, *Wykked Wyves and the Woes of Marriage: Misogamous Literature from Juvenal to Chaucer* (Albany: State University of New York Press, 1990); and Linda Woodbridge, *Women and the English Renaissance: Literature and the Nature of Womankind, 1540*–1620 (Chicago: University of Illinois Press, 1984).

12. See, e.g., Henry Lea, *History of Sacerdotal Celibacy in the Christian Church* (London: Watts and Company, 1932); Roman Cholij, *Clerical Celibacy in East and West* (Leominster, Herefordshire: Fowler Wright Books, 1988).

13. Geoffrey Chaucer, *The Riverside Chaucer,* ed. Larry D. Benson, 3rd ed. (Boston: Houghton Mifflin, 1987).

14. *The Vision of Piers Plowman: A Complete Edition of the B-Text,* ed. A.V.C. Schmidt (London: J.M. Dent & Sons, 1984).

15. See Mary Carruthers, "The Wife of Bath and the Painting of Lions," *PMLA* 94 (1979): 209–22.

16. At the end of "The Tunnyng," Skelton suggests by his emphasis on accounting and the "tayle" or tally that he may have Chaucer in mind again:

> Suche were there menny
> That had not a penny,
> But, whan they shoulde walke,
> Were fayne with a chalke
> To score on the balke,
> Or score on the tayle.
> God gyve it yll hayle,
> For my fyngers ytche.
> I have wrytten so mytche
> Of this mad mummynge
> Of Elynour Rummynge.
> Thus endeth the gest
> Of this worthy fest.
>
> (611–23)

17. George Puttenham, *The Arte of English Poesie,* [1589] facsimile (Kent, OH: Kent State University Press, 1970), 197.

18. Cf. R. Howard Bloch, commenting on Tertullian's misogyny in "Medieval Misogyny" (*Representations* 20, Fall 1987, 13): "The affinity between gold, the product of excess labor, "the arts," and women constitutes an economic nexus taken as a given; their natures, by definition inessential and antinatural, attract each other because they partake coevally in a scandalous excess that offends."

19. I do not have the original text, which is presumably in Latin, but R. E. Latham's *Revised Medieval Latin Word-List: From British and Irish Sources* (London: Oxford University Press, 1989) contains the following entry:

tip/ulator 1391, 1553, **-lator** 1539, **-pilator** 1603, 'tippler', retailer of ale and wine; + **tirpillatrix,** ale-wife 1547; **domus-ulatoria,** ale-house 1661; **-lo** 1371, **-ulo** 1507, to 'tipple', keep an ale-house.

The Oxford English Dictionary defines "tippler" as "a retailer of ale and other intoxicating liquor; a tapster; a tavern-keeper. *Obs.*" It lists this 1478 entry in the records of the borough of Nottingham: "Fines pro licentia merchandizandi Alicia Bult, tipler, iiij d."

20. "Eleanor Rumming," *Times Literary Supplement* 26 Oct. 1946: 521.

21. Regraters, forestallers, and engrossers were universally condemned from the middle ages through the sixteenth century. They are "middlemen" (figured as female here), though not in the obvious sense: J.E.T. Rogers, in his *History of Agriculture and Prices in England: 1259*–1793, Vol. IV (London: Oxford University Press, 1882), did not find that prices varied with quantity (i.e., there was no difference between "wholesale" and "retail" price). Buyers who bought goods for resale in the same market (regraters), who secured commodities in advance of market arrival (forestallers), or who bought up the entire supply of one commodity in order to corner a market (engrossers), produced illegitimate profits at the expense of the consumer.

22. *The Book of Margery Kempe,* ed. S.B. Meech, Early English Text Society O. S. 212 (London: Oxford University Press, 1940), 9–10. Characters silently regularized.

23. The *Breviary* of Robert Rogers (d. 1595): see *The Chester Mystery Cycle: Essays and Documents,* ed. R.M. Lumiansky and David Mills (Chapel Hill: University of North Carolina Press, 1983), 200, 265, 45–47.

24. *The Chester Mystery Cycle: Volume 1, Text,* ed. R.M. Lumiansky and David Mills, Early English Text Society S. S. 3 (London: Oxford University Press, 1974).

25. III.iv.30–32 in *The Riverside Shakespeare,* ed. G.B. Evans (Boston: Houghton Mifflin, 1974).

26. Andrew Boorde, A *Compendyous Regyment or A Dyetary of Helth,* [1542] ed. F.J. Furnivall, Early English Text Society E.S. Vol. X (London: EETS, 1870).

27. See Scattergood's note to lines 355–62 (451) and *The Calendar of State Papers: Foreign and Domestic, Henry VIII,* Vol. II, Part II, 1031.

28. *Capital: A Critique of Political Economy,* [1867] trans. Samuel Moore and Edward Aveling, ed. Frederick Engels, Vol. I (New York: International Publishers, 1967), 79.

29. For example, see two cases from the Year Books of Edward IV in J.H. Baker and S.F.C. Milsom, *Sources of English Legal History: Private Law to 1750* (London: Butterworths, 1986), 98–100; William Blackstone *Commentaries on the Laws of England,* [1765–69], Vol. I, facsimile (University of Chicago Press, 1979), 430–33 on unity of person in marriage; Frederic Pollock and Frederic William Maitland, *The History of English Law: Before theTime of Edward I* [1895], 2nd ed., Vol. I (Cambridge: Cambridge University Press, 1968), 482–85; but see also, e.g., Carruthers (above n. 15) who emphasizes how much room there is for woman's volition in actual economic and legal practice. I discuss Langland's model of agency relations in a forthcoming essay on Mede's marriage litigation.

30. See Lester K. Little, *Religious Poverty and the Profit Economy in Medieval Europe* (Ithaca, NY: Cornell University Press, 1978), on the relation between economic change and the growth of religious mendicancy and voluntary poverty.

31. See Jacques Le Goff, *Time, Work and Culture in the Middle Ages,* trans. Arthur

Goldhammer (Chicago: University of Chicago Press, 1980).

32. Though "The Tunnyng" is (and should be) taught next to Dunbar's "The Tretis of the Tua Mariit Wemen and the Wedo," Skelton's poem is clearly related to the genre of the gossip or alewife dialogue: see *The Poems of William Dunbar,* ed. James Kinsley (London: Oxford University Press, 1979), 260–61 for bibliography.

33. Lewis, 143. But see the assessment of the ways in which Skelton extends Chaucer in A. C. Spearing's *Medieval to Renaissance in English Poetry* (Cambridge: Cambridge University Press, 1985) 224–77.

34. Cf. Spearing, 242:

> Stanley Fish has claimed that "the locus of a Skelton poem is the narrator's mind; and since the drama is internal, it will reveal itself to a reading which attends to the psychology of the speaker and proceeds from there to a consideration of scene, which moves, in short, from the internal to the external."[29–30] It seems to me, though, that the structure of a Skelton poem is combinatory rather than organic, and that the persona is one means among others of bringing together the various elements of which it is made up. To think of Parott, above all, as possessing a unitary "mind" or "psychology" is to obscure Skelton's purpose.

35. Greg Walker, *John Skelton and the Politics of the 1520s* (Cambridge: Cambridge University Press, 1988).

GLEANINGS

NATHANIEL WALLACE

Talus: Spenser's Iron Man

DISCUSSIONS OF Spenser's narrative of justice, Book V of *The Faerie Queene,* have been especially concerned with the justice of the narrative—the issue of its looseness or underlying coherence—as well as with the justice *in* the narrative—the reasonableness of the various judgments and punishments meted out during the adventures of Artegall and Britomart. Not surprisingly, commentators have sought to correlate the success or inchoateness of the two elements.[1] Placed in the context of such debate, the figure of Talus seems an allegorical curiosity illustrating the administration of justice and is ostensibly of limited import in evaluating the narrative or its ruling virtue. Yet in a crucial but overlooked stanza, the iron man prompts a reassessment of the nature of justice in *The Faerie Queene.*

Toward the end of Canto vii, after passing a night in the temple of Isis, Britomart proceeds with Talus to the land of the Amazons, where she succeeds in slaying Radigund and freeing her lover. Faced with Talus's slaughter of the offending queen's followers, Britomart commands an end to carnage and revenge. The iron man's powers have not been found excessive previously, and the incident can be viewed as the appropriate close of a self-contained episode that began with the exclusion of Talus from the temple of Isis (vii.3.9). Both the beginning and concluding actions signal the iron man's disassociation from equity and mercy, moderating factors that are linked to Isis (3.4, 22.6–9) and are among the varied aspects of justice displayed by Britomart in Canto vii.[2]

Yet the succeeding stanza, through a subtle pun, disturbs this sense of stability and resolution:

> Tho when she had his execution stayd,
> She for that yron prison did enquire,
> In which her wretched loue was captiue layd:
> Which breaking open with indignant ire,
> She entred into all the partes entire.
> Where when she saw that lothly vncouth sight,
> Of men disguiz'd in womanishe attire,
> Her heart gan grudge, for very deepe despight
> Of so vnmanly maske, in misery misdight.
> (V.vii.37)

The repeating phoneme, "ire," prominent as the crucial "b" rhyme of the stanza, acquires priority of interest as very much a word in its own right and as echo of "iron." The unexpected overlapping of significations is intriguing.

If Talus is the man of ire and Artegall a prisoner of ire (of Radigund's if not his own), then several things are suggested about the nature of justice as well as of moral error in Book V. First of all, it is oversimple to identify Talus exclusively with the wrath of God and thus conclude that the tensions resulting in the program of justice from the iron/ire equation are entirely dissipated; such as interpretation is appealing in view of Talus's former office as groom of Astraea, goddess of justice and mentor of Artegall in "all the depth of rightfull doome" (i.5.3). Nor, amid the multiple functions of Spenserian personnel, does Talus's alternate identity as *lex talionis* fully justify even as it explains much of the ire evident in the workings of retribution. Rather, the conjunction of "iron" and "ire" tends to accentuate the extent to which the intemperance of anger is implicated in many of the crimes and at least some of the judgments in Book V. Thus, Artegall and the Sarazin wax mutually wroth (ii.11–12); the populist Gyant is deeply angered at the very nature of things before Talus casts him from a cliff (ii.37–49), and Britomart as well as Radigund enter combat with such "great fury" that "both their skill forgot" (vii.29.4).

The question of narrative coherence in Book V cannot, perhaps, be fully resolved, partly because the iron/ire equation suggests discord within the concept of justice, a tension between justice both as social equilibrium, allowing people to enjoy what is rightfully theirs, and as discomfort inflicted upon those desiring more than they are entitled to. It was a quandary to which reflective minds of the sixteenth century were sensitive. While he assents to the efficacy of punishment, Richard Hooker finds no intrinsic merit in the *lex talionis* and emphasizes "that which should cause even hearts of stone and iron to relent, we do not find God in Scripture so often rejoicing over the righteous, as shedding forth tears of kindness in the bosom of sinners penitent" (628). Such a perspective was hardly unique to Hooker,[3] and even if Spenser did not share it, his text inherits a debate over justice and its status. At the same time, complications of this sort insure that Book V will never be read as just a narrative.

South Carolina State University

NOTES

1. The argument for coherence in Book V is effectively advanced by R.J. Manning. For a contrasting view, see Judith H. Anderson, "'Nor Man It Is': The Knight of Justice in Book V of Spenser's *Faerie Queene*" (Hamilton 447–70).
2. James E. Phillips's discussion of the components of justice remains valuable. See "Renaissance Concepts of Justice and the Structure of *The Faerie Queene,* Book V" (Hamilton 471–87, especially 473).
3. A related point of view is thoughtfully expressed by Montaigne in *Essais* II.11 ("De la cruauté"), especially 410–12 and 414.

WORKS CITED

Hamilton, A. C., ed. *Essential Articles for the Study of Edmund Spenser.* Hamden, CT: Archon Books, 1972.

Hooker, Richard. "A Learned Sermon of the Nature of Pride." *Works.* 7th ed. Ed. John Keble, R. W. Church, and F. Paget. 3 vols. Oxford: Clarendon, 1888. 3: 597–642.

Manning, R. J. "Deuicefull Sights: Spenser's Emblematic Practice in *The Faerie Queene,* V.1–3." *Spenser Studies* 5 (1985): 65–89.

Montaigne, Michel de. *Oeuvres complètes.* Ed. Albert Thibaudet and Maurice Rat. Paris: Gallimard, 1962.

Spenser, Edmund. *The Faerie Queene.* Ed. Thomas P. Roche, Jr. English Poets Series 6. New Haven: Yale University Press, 1981.

Index

Contents of Previous Volumes

VOLUME III (1982)

VOLUME IV (1983)

VOLUME VII (1987)

VOLUME VIII (1990)

VOLUME IX (1991)